An Endless Quiet Valley

An Endless Quiet Valley
A Reappraisal of
John Masefield

by
Paul Binding

Logaston Press

LOGASTON PRESS
Little Logaston Woonton Almeley
Herefordshire HR3 6QH

First published by Logaston Press 1998
Copyright © Paul Binding 1998

Hardback: ISBN 1 873827 35 0
Paperback: ISBN 1 873827 30 X

Set in Times by Logaston Press
and printed in Great Britain by
Biddles Ltd

for
Francis King
with affection and admiration

Contents

Acknowledgments

So many people to thank, but here I will record my debts to the poet's nephew, William Masefield of Ledbury, for his helpfulness and hospitality; to Philip Errington of University College, London and the John Masefield Society for his extraordinarily attentive reading of the manuscript. I wish to acknowledge that the permission to quote John Masefield's work has been kindly granted by The Society of Authors as the Literary Representative of the Estate of John Masefield; permission to quote Rudyard Kipling's work has been given by A.P. Watt Ltd on behalf of The National Trust; also by A.P. Watt Ltd. to quote Y.B. Yeats; permission to quote Terry Coleman's *The Railway Navvies* by Peters Fraser & Dunlop Group Ltd.; to quote Auden and Ezra Pound by Faber and Faber; and I express my thanks to Felix Watkins for permission to use and to refer to Alfred Watkins' manuscript. I also wish to acknowledge The Board of Trustees of the National Museums and Galleries on Merseyside (Merseyside Maritime Museum) for the illustrations of the *Conway* and Liverpool Docks; and to Hereford Museum for the Watkins Collection photographs.

I also wish to thank Mark Todd, for his kindness, not least in the matter of many expeditions in the Masefield country; and, of course, to my publisher, Andy Johnson, for his enthusiasm, patience and thoroughness. I would also like to express my gratitude to Sir Julian Critchley; Simon Dorrell for the cover illustration; Brian Byron for the map of Ledbury District; Caroline and Simon Gourlay; and Mirrabel Osler for support and thoughtfulness during the time of writing this book.

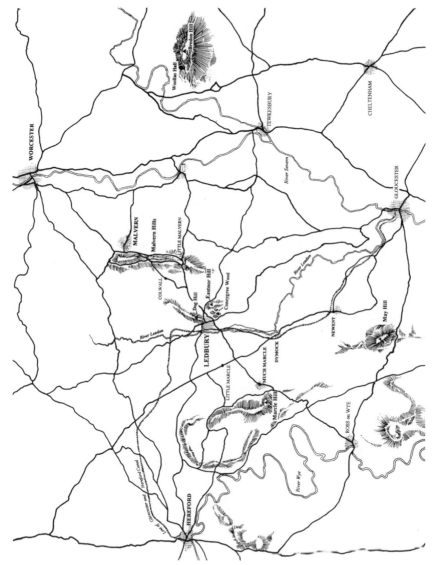

Map of the area around Ledbury, illustrating places mentioned in the text

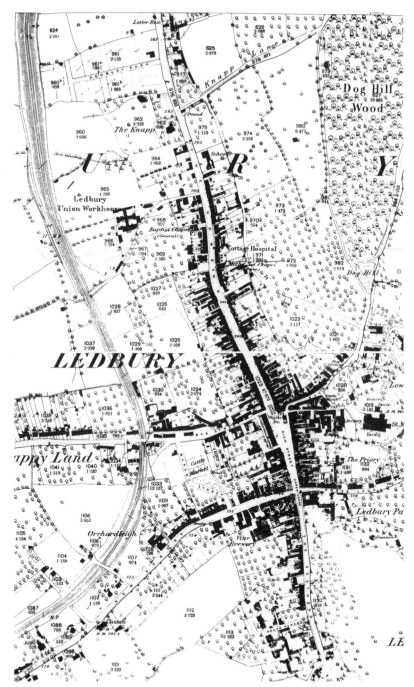

1st edition 25 ins OS Plan of Ledbury (1887)

CHAPTER I
'A Corpse Who Recovered Life'

My life has been in three scenes, one of great happiness, one of
horror, terror, shame and disgrace beyond all telling, and then, one,
a long one, of an interest, a steady joy and peace for which no words
of mine can suffice. I do not know enough of this life of ours to be
able to explain why the second scene was allotted to me. I was a
young man at the time, wicked, no doubt, with the usual folly of the
young, but not so wicked, as I see myself, as to deserve such fate.
Without that second scene the third could not have been; this too I
know. Wise men in the land where I had lived have told me, that I
was receiving punishment for something done in a past life. One or
two of them have said that I was being prepared by destiny to a new
fate, and that all, to whom life is to be full, or significant, must first
pass through a furnace of suffering. It may be so. One told me that
I was blessed among men, to have gone through a Hell in my life-
time. That, too, may be so. He said that fire cleanses, and that
sorrow purifies and ennobles. I know that my fire did not cleanse
me, nor my sorrow ennoble. The fire smouldered in me for years,
filling me with smoke of blackness and bitterness; my sorrow made
me angry, cynical and savage. It gave me hatreds which even now
are hideous in me.

So declares Ned Mansell at the beginning of John Masefield's novel, *Dead
Ned* (1938), published in the author's sixtieth year. Set in the late eighteenth century, it is the story of a well-meaning, serious, hard-working
young man who, after a sequence of misapprehensions and betrayals, is
arrested, tried and finally hanged for a murder he didn't commit. But he
survives the hanging, and friends enable him to escape the country. In the

1

sequel, *Live and Kicking Ned* (1939), Ned wins through, after appaling hardships, to a new purpose for living, returns to England and clears his name, to find himself 'with Wife, Friends and Fortune, the Rose revived, Ned alive and the bright road clear before me.'

What is remarkable in Ned's story is the extreme cruelty of his misfortune. Strung up at Tyburn, the execution blessed by the chaplain, and the broadsheet-hacks standing by to make their erroneous reports, he is put to death by society's wish and command:

> I died denying Providence. If Providence could watch unmoved the misery of a boy unjustly hanged I reckoned that I would have none of it. I died hating men, loathing life, longing to be quit of it for ever, yet in terror of what might be to come. If you think that you would have died in nobler temper, do try it.

But Providence has (it turns out) ordained not only Ned's unjust hanging but his deliverance as well, implemented through the courage of a few exceptional men.

What is remarkable in the Prologue to the story, however, is Ned's insistence (which is Masefield's also) that, contrary to the conventional, Christian view-point, all the suffering undergone did *not* improve his character. Rather, what he had to endure has created wounds which have continued to fester in his soul. Ned impresses on readers, vitiating his description of his present life as one of a 'steady joy and peace', that even now he is possessed by 'hatreds which are ... hideous in me.'

While it is always dangerous to confuse the narrators of novels with their creators, in the case of Ned Mansell and John Masefield there are parallels so strong as to be impossible, with hindsight, to ignore. After *Dead Ned* and *Live and Kicking Ned*, Masefield dedicated the greater part of his writing life to the re-creation of his earlier years, those before he knew literary fulfilment and success, suggesting that the novels were works of important self-confrontation and release.

For instance, *Some Memories of W.B. Yeats* (1940) is a tribute to the principal literary mentor of Masefield's young manhood. His next two volumes of poetry have largely autobiographical concerns: *Gautama the Enlightened and Other Verse* (1941) attempts to explain the course of life in other than those Christian terms rebutted in the opening to *Dead Ned*; *Wonderings (Between One and Six Years)* (1943) explores

2

that 'first scene ... of great happiness', a scene he was further to evoke in prose in his last published work of all, the marvellous *Grace Before Ploughing* (1966), a sequence of vignettes of his childhood world. Shortly after the Ned novels came two lively reminiscences of youthful experiences, *In the Mill* (1941) and *New Chum* (1944). In 1952 he produced his nearest to an autobiography proper, *So Long to Learn*, an account of his development as a writer, more particularly as poet. So at the very least we can view *Dead Ned*, together with its sequel, as a precursor to works in which he examined himself and how he had spent his life. In this light, its eighteenth-century pastiche subtitle, acquires significance: 'The Autobiography of a Corpse/ Who recovered Life within the coast of Dead Ned/ And came to what Fortune you shall hear.'

Yet to the outside world it must have seemed that Fortune had dealt with Masefield with outstanding open-handedness. In 1930 he was appointed Poet Laureate, the then Prime Minister, Ramsay Macdonald, having asked him in the most honourific terms if he might put his name forward to King George V whose favourite poet Masefield reputedly was. His *Collected Poems* (first edition, 1923) had enjoyed phenomenal success on both sides of the Atlantic, selling over 200,000 copies. He had married Constance de la Cherois Crommelin in 1903, and was the father of a daughter, Judith, born in 1904, and a son, Lewis, born in 1910. He knew domestic security, had a large readership and a public position consequent on a sizeable, various and well-received *oeuvre*. It would be possible to go further, and say that the John Masefield of *Dead Ned* was one of the most famous people in the entire English-speaking world. But his hero's words suggest an unhappiness, even an insecurity, living on in him, the stubborn presence of a difficult past, phases of which he can still think of as 'a furnace of suffering', 'a Hell', and for which the appropriate metaphors are an innocent youth hanged through the calumnies of the malicious and the duped, and a corpse painfully and secretly revived.

2

All who met John Masefield in his Poet Laureate years commented on his courteous, considerate manner, on the beauty of his voice, particularly when speaking poetry, and on the handsomeness of his appearance. But if his outward form—and, for that matter, the elegance of the work

3

he turned out in his public capacity—masked darker inner preoccupations and memories, which went unrecognised, it's also true to say that the very fame that he enjoyed was something of an illusion. For it was fame without reputation. And he had far too keen a mind not to be aware of this.

The year in which *Dead Ned* came out saw the publication of George Orwell's *Homage to Catalonia*, Graham Greene's *Brighton Rock*, Cyril Connolly's *Enemies of Promise*, and Hemingway's *The Fifth Column and the First Forty-Nine Stories*, all of which take the pulse of their tormented age and reveal their authors striving for an appropriate style—plain, vernacular, flexible yet nervous—to convey its tensions, its debates and its needs. More interior in preoccupations were Virginia Woolf's *The Years* and Elizabeth Bowen's *The Death of the Heart*, in both of which an essentially feminist vision exposes the limitations of the conventional world on the edge of a great abyss. There also appeared in 1938 two major new dramatic works by poets, W.H. Auden's collaboration with Christopher Isherwood, *On the Frontier*, and Stephen Spender's *Trial of a Judge*, together with a new volume of poems, *The Earth Compels*, by their friend and contemporary, Louis MacNeice; all three productions yield nothing to the novelists in their intense engagement with the world of that time. No publication by a poet, however, was of greater significance than the *New Poems* of Masefield's older mentor and friend, W.B. Yeats. 'The Gyres', 'Lapis Lazuli', and 'What Then?' not only demonstrated the great modernist heights Yeats (born in 1865) had attained, they became, almost from their first appearance, touchstones by which later generations have evaluated poetry.

Yeats was to die the following year, on 28 January 1939. A month later the dominant poet of his generation, W.H. Auden, wrote 'In Memory of W.B. Yeats':

> What instruments we have agree
> The day of his death was a dark cold day.

The poem is in part a salute to Yeats' art, in part a valediction to the hegemonic idea of the Thirties that literature in general, and poetry in particular, could be a weapon in the service of political and social justice:

For poetry makes nothing happen: it survives
In the valley of its making where executives
Would never want to tamper, flows on south
From ranches of isolation and the busy griefs,
Raw towns that we believe and die in; it survives,
A way of happening, a mouth.

Auden gave no thought, in this commendation of poetry as timeless and time-defying, to Yeats' younger one-time protegé, who had indeed, when writing of the invasion of the private by the public/historic, used the valley as a metaphor for the containment of the human spirit—in 'August 1914':

An endless quiet valley reaches out
Past the blue hills into the evening sky;
Over the stubble, cawing, goes a rout
Of rooks from harvest, flagging as they fly.

For, in Auden's imagery, Masefield's work had, as far as a serious readership was concerned, ceased to flow on south, was an articulating mouth no longer, had not survived.

It would be fair to say that not one of the writers of 1938 just cited would have been taking note of what Masefield was currently up to, nor would any of their admirers. The people who went on buying, or who treasured their copies of, his phenomenally best-selling *Collected Poems* would have been for the most part (and fairly self-consciously at that) middle-brows, as cautious about culture as they were about politics, as unanxious to commit themselves to the experimental, the questing, the intellectually provocative as they were to take stands about social injustice or events in Spain, Italy, Germany. The fame that Masefield enjoyed was essentially that of a man with an honourable past; by sixty he had become a relic.

John Masefield lived on until 1967, dying twenty days short of his eighty-ninth birthday. Now, with the passing of time even his fame has diminished, though his name is still a well-known one, included more often than not perfunctorily in literary histories, while his reputation— outside circles of dedicated enthusiasts—scarcely exists. 'Sea-Fever' and 'Cargoes', two uncharacteristic and undistinguished if rhythmically pleasing poems and the (still appealing) children's stories, *The Midnight Folk* (1927) and *The Box of Delights* (1935), are all that the average

5

student or reader of English Literature is familiar with. Specialist book-sellers report a decline in recent years in demands for his books; the few consistently asked for—the prose-works *Gallipoli* (1916), *The Old Front Line* (1917), the portrait of the writer's old training-ship *The Conway from her Foundation to the Present Day* (1933) and the related *New Chum* (1944)—being sought by those fascinated not so much by John Masefield as by the First World War and British ships. If ever there could be said to be a corpse among twentieth-century writers of stature, Masefield is as good a candidate as any. The motto Masefield affixed to his 1938 novel, a traditional jingle, comes to mind:

> And since it's only Ned,
> Who was alive and is dead,
> There's no more to be said.

But there is, and a great deal. At its finest Masefield's work has the vitality and universality of great art. Yet it amounts to a very small propor-tion of his huge output, to say which is not to deny considerable interest to many other of his copious productions. This small proportion constitutes a unique contribution to English Literature, one of its triumphs, and is in real need of advocacy today; it is (more or less) coincident with what seized the imaginations of the reading public of the times, shocking and inspiring them, and certainly begins with the work that forced the name John Masefield on its attention: *The Everlasting Mercy* (1911). Masefield himself wrote in *The Ledbury Scene as I have used it in my verse* (1951): 'I shall begin (as I feel that I, myself, began as a writer) with the tale in verse called *The Everlasting Mercy*.'

Appearing in the prestigious *English Review* in October 1911, and published in book-form the following month, it had a *succès d'estime et de scandale* such as happens at most only once or twice a decade. It was everywhere discussed, it found fervent eloquent admirers and fervent eloquent detractors, it moved many people, it disgusted others, it was quoted from pulpits, and it made pundits aware that the English could, like the French, become excited about poetry if it touched a nerve—as *The Everlasting Mercy* so patently did—if it possessed, in almost equal measures, freshness, sensitivity and vigour. A comparison springs to mind at once with the poets of the Auden generation at the start of their careers, Spender, MacNeice, Day Lewis, and Auden himself, though in point of fact none of these experienced quite the sudden notoriety, the rocketing into fame that Masefield did. There had arrived, it was felt, something both boldly new to the point of being sensational but also undeniably serious, brilliant yet demotic, a fitting creation to mark a new era (George V was crowned on June 23 1911). Though Masefield had been productive, published and even critically appreciated relatively early, nothing in his previous writings had prepared readers for this work.

Masefield proceeded to follow it with three other long narrative poems, *The Widow in the Bye Street* (1912), *The Daffodil Fields* and *Dauber* (both 1913). He was never to sustain such intense creativity again; four works in succession, clearly the work of the same imagination yet each an individual work, each doing successfully something no one had attempted before.

☆   ☆   ☆

On August 4th 1914 Britain declared on Germany; the crowds cheered their way through the London streets and sang the National Anthem outside No 10 Downing Street and Buckingham Palace. Masefield in 'August 1914' recorded the outbreak of the Great War in a country context (Berkshire, his then home):

> How still this quiet cornfield is to-night!
> By an intenser glow the evening falls,
> Bringing, not darkness, but a deeper light;
> Among the stooks a partridge covey calls.

But even here, disturbing a scene as peaceful and numinous as a landscape by Samuel Palmer (and evoked the more effectively for that subtle and unexpected use of the comparative, 'intenser'), the news of the declaration of war is palpable, and it could not be doubted that

>   ... [it] meant
> The breaking off of ties, the loss of friends,
> Death, like a miser getting in his rent,
> And no new stones laid where the trackway ends.

The Great War, like the Holocaust, like the dropping of the Atom Bomb on Hiroshima and Nagasaki, is an event not just in human history but in human consciousness, a constituent of the Western

7

psyche. In 1916, half-way through it, Masefield published a sequence of *Sonnets*, searching, ruminative, metaphysical, concerned with eternal realities in the face of personal and national distress. At the same time they lack the disturbing intensity, vitality, especially in their language, not only of Masefield's own preceding narrative-poems but of contemporaneous work, above all that of the poets actually partici- pant in the war and (for the most part) published after it: Siegfried Sassoon, Wilfred Owen, Isaac Rosenburg, Ivor Gurney. Of poetry overtly about the war Masefield produced none, his energies going into prose-works which involved painful—if essentially circumscribed— witness of its terrible progress. But the cataclysm of the War, which conditioned the sensibility and preoccupations of the decade that followed the Armistice, divided Masefield from his creative self at its fiercest and most personal, just as it forced an unbridgeable breach in the reading public itself; its most serious members would, after so huge a trauma, not want what Masefield had given them.

Masefield's interpretation of the needs of the post-War world was idiosyncratic. In 1919 he produced what has proved his most popular single work, and by many (writer and Masefield critic, Muriel Spark, among them) his most admired: *Reynard the Fox*. In this narrative poem he took for his model, both in scheme and in use of the rhyming couplet, Chaucer's 'Prologue' to *The Canterbury Tales*, as he had turned before the War to Chaucer's *Troilus and Criseyde* for his poems of the passionate lives of individuals, *The Widow in the Bye Street*, *The Daffodil Fields* and *Dauber*. There was an ideological motive for his decision. Fractured, war-shattered England was to be united through art with an earlier epoch of social cohesion and common faith. In impor- tant respects his thinking here was that of one of the idols of his youth, William Morris, and of his own older contemporary, G.K. Chesterton; the Middle Ages should inspire the regeneration of England. Belief and poem were borne of concern for the contemporary social fabric, but even so could not, to those equally but differently concerned, fail to seem tinged with reaction. The accusation of artistic conservatism clung, unjust though in many respects it was.

With *Reynard* Masefield's career as a seriously read, critically discussed poet in rapport with the times in effect comes to an end, though admirers of *King Cole*, such as myself, would extend the period to include this 'adult fairy-tale' of 1921. Composed again in the 'rhyme royal' of *Troilus and Criseyde* and Masefield's masterpieces of 1912-13, this narrative poem with its circus setting shares, maybe unwittingly, many of the attributes of key modernist works: Picasso's *Les Saltimbanques* (The Acrobats) with Rilke's salutation to them in his *Duino Elegies*; Falla's *El Retablo de Maese Pedro* (Master Peter's Puppet-Show) and the cross-media creations of Jean Cocteau for whom the circus was so important.

The following year, 1922, is, by general consent, the *annus mirabilis* of modernism: Eliot's *The Waste Land*, James Joyce's *Ulysses*, D.H. Lawrence's *Aaron's Rod*, *England, My England* and *Fantasia of the Unconscious*, Edith Sitwell's *Facade* and Virginia Woolf's *Jacob's Room*, literary achievements the twentieth century would be unimaginable without. Masefield could no more stand up against this mighty and purgative tidal-wave than could such Georgians as Edmund Blunden and John Drinkwater with whom he has subsequently often been compared, and even lumped, despite the radical and obvious differences between them.

From then on Masefield devoted himself principally to fiction for which 'romantic' is perhaps the aptest term; the word is not intended disparagingly. *Sard Harker* (1924), *Odtaa* (1926) and *The Bird of Dawning* (1933), issued in large print-runs, were immensely popular, and have their admirers today (though none of these novels is at the time of writing in print). But they are nowhere near the literary mainstream either as represented by the modernists or by those middle-ground or popular writers who, at one level or another, dealt (at any rate purportedly) with the society and issues of the day: Galsworthy, Maugham, Priestley etc. The same goes for the volumes of poetry he produced, for all the beauties to be found in them, whether the Arthurian *Midsummer Night* (1928) or the very various *A Letter from Pontus and Other Verse* (1936) is under consideration.

To one genre, however, Masefield was generally agreed to make not just a significant but a unique contribution in the between-the-wars period—literary fiction for children. *The Midnight Folk*, reputedly the author's favourite among his books, and *The Box of Delights* to a certain extent build on Masefield's achievement of 1910 in this field, *A Book of Discoveries*, which he dedicated to his daughter, Judith, but go far beyond it in sophistication of artistry. Both books, the latter a great success when dramatised in the '50s for radio and the '90s for television, are distinguished by a richness of invention and use of language which make them—together with the work of Hugh Lofting and Arthur Ransome—one of the few true links between the great Victorian and Edwardian classics and those of the post-Second World War era, 'the Second Golden Age of Children's Books', of C.S. Lewis, Mary Norton, Philippa Pearce, William Mayne and Alan Garner. They relate intimately to Masefield's earlier life, to the happy and the unhappy in almost equal measure, plundering as they do experiences of his now remote-seeming past, if magically translating them. Together with *Dead Ned* and *Live and Kicking Ned* (which indeed have found both young and adult readers; Penguin Books reissued the stories in the 1970s under their Puffin imprint), they deserve currency today. Interestingly the Ned novels show Masefield coming to terms not only with his own past, but with his own country's. His detestation of Imperialism, his feeling that Britain should feel creative guilt for its crimes against Africa perpetrated through the slave trade bore fruit in these novels which I view as ancestors (if at one removed) of such contemporary achievements as Caryl Phillips' superb *Cambridge* (1991).

Ned Mansell's story made Masefield re-consider his own, and no one interested in Masefield should neglect *In the Mill*, *New Chum*, *So Long to Learn* and *Grace Before Ploughing*. But a caveat should be given. Yes, Masefield appears to have had total recall; he could bring scenes from his past alive in both atmosphere and detail. But as he got older, his outlook became more generally mellow or benign, reflected in a prose-style Muriel Spark in her *John Masefield* (1953) aptly calls 'Addisonian', after Joseph Addison (1672-1719) with his Augustan cultivated style, consciously equally aptly adding: 'I do not really think Masefield was quite so Addisonian as all that.'

He surely wasn't. The testimony to the life he knew in Herefordshire, in Liverpool, at sea, and down and out in New York and London, is in truth not contained in these comparatively genial memoirs, for all their plenitude of interesting anecdotes, but rather—sometimes directly, sometimes at one or two removes—in the best of his creative work. And there we find another vision entirely, an uncomfortable, troubled and troubling one, open to and outraged by pain and gratuitous suffering, offering us no tidied-up view of human nature either in its individual or social manifestations, particularly the last. There is something curiously and stubbornly anarchic in Masefield's strongest pieces.

10

The caveat is less necessary for that swan-song to his *oeuvre*, *Grace Before Ploughing* (1966), a book unlike any other yet poetic and atmospheric, which in its sharp cameos of early childhood, combines (to take parallels from Masefield's home-country) the interest in an actual locality of Francis Kilvert with the visionary insight of Thomas Traherne. It gives us a key to the still centre that sustained Masefield throughout his long writing life.

3

Masefield was a man of many paradoxes. They tend to dissolve with closer analysis, since public image has too often distorted the complex reality of man and writer. A celebrant of the English countryside and its traditions, he made it clear in autobiographical writings that the past had witnessed the intolerable misery and poverty of too many people, and that he didn't regret its passing. A spiritual man, whose first famous work apostrophises the antiquity and traditions of the local church and concerns a religious conversion, he was by conviction anti-clerical, refusing to have his children baptised and disliking weddings. Drawn to Buddhism from his young manhood, unusually sensitive to pain wherever experienced (he found Isaac Walton's descriptions of angling hard to stomach), and, during his late teens, a vegetarian on moral grounds, he could write of fox-hunting as late as 1924: 'To all Englishmen who have lived in a hunting country, hunting is in the blood, and the mind is full of it. It is the most beautiful and the most stirring sight to be seen in England.' Yet the author of *Reynard the Fox* turned against the activity at the centre of his poem, quarrelled with his county neighbours over the issue, and praised his late son, Lewis, (who had died in 1942) with the words: 'He loathed cruelty of any kind; the hunting of animals and the shooting of birds, for what is called "sport" seemed to him the recreation of savages.'

He was a great lover of women, whose virtues he found superior to men's, he was closer to his sisters than to his brothers, and his decidedly chivalrous admiration did not prevent him from being an ardent public champion of their legal and political rights, yet he was unable to draw any feminine characters, and his best productions centre on masculine predicaments.

He was a devotee of Shakespeare, on whom, though an auto-didact he was to write a respected book, but loathed the character and attitudes of Henry V and believed that Shakespeare did so too. He was widely represented as English of English, but he was soaked in French and Russian literature, and admired, for differing reasons, Racine and Baudelaire as much as any writers of the past, while as a young man his chief mentors were Irish—W.B. Yeats and his brother, Jack, the painter, and John Millington Synge.

Some of these paradoxes were beneficial to his art, others detrimental, and account for the shortcomings and limitations of his *oeuvre*.

One area of tension there is not. Masefield, much as he may have benefited from the literary associates of his early twenties, never cared for city life. It stifled him; in distinction he was stimulated by the country to which by birth and boyhood he belonged. And, though he never returned to Herefordshire to live, Ledbury and its surroundings were indissolubly linked to his imaginative powers. With the exception of *Dauber*, which however has an extremely important flash-back to the Gloucestershire countryside, all his major works relate to the land he knew when young; their topography, traditions, problems and characters were essential spring-boards for his most daring flights of imagination.

This makes a look at his formative years indispensable. A cautionary note before any such examination is undertaken, is supplied by a poem that Masefield wrote between submitting *The Everlasting Mercy* to *The English Review* and its publication—called simply 'Biography'. It's a little odd that he should have written these lines when he did; it's as if he knew in some part of his being that fame was soon to be his, and great fame at that, which would appropriate him and obfuscate important features of his personality and past. We can even find, with hindsight, hints at the likely impermanence of this fame:

> When I am buried, all my thoughts and acts
> Will be reduced to lists of dates and facts,
> And long before this wandering flesh is rotten
> The dates which made me will be all forgotten;
> And none will know the gleam there used to be
> About the feast-days freshly kept by me,
> But men will call the golden hour of bliss
> "About this time" or "shortly after this".

What addresses itself to the most creative elements of the psyche, he is emphasizing, cannot be tied down to external events and dates; it defies crude measurement, neat laws of cause and effect.

> Years blank with hardship never speak a word,
> Live in the soul to make the being stirred;

The happier experiences (and 'Best trust the happy moments' is the poem's somewhat Stevensonian concluding exhortation), far from being part of a an upward-reaching ladder belong to that buried secret life that links one to the timeless.

> This many pictured world of many passions
> Wears out the nations as a woman fashions,
> And what life is is much to very few,
> Men being so strange, so mad, and what men do
> So good to watch or share; but when men count
> Those hours of life that were a bursting fount,
> Sparkling the dusty heart with living springs,
> There seems a world, beyond our earthly things,
> Gated by golden moments, each bright time
> Opening to show the city white like lime,
> High-towered and many-peopled. This made sure,
> Work that obscures those moments seems impure,
> Making our not-returning time of breath
> Dull with the ritual and records of death,
> That frost of fact by which our wisdom gives
> Correctly stated death to all that lives.

Nonetheless, if we are to understand the extraordinary breakthrough that was *The Everlasting Mercy*, with which Masefield begins his claims on posterity—and it is an aim of this book to make him appear bold, innovatory and shocking again—a certain amount of biographical matter is not to be avoided. Nor is a look at Masefield's works leading up to that masterpiece of 1911. After all, exhaustion would have played a part in the despair out of which the narrative poem was born, and the exhaustion cannot be altogether unrelated to his prodigious productivity, the fruits of which are by no means without interest. While individually each has imperfections, collectively they add up to a most impressive list: three volumes of poems, *Salt-Water Ballads* (1902), *Ballads* (1903), *Ballads and Poems* (1910) this last largely derived from *Ballads* and *Salt-Water Ballads*; six novels, *Captain Margaret* (1908), *Multitude and Solitude* (1909) *Martin Hyde: The Duke's Messenger* (1910), *Lost Endeavour* (1910), *Jim Davis* (1911);

two major plays, *The Tragedy of Nan* (1909) and *The Tragedy of Pompey the Great* (1910); a children's story, *A Book of Discoveries* (1910); five books of prose, *A Mainsail Haul* (1905), *Sea Life in Nelson's Time* (1905), *On the Spanish Main* (1906), *A Tarpaulin Muster* (1907) and *My Faith in Woman Suffrage* (1910).

The author of these must have possessed a formidable capacity for hard work, a relentless intellectual curiosity, an imaginative energy—and an unquenchable love of the act of writing. None of these qualities was ever to desert him.

CHAPTER II
'Milestones Upon Time'

John Masefield (known in his boyhood as Jack) was born on June 1st 1878 in Ledbury in Herefordshire. He was later to describe his birthplace thus:

> Mine was a little town of ancient grace,
> A long street widened at a market place,
> Crossed, in its length, by two transversal ways
> Doubtless the course of brooks in ancient days.
> Within the width, a market building stood
> Propped upon weathered quarres of chestnut wood.
> In nearby lanes, where rotting tan-pits stank
> Prince Rupert's horse had broken Massey's rank,
> And sent him flying in our civil war;
> Men find the bullets still, in beam and door.
> > Rude leaden lumps, last relics to survive
> > The agony and rage of men alive.
>
> The little town was pleasant to the sight,
> Fair, with half-timbered houses, black-and-white,
> Shops, taverns, traffic, market on the street,
> And cobbled paving, painful to the feet.
> Slowly I came to know it, but at first
> Judged of it only, by its best and worst.

These lines, if not among Masefield's most verbally inspired, nevertheless not only give an accurate and vivid enough impression of Ledbury, they also convey important features of the poet's response to it. He has a clear and factually sound view of the town, which if 'little' was, and is today, one of the important towns of Herefordshire. He knows what makes such a community tick and both the good and the more disagreeable aspects of this; the unexpected 'where rotting tan-pits stank', referring to Ledbury's leather industry, is very characteristic of him. At the same time his is a palimpsestic approach; the layers of the past are always visible to Masefield, one behind the other, (just as they are tangible to those minded to look, such as the men who find bullets in old beams). Ledbury saw fierce fighting in the Civil War ('our civil war' as Masefield here and elsewhere calls it, almost casually, without the drama of capital letters); at the Battle of Ledbury in April 1645, Prince Rupert and his supporters made their way through the gardens of Masefield's own native part of the town, The Homend, in order to cut off the Parliamentarian Colonel Massey's retreat towards Gloucester, of which he was Governor. The boy that John Masefield had been could not conveniently consign experiences to the history book, and neither could the man he grew into; what Ledbury people went through in the past is still real to him. At the same time, Masefield, interested in self and the nature of experience, is able to recall here the sensory impact of the place—the cobbles 'painful to the feet'—and to admit that his appreciation of the life of the town was a gradual business, which involved unlearning as well as learning, requiring as it did a child's tendency to see people and their lives in terms of simplistic contrasts.

John Masefield's father, Edward, was a solicitor in Ledbury as his father had been before him. The family firm continues to this day in the care of Edward's grandson, William, and great-grandson, Charles, and in the same long, low, brick premises in Worcester Road which has contained it since approximately 1830. (The house, originally a private dwelling, dates from the early eighteenth century.) It's only in the last twenty years that a partner who isn't a Masefield has been taken into the practice. Masefield's mother, Caroline Louisa Parker ('Carrie'), was the daughter of the vicar of Great Comberton in Worcestershire; her early death meant that his recollections of her were to be only partial and coloured by a bemused regret he never quite lost. In his *Ballads and Poems* of 1910, Masefield paid homage to her in a poem 'C.L.M.' which has something of the sad dignity of William Cowper's more famous 'Lines to his mother's picture':

> Down in the darkness of the grave
> She cannot see the life she gave,
> For all her love, she cannot tell
> Whether I use it ill or well,
> Nor knock at dusty doors to find
> Her beauty dusty in the mind.

If the grave's gates could be undone
She would not know her little son,
I am so grown. If we should meet
She would pass by me in the street,
Unless my soul's face let her see
My sense of what she did for me.

There is a subdued guilt here as well as sorrow, and a sort of nostalgia for what could never be. There's also, if only nascently, a wish on Masefield's part to elevate his mother to the position of supreme moral arbiter, a wish which, whenever first manifest, had marked psychological repercussions on his life. Masefield came to believe he had inherited his feeling for poetry from Carrie.

☆　　　　　　　☆　　　　　　　☆

Masefield was born, third child and second son (two other sons and daughters were to follow), in The Knapp, the large house Edward Masefield had had built some years before, in Victorian half-timbered style, on the road called The Homend that leads northwards out of Ledbury, 'though,' said the writer later, 'I am not sure I was born there ... I leave that to others.' (The reasons for his doubt are obscure.) The Knapp was then on the very edge of the town, belonging as much to the countryside as to the town proper. Its view and its atmosphere were to stay with him always:

> I suppose that I first looked out of its western windows on an orchard, a more distant field, a long clump of elms with a great rookery in its forty or fifty trees, a canal that flowed, as I thought, from Paradise to Heaven, though some have doubted this, and then miles of woodland that barred much of the main view.
>
> In the fields beyond the canal, in wet weather, a wide reddish smudge would appear, which I was told was the floods. In ordinary seasons I looked beyond these fields to a wooded hill, and to the left, or south of this hill to a more distant, less wooded hill, which I was told was Marcle. ... Of Marcle, I will only say here, that when it was going to rain it looked very clear, and in the clearness a new land appeared beyond it.
>
> I was told that the new land was Wales, and that these were the Black Hills. ...
>
> Much nearer to me, in a middle distance of about 200 yards, there stretched visibly one of the wonders of the world, the Gloucester and Hereford Canal, which made a straight course north at that point for a marvellous mile or two.

At its southern extremity, this canal joined the Severn and provided Masefield with his first sight of boats, boatmen and their cargoes. At four and five years of age he watched the canal being drained and filled up, to make room for a southward-running railway (closed in 1959 and long pulled up). What he witnessed then remained strong and distinct in his memory; throughout his life he retained a sense of the *genius loci*, the spirit of a place, that all of us know in childhood but which often gets buried in conventional living.

Afterwards he was to say he never knew anywhere quite so thoroughly as he did the immediate vicinity of The Knapp, but in fact his knowledge of the whole Ledbury neighbourhood was intense and intimate. This is evident in any examination of *The Everlasting Mercy* which is, among other things, an emotionally compelled return to the country of his earlier years.

Ledbury is the centre of a richly farmed countryside, mixed farming, but a peculiar fame attaches to the orchards, both apple (with cider apples a speciality) and pear. 'Cider and Herefordshire have been synonymous for centuries,' says the official local guide proudly, there are cider and apple festivals, Hereford and Much Marcle contain well-known long-established cider companies to which much local produce is sent, while perry, made from perry pears, is probably more popular now than in Masefield's day. Hop-growing, principally to the north-west of the town, is another feature of local agriculture, and Masefield as a boy relished the September hop-picking when so many folk (not all of them 'desirable characters') converged on the neighbourhood, often from big towns:

> The pickers were always kind and welcoming to us and we enjoyed it all, save one thing—that the pickers insisted on: we had to be put into the crib.
>
> There were many cribs in each hop-yard. The crib or cratch, an open trough, I suppose about nine or ten feet long and two feet across, is a kind of elongated manger made of canvas secured to a wooden frame; it stands about as high as an ordinary table. The hop-vines are brought across the crib and the pickers pick the hops from the vines into the crib ... It was the law of the hop-yard that every picker must be put into the crib before he could be allowed to pick. This was the old custom of the yards, and was always exacted. Such customs exist in many kinds of harvest from very ancient times, to mark a propitiation or a thanksgiving ...

At the start of the growing season townspeople would come into the neighbourhood to pick the spring flowers, particularly daffodils, for the shops and markets. They are referred to in an early stanza of one of his greatest works, *The Daffodil Fields*.

To the west—from the nursery windows of The Knapp—Masefield could look out over an abundantly orcharded, intensely cultivated land, framed by Marcle Ridge; to the east the prospect is quite different. Above Ledbury two wooded hills rise, both familiar to lovers of Masefield's poetry, Dog Hill and Coneygree Wood, and beyond the latter, Eastnor Hill. Behind these, four miles or so from Ledbury at the nearest point, there rear the Malvern Hills, an abrupt precipitous ridge resembling, as do its geological kin further to the north in Shropshire, some huge beached cetacean. The steep road connecting Ledbury to the southern end of the hills is called Chance's Pitch and is supposedly haunted by the coachman and guard of a coach and four that fell off it; above looms the Herefordshire Beacon or British Camp, 1,000 feet high.

There are further hills to the south of Ledbury, guarding the entry of the Severn into the Bristol Channel. One of the more remarkable of these, just below Newent, is May Hill of which an enticing view can be had from Ledbury. Certainly young Jack Masefield felt enticed:

> The hill, I suppose, would be about seven miles from us, and at that distance it gave to us, on any clear day, a most vivid image of a man ploughing with a yoked team. No one could be in any doubt that at the top of the hill, facing the distant Severn (due south) a giant ploughman drove a team that never got any further.
>
> The grown-up observer knew that the ploughman, the plough and the team were distant trees, but the little child thought that they were real ploughing figures, and giant figures. I know that they produced on myself an impression of enormous size, splendour and reality.
>
> What if those figures were to come down and command men to do their bidding and bear a hand at ploughing the hill?
>
> The impression that those giant figures were real, yet beneficent, was most real to me, and I could not doubt it for several early years.

In his watershed work, *The Everlasting Mercy*, 'the May Hill ploughman' epitomises the benign force of the title.

In an account of their early years, Jack's older sister, Ethel Ross, wrote in a piece published by *The Author* in Spring 1993:

My earliest recollections are of clambering up on the broad nursery seat with Jack and watching storms of rain coming across the hills while we chanted in a gradually increasing yell. 'Now it's coming across the hills; now it's coming across the fields; now it's in in the garden, and now it's *here*!'

Jack and I were next to one another in age, and soon allies and confederates in all mischief; our old nurse used to say that 'Master Jack wouldn't be half such a handful if Miss Ethel didn't spoil him so'—from which I gather that Jack was generally ringleader and that I merely aided and abetted.

The garden was a great joy: there were little grass banks you could slide down, and two great yew trees which had grown together in such a manner that they made a great green tent where it was dry enough to play in all but the very wettest weather. The boys' great game was to climb up one trunk and down the other. Round about we built houses and churches and forts of sticks and twigs, and arranged elaborate funerals for dolls, mice, kittens and such small game. Jack usually officiated, draped in one of my pinafores ...

Jack was a favourite with everyone. He really was a beautiful little boy, with great solemn hazel eyes and lovely curls. The servants all adored him. He devoured poetry ...

Throughout his *oeuvre*, though particularly as he grew older, Masefield recreated his early childhood experiences in something of the spirit of Henry Vaughan's 'The Retreat' or William Wordsworth's 'Immortality Ode'. With the first, born in 1621 just over those 'Black Hills' (actually called Black Mountains) he could have said:

> Happy those early days, when I
> Shined in my angel-infancy!
> Before I understood this place
> Appointed for my second race,
> Or taught my soul to fancy aught
> But a white, celestial thought; ...
> When on some gilded cloud, or flower,
> My gazing soul would dwell an hour,
> And in those weaker glories spy
> Some shadows of eternity;

Grace Before Ploughing (1966) from which all the prose passages in this chapter have been taken, begins quite simply:

For some years, like many children, I lived in Paradise ...

But this Paradise was to be irrevocably violated. Five months before Jack's seventh birthday Carrie Masefield died, as a result of giving birth to a second daughter, Norah. And with her died—to an extent that could not at the time have ben predicted—security and any kind of solidity of happiness.

2

A governess was installed in the household, an unsympathetic woman for whom Jack conceived a literally violent hatred: in a frenzy of anger he was to plunge a fork into her arm 'with intent to kill', an episode he later recounted to W.B. Yeats, who would subsequently introduce him to friends as 'my murderer'. Later still, as readers of *The Midnight Folk* are unable to forget, he made a governess (Miss Pouncer) an agent of evil.

Then, when Jack was eight, the family moved from The Knapp to his late grandfather's house, the capacious Priory, right in the heart of old Ledbury. Its large garden bordered the churchyard of the basically fourteenth-century St Michael and All Angels, while on another side stood the eighteenth-century premises of the family firm. The body of the house, as distinct from its later 'modern' wings, was extremely old—'Tudor, possibly; most of the older part was of the seventeenth century.' The Priory was to work on Jack's unusually heightened awareness of the past, but the move there also emphasized the broken nature of his family life (even though he had, in point of fact, visited The Priory at least twice-weekly for most of his life). He came to be both fond of and indeed grateful to the house, but it was also to be the scene of great unhappiness. Of course, in a large family, well-known and long-established in the locality, there must have been activity and even merriment—and we have testimonies to this—but the overall impression we form of the young Jack Masefield (the stronger if we draw on the imaginative legacy of these years, which he was so repeatedly to mine) is of a solitary, independent boy, perhaps broody by inclination.

> The change in my home made a great change in my habits. I was now permitted to wander out by myself; and wandered forth much oftener than was permitted. I had all a heavenly new country to explore and make mine. Five hundred yards took me into the woods, from which I could reach a wilderness of old quarries, poor pasture, springs, brooks and tempting distance. In fine weather, when alone, if I were not in the Church or churchyard, lost in dreams, and studying the epitaphs, I was in these wilds.

His curiosity about the Herefordshire countryside around him grew into informed passion—for history (especially Roman and pre-Roman; the two boys in his first work for younger children, *A Book of Discoveries*, share his longings to know more about it), and for natural history (he was zealous in his pursuit of geology, the nearby quarries yielding many and rare types of fossil). The love, and concern for animals and birds (moles, deer, foxes; cats, guinea-pigs; swallows, peewits, corncrakes) and plants ('the pale blue chicory', wild geraniums, toad-flax, clover-cop and wild hops) were strong early, never to desert him; they are a marked feature of his writing from the first. Individual places demanded knowing and exploring: Coneygree Wood on its overhanging hill, and the stream that flowed down from there to pass Hall House Farm with its famous daffodil fields, rivalling those round Dymock just down the road, Eastnor with its castle, and the Malverns at hand. He came to have a developed feeling for the whole Marches area, down to the Severn estuary on the one hand, up to the wilder Shropshire hills on the other, including their isolated outpost, The Wrekin. Shropshire, where the Masefields had family, appealed to Jack strongly, some of his work would suggest that he himself emanated from the county. Though, at his own admission, he drew on Hall House Farm for his *Daffodil Fields*, he actually translates the Herefordshire people of the poem to Shropshire, and the opening of *The Widow in the Bye Street* places Ledbury in the other county, too!

In all his ramblings round Ledbury he was intensely mindful of the poverty in which so many of its inhabitants had to live, their cramped dwellings, their undernourishment, their scanty clothes, their all-too-frequent shoelessness. Later he would write:

> I never crossed the town without the sight
> Of withered children suffering from the blight.

Just on the edge of Ledbury itself, near the station, were the Hunt Kennels, something of a lodestar for Jack, and for his brothers too, who were often hanging around there. Fox-hunting, that activity he was eventually to reject for compassionate reasons, at that time absorbed people from all strata of Ledbury society. He was later able to remember, as Muriel Spark records in her *John Masefield*, individual hunts and what happened on them, but always felt an empathy with the fox, an emotion which in the end won out. One imagines that one of the boy Masefield's ideals is embodied in the character and practices of the landowner, Mr Hampden, in *A Book of Discoveries*:

> The owner of that estate loved all wild creatures. ... His chief pleasure was the study of the wild life on his estate. He knew it better than any landlord. Most of the landowners of England value the life on their estates merely because they have pleasure in blasting it out with guns. Mr Hampden valued it because because he saw in every little mouse and warbler something living and lovely, with a tiny brain and knowledge of the world, which became more wonderful the better he came to know it. He got more pleasure and knowledge from his woods than the killing man could understand. Birds followed him for crumbs and currants whenever he went for a walk. A robin would perch upon his shoulder. Squirrels would come to him for nuts. He always wore soft hide moccasins when in the woods, so that he might walk noiselessly. Creeping gently, he could often surprise a vixen playing with her cubs, or see an otter at dinner, or a weasel hunting. He knew the birds and their habits; the insects, the plants loved by them; the trees where the squirrels nested; the springs where the woodcock fed. Nature was a never-ending wonder-book to him.

It has to be said, however, that the two boys of the book have to be converted to this point of view from a very different attitude to Nature.

☆   ☆   ☆

A few miles to the east of the Malvern ridge, and in sight of it, lay what Masefield in *Grace Before Ploughing* spoke of as his 'second Paradise': Woollas Hall, the great Jacobean manor belonging to his godmother, his mother's great friend, Miss Flood, where he was a welcome and intensely appreciative visitor. A beautiful-aspected house built of gold-green stone, it is situated on the north-west flank of Bredon Hill. Were not the whale-like ridge of the Malvern Hills in the way, you could look across from it to the hills above Ledbury itself. Miss Flood recognised—as almost no one else seems to have done, at least not in these terms—just how imaginative and unusual a boy Jack was, ('the romantic boy' he was called in his home-town) with his continuously developing love for books (plentiful at The Priory, but even more so at Woollas Hall). Jack was not just a devourer of books but someone through the crucible of whose mind their contents would be translated—histories, romances and travelogues, the classics of world literature, as well as bound and unbound magazines. In the latter he

23

could read, for instance, the annals of cricket matches ('The Australians in England in 1882'; 'The Australians in England 1884'). Masefield was fond of the game, though he was never the ardent or accomplished cricketer such as other boys in his family were.

Later Masefield wrote of himself in *Grace Before Ploughing*:

> I am told that I learned to read at an early age, and that I enjoyed reading more than most children.
>
> I do not know if this were so, but I know that I found that I could tell myself stories at a very early age.
>
> I was in the garden one day, standing near a clump of honey-suckle and looking north. As I looked, I became aware, for the first time, that I had an imagination, and that I could tell this faculty to imagine all manner of strange things, and at once the strange things, especially fantastic things, would be there in multitude to do my bidding. If I told them to put on armour and conquer France, or save Joan of Arc from being burned or Mary Queen of Scots from Fotheringay, the thing would be done, and if I disliked the doing, I had but to suggest a better method, and at once the figures for the new scene were there, perfect in form and costume, armed and horsed and with colours flying.
>
> The faculty was extraordinary to me, and of such inner delight that I could not mention it to anyone.

There is a note of regret, and of foreboding too, in this last sentence, and justifiably so. For these years at The Priory, for all their delights and inspirations, were enshadowed ones. The shadows were cast not just by the past, by the tragedy of Carrie's death in January 1885, but by Edward Masefield's gravely and chronically deteriorating mental and physical health. This was, to a considerable degree, brought about by his awareness of his own father's gross mismanagement of the family money—misman-agement on a considerable scale. The situation his sons and daughters would have to face when they put childhood behind them was by no means what he'd expected for them. It seems improbable that a sensitive and observant boy such as Jack would not have been aware of the symptoms of his father's decline, even before its irreversibility was obvious, however little he may have understood about its origin. And in a small town like Ledbury there would would have been talk to overhear; Masefield's readers won't forget the clacking tongues of Mrs Gossip and Mrs Tattle in *The Midnight Folk*.

Early in 1890 Edward Masefield, for some while a danger to himself, became an inmate of a Gloucester hospital. In 1891, unbalanced in mind, he died.

'A furnace of suffering' was how the narrator of *Dead Ned* saw the second, all-important phase of his life. The image comes from the smithy, and, in point of fact, in 'The Blacksmith', a strange, ambiguous poem written during the Great War, Masefield had already used this image to describe someone captive in his life, yearning and needing to break out, to know a fuller self-realisation, a more complete picture of the world. It seems pertinent to Masefield's unhappy adolescence:

> He felt his very self impelled
> To common uses, till he cried:
> "There's more within me than is tried,
> More than you ever think to weld.
>
> For all my pain I am only used
> To make the props for daily labour;
> I burn, I am beaten like a tabour
> To make men tools: I am abused.
>
> Deep in the white heat where I gasp
> I see the unmastered finer powers,
> Iron by cunning wrought to flowers,
> File-worked, not tortured by the rasp.
>
> Deep in this fire-tortured mind
> Thought bends the bar in subtler ways;
> It glows into the mass, its rays
> Purge, till the iron is refined.
>
> Then, as the full moon draws the tide
> Out of the vague uncaptained sea,
> Some moony-power there ought to be
> To work on ore; it should be tried.
>
> By this fierce fire in which I ache
> I see new fires not yet begun,
> A blacksmith smithying with the sun,
> At unmade things man ought to make.

Life is not fire and blows, but thought,
Attention kindling into joy;
Those who make nothing new destroy:
O me, what evil I have wrought!

Oh me!" and as he moaned he saw
His iron master shake; he felt
No blow, nor did the fire melt
His flesh, he was released from law.

He sat upon the anvil top
Dazed, as the iron was dazed; he took
Strength, seeing that the iron shook;
He said: "This cruel time must stop."

3

After their father's death, Masefield and his younger siblings stayed on at The Priory under the guardianship of their childless Uncle William and his wife Aunt Kate, Uncle William having been Edward's partner in the firm. Aunt Kate (the Masefield family is firm on this point even today) didn't care much for children at all, and undoubtedly resented her new responsibility, but—singling him out from the others—she was positively antagonistic to Jack, with his temperament that was at once dreamy and idiosyncratically adventurous. She was contemptuous of his imaginative abilities (he was already a good story-teller to other children, especially his younger siblings) and his taste for reading, so fostered by Miss Flood in his 'other' home, seemed to her downright unhealthy.

Three years before, when ten years old, Masefield had been sent away as a boarder to Warwick School, where he was at first extremely unhappy, even trying to kill himself by eating laurel leaves. To cite Ethel Ross again:

> He was sent to school at Warwick, and there I'm afraid he was not at all happy. He was at the same time backward and precocious, shy and trusting, solitary and friendly, and the young barbarians gave him a bad time, at any rate to begin with. He never mentioned those school days to me afterwards, and I have never been able to trace any mention of them in his books.

For all this, he enjoyed many of the activities available at Warwick, though he thought of himself later as essentially an 'indolent' schoolboy.

Now, It was decided that his school-education should be terminated, and it was his aunt's idea that he should be sent for training for the merchant navy; the Royal Navy would cost too much! The famous Liverpool 'school-ship' H.M.S. *Conway*, which was permanently moored in the Mersey, was chosen.

How this decision appeared from the decision-makers' point-of-view can be glimpsed in a manuscript that indefatigable man of Herefordshire, Alfred Watkins (1855-1935), photographer, author of *The Old Straight Track* and 'discoverer' of ley-lines, left behind him. In *The Masefield Country* (1931)—written, of course, when the poet was still alive and indeed had thirty-six more years left to live:

> I give a conversation I had with a Ledbury farmer the other day, who (like me) is a score or more years older than the poet. I jotted it down the same day.
> '... Young John—yes, I remember him—his Uncle William, who had no chicks of his own, had brought up all Edward's children in his own house, and once when I met him in the street, he said to me: "That lad John settles down to nothing. I don't rightly know what to make of him." But there'—said my farmer friend—'what could you expect? Of course he was not built like the others; he could see right through things, whether it was a horse, or a dog, or a man's character, or fields and trees, or things about a farm. And put it down on paper into the bargain. Nothing but getting away from lawyers' offices and stools would do for his sort. So William saw that he was 'prenticed into the merchant shipping, and we didn't hear of him for a few years.'

Ethel Ross says:

> We were a family of very square pegs, and most of the holes we were expected to fit were round. Jack's name being Jack, he was expected to become a sailor, and was sent off to the training ship *Conway*. I don't think he had the least desire for the sea ...

Masefield entered his teens with a sense of severance from what was dependable and sustainable in existence. The premature deaths of both parents, with the prior breakdown and mental instability of his father, a revision of financial probity and prospects, with all that that implies for social identity as well as personal needs and ambitions can, in addition to

27

the distressing nature of the happenings themselves, shake, sometimes beyond bearing point, the security of a young person, who, to cope with the demands that growth towards adulthood desperately entails, requires stability, and a sense of solidarity with others. In Masefield's case this was denied him by his being taken away from school which, whatever its limitations, was a known entity he shared with others, compounded by the separation from his Ledbury contemporaries. The young do not like to feel cut off from their kind, even if they are (or appear) solitary and independent. They also need to be liked. And it is all too clear that Aunt Kate did *not* like Jack, and behaved accordingly. It is worth noting, even at this juncture, that the central figures of Masefield's best-known works — Saul Kane (in *The Everlasting Mercy*), Dauber, Reynard the Fox himself, Kay Harker (in *The Midnight Folk* and *The Box of Delights*), Ned Mansell — have only themselves to rely on; theirs are the quests and tests of someone, always a male, on his own. There is something else important to stress as Jack sets off for H.M.S. *Conway*: life was conspiring to detach him — to a very unusual and, as it turned out, a creatively fruitful extent — from that indomitable mesh-like feature of English life: the class-system.

His family were, and had long been, prominent and highly regarded in the district, solicitors forming the very backbone of small town society. The Knapp and The Priory are houses of substance, while Woollas Hall proclaims itself in its sequestered eminence and architectural handsomeness, as a home of gentry, of the squirearchy. But now the young Masefield was made to feel the absence of any money to sustain him for further education. Unlike so many boys of his background he had *not* gone to a traditional-style public-school (nor even to a local school which would have integrated him with his immediate environment). He was *not* to go to university (something that was to be a matter for regret to him later on), he was *not* even to go into the Senior Service, the Royal Navy, that bastion of the Imperial Establishment, but would, through his trainee-ship, be associating with boys and men who would come from sections of society to which The Knapp and The Priory would be entirely foreign. There is no evidence how Jack Masefield himself responded to his situation in this respect; the tone of *New Chum* is thoroughly democratic. But one story it tells of Masefield's relationship to his fellow trainees on the 'school-ship' must, I think, have class undercurrents. A boy who'd been notably hostile to Jack found out that he too came from the Marches of Wales, and that their mothers had known each other. As a consequence he changed his attitude and became a friend.

Masefield tells us he wasn't homesick during his first term on H.M.S. *Conway*, and doesn't appear to have been homesick later either, though he greeted holidays back in Ledbury warmly enough. The latter part of his youth was to be sensationally unlike that of the average Herefordshire professional man's son. With the onset of his teens Masefield broke out of the moulds of the English class hierarchy about as effectively as one from his background could ever have done. It explains his remarkable ability to cope with New York City in his late teens, the range of his London acquaintance on his return, and the important role played by Ireland in his young manhood, Ireland offering a mirror in which to view England as perhaps no other country could.

New Chum (1944), written over fifty years after the experiences it describes, is a work of the most astonishing and kinetic liveliness, though the patina of kindliness that the elderly Masefield put on the scenes and people of distant years cannot be discounted. Readers accompany the boy Jack to the Mersey-docked ship, and follow him through his first term there (his training lasted two and a half years), to the point when he ceased to be a 'new chum'. They share his hopes, excitements, bewilderments, disappointments and general enlargement of knowledge—of ships and shipping, of other people, of himself, of life. More than half the book concerns itself with Jack's first three days on board, so intense and (one assumes) so precise is the author's recollection of that time of initiation. The very opening of the memoir suggests the young hero of a folk-tale journeying forth in ardour and ignorance for a wider world than that of his home-country, and with imminent hard lessons to learn that as yet he can't so much as guess at; Jack's knowledge of ships and their demands came principally from *Boys' Own Paper*:

> I set out to join H.M.S. *Conway* on a fine sunny morning a fort-night after the September term had begun. As I had been exposed to an infection of chicken-pox, the ship had refused to receive me sooner. The *Conway* autumn term always begun very early, about the 9th; and in that lovely weather my extra fortnight of holiday had been welcome to me. Had I known what disadvantages it would bring me for the next two years, I should have changed my tune.
>
> As I walked to the station, I thought with joy that that night I should be sleeping in a hammock over my own sea-chest, which would contain not only the blacking-brushes, with which I should be able to polish my own shoes, but my "knife, fork and spoon, with

name engraved", "a jack-knife with lanyard", a pair of sea-boots; Raper's Navigation and Tables, and many articles with strange names, a jumper, a pair of bluchers, white drill trousers, blue Crimea shirts, and one superfine uniform for Sunday. I have set down the things in the order in which they pleased my expectation; hammock and sea-chest certainly first, Sunday uniform last. I did not know what Raper's Tables might be. I think I expected some snug and neat kind of mess table, which folded up when the mess-mates had finished. I was thirteen years three months and three weeks old; expectation was lively in me; as someone says of Shakespeare, "he had the Phantsie very strong".

The 'Phantsie' was to be a source of both sorrow and happiness during the next two and a half years. From *New Chum* we build up a picture of Jack Masefield as a trusting sort of boy, sufficiently romantically excited by the prospect of living and working on board a ship, despite all the tales he'd heard of the bullying and for which he was, time and time again, unprepared. That hammock of which he was so proud was repeatedly let down from its hooks in his first days, sometimes several times a night. Tricks and games were played on him and on other raw trainees, especially on visits ashore—to the football field, where the older boys would ride the younger ones as ponies, goading them into races, or to the swimming baths where duckings were a constant threat—while during religious services or lectures a pin surreptitiously and painfully jabbed in the bum was the danger. All around him—as would be obvious to almost anyone but delib-erately blinkered models of late Victorian rectitude such as his uncle and aunt—he encountered cursing, cuffing, verbal abuse in the foulest language, personal disparagement of one kind or another. (The dialogue in his memoir is extremely convincing in its rhythms, and echoes familiarly today, even though it's rendered without our contemporary licence to reproduce certain very common obscenities.) Some of the older boys would boast, both threateningly and enticingly, of sexual and semi-crim-inal exploits in Liverpool and elsewhere, stories by which Jack (he recounts being their captive audience during a spell in the sanitorium) could not help being fascinated, with all an adolescent's appetite for learning of illicit adventure.

At the same time he appears to have been a pretty resilient sort of youth, the resilience deriving from an inner life (even though his powers of inven-tion had temporarily ceased, a source of sorrow to him). The new tasks, the questions posed by the life all around him on H.M.S. *Conway*, and in Liverpool beyond absorbed him; he was often zealous beyond requirement. On the whole he got on with his fellows easily, the more easily (one suspects) for a certain reserve, for an aura of privacy. But he was not so private that he kept his remarkable story-telling powers to himself. If he could no longer invent, as he had for so many years been accustomed to do—surely a result of his feelings of loss and betrayal—his 'Phantsie' enabled him to relate the inventions of others in a lively and appealing enough manner, and he was holding the interest of his ship-mates with ghost-stories, tales of murder etc within twenty-four hours of his arrival.

A trainee was expected to learn—and practise—all aspects of a seaman's life, from the humblest and most basic such as swabbing the decks, to the arts of navigation and astronomy, by both of which Masefield was fascinated. Indeed their fascination was never to die for him, long after the dictates of a nautical life were the stuff only of memories. The *Conway* was a sailing-ship, and had been built as a naval vessel. 'Our rig and routine were naval, dating from 1865-70; the men who taught us had been ship-mates with the old gear and stood for the old routine.' Yet the boys were not being trained for a naval life, nor could their ship compare with the big four-masters they could see in dock on the Mersey, nor with the steamers which had already taken over the majority of the routes. But Masefield relished a physical relationship with the *Conway*; particularly he liked climbing the cross-trees of her masts, an activity he'd long dreamed of doing. Here the tastes of an active, adventurous boy and of the aesthetically sensitive embryonic artist converge, for, throughout *New Chum*, like a melody in some tone-poem, Masefield conveys to us his rapture at seeing from these heights the River, as he invariably calls the Mersey, with Liverpool on the one bank, Birkenhead on the other:

> I have told of my joy in being aloft. That heart would have been
> dead indeed who could not find beauty in the River. At all seasons,
> at all states, the River was beautiful. At dead low water, when great
> sandbanks were laid bare, to draw multitudes of gulls; in calm,
> when the ships stood still above their shadows; in storm, when the
> ferries beat by, shipping sprays, and at full flood when shipping put
> out and came in, the River was a wonder to me. Sometimes, as I sat
> aloft in the cross-trees, in those early days, I thought how marvel-
> lous it was, to have this ever-changing miracle about me, with
> mountains, smoky, glittering cities, the clang of hammers, the roar

and hoot of sirens; the miles of docks, the ships and attendant ships, all there for me, seemingly only noticed by me, everybody else seemed to be used to it by this time, or to have other things to do.

The burgeoning seaman and the aesthete combined again in his delight in the 'setting-in' book. As this last can be considered a milestone in his development, the whole passage recounting it is worth quoting:

On the main deck, many happy men had pulled out desks and forms under the heavy, swinging copper lamps; ... about three of the silent workers little groups of men stood intently watching what was being done. I timidly asked another new chum, who had all the superiority of fourteen days seniority what was the interest of the nearest group. He said, "It's ... doing a ship in a setting-in book." I asked if I might be allowed to look ... and perceived a senior, whom I had noticed already elsewhere, drawing a ship in full sail on the pages of an exercise book. He was using a crow-quill pen and a little pan of Indian ink. ... All the dozen men watching him felt as I did, that we were watching a miracle; ... I went cautiously to see the work of other artists: one of them was painting in water colour. ... [He] asked if I painted. I said: "No; I was afraid not."

"You ought to paint," he said, "every sailor ought to paint; or at any rate make records in neutral tint ..."

"Please, will you tell me what that is?"

"It's very simple; a little blue, a little red, and a little brown, all mixed. Did you ever see a setting-in book?"

"No; never."

He held up the book in which he was painting, slantingly to the light, so that he could be sure that the page was dry; he then handed it to me. "This is a setting-in book," he said. "You set into it examples of how you work out your different sights. Generally, you don't begin one till you're a Quarter Boy, but if you're wise, you'll start one now.'

I looked at the book with interest and admiration; and at once began to long for one of my own; for it was not only a record of knowledge painfully won and exquisitely written down, but an album, illustrated by the choicest artists in the ship, and made precious by the signatures and apothegms of eminent officers and shipmates. One such sentence caught my eye; it was signed by one whom I already knew to be the toughest character on board: "Love is sweeter than sugar."

In itself, the setting-in book was a handsome large quarto manuscript book, having unlined pages of choice paper, and strongly
bound in some black leathery substance. It cost about seven
shillings and sixpence. into this, with great care, with much careful
ruling, and the occasional use of coloured inks, the man "set-in" or
wrote out examples of every calculation by which a ship's position
could be determined. If the owners were keen seamen, and many
men were, they did not stop at Navigation; they added Meteorology,
Rule of the Road, and even interesting points of seamanship. When
a book had been filled in by a conscientious man, he learned much.
... More than once in after years, old Conways asked me for the loan
of my book, so that they might have a guide to the various problems. I believe that it is now many years since setting-in books were
brought to an end, having served their turn. On the whole, in my
time, they were among the best things in the ship; they made the
gathering of knowledge a work of art, and brought art to the gracing
of knowledge.

The poet is a 'maker', and this is the earliest glimpse we have of
Masefield's delight in 'making'. His admiration for the young masters of
the 'setting-in book', an admiration he evidently shared with most of the
young crew, anticipates his later admiration for the skilled practitioners of
all crafts and art—painters, musicians, actors and set-designers, and
speakers of verse—and his belief in the ubiquity of the creative impulse.

But in his rhapsody over the view from the River and even over the
'setting-in book', he reveals himself as concerned essentially with the solitary pursuit or pleasure. Not infrequently in Masefield's re-creations of his
adolescence, both direct and oblique, one has the sense that he's close to
nobody. Emotional desolation deriving from childhood traumata? Or a
natural disposition? Insofar as a sensible distinction can be made between
the two, the poems and novels make one incline to the latter answer. But
in *New Chum* he touchingly does describe his feelings, part friendship, part
hero-worship, for three seniors on board the *Conway*: 'H.B.' (H.B.
Meiklejohn), Dick and Bill, the latter a brilliant exponent of the art of the
'setting-in' book, and his instructor in meteorology. All three young men
come across as real specimens of human goodness, in whose later fortunes
Masefield took active interest not least out of gratitude for a friendliness
the full value of which they could not have appreciated. Bill—who was to
die early and the memory of whom haunted him—brought out in
Masefield a too often repressed human warmth:

My friend said to me: "... What makes you interested in weather?"

"You do."

He was pleased by this. "All right," he said. "I'm keeping the log at present. If you like you shall help." Did I like to help, "to help", a mixture of Phoebus Apollo, Leonardo da Vinci, Sophocles, Sir Isaac Newton and Captain Cook? He showed me how to read a mercurial barometer, how to take the wet and dry bulbs, how to draw a bucket of water for the spec-grav readings. ... He taught me the different sorts of clouds, and roughly what each meant. He persuaded me to watch the upper clouds for him, and to observe the directions of their drifts. Sometimes, I had the extraordinary interest of doing these things with him.

The privilege of doing these things for him and with him was an enchantment to me. Then, in the nick of happy time, a kind friend sent me a pound of butter. I had learned to be a little cautious about tuck. I did not tell the world, now that I had some tuck; no, I put the butter in my chest with my sea boots, where people would not be likely to look for butter. But I learned that my new friend loved having bread and butter at dinner, when the ship supplied neither; so, while the butter lasted, I brought him some for dinner, each day. One could always lay in a store of bread at breakfast. I used to take an extra "share" at breakfast, that is, about an eighth part of a big loaf. Tucking this into my tunic, I took it to my chest, where with a jack-knife I gouged a hole in the crumb, filled the hole with a blob of butter, and stopped the hole with a crumb again. I did this privily, when men were not about; then at dinner, I could hurry to the godlike being's mess, and hand him the salted gold-mine of the share of bread ...

I asked him what name I was to call him; which would be permitted; he said: "Bill."

It was a great sadness when he learned that Bill was soon to sail away from Merseyside and the *Conway* and join a new 'elegant' clipper. Masefield's account of how he was given leave to see the ship off, how he ran to witness the leaving at Pierhead—and failed to be in time to wave Bill goodbye as he desired, shows his boy's largeness of heart—and its empty chambers.

He would seem to have much to be grateful to the *Conway* for, and gratitude seems to have been his predominant feeling for the training-ship, even publishing in 1933 a history of it. And in his 'Biography' of 1911 this emotion is made explicit. He is thankful for:

> The gift of being near ships, of seeing each day
> A city of ships with great sails under weigh;
> The great street paved with water, filled with shipping
> And all the world's flags flying and seagulls dipping.

And he devotes a whole later section of the poem (informed by a light humour as unusual for him at that time as the emotional tone of the writing about Bill was later) to the gleeful yearly race between the crew of his ship and that of another cutter from London:

> And the curse quickened from the cox, our bows
> Crashed, and drove talking water, we made vows,
> Chastity vows and temperance; in our pain
> We numbered things we'd never eat again
> If we could only win; then came the yell
> "Starboard," "Port Fore,' and then a beaten bell
> Rung as for fire to cheer us.

Nor did all these experiences prevent him from reading, and it is clear that Masefield read in a peculiarly intent and receptive way. A copy of *Treasure Island* made him see his fellows with fresh eyes for he could find among members of the crew the character-types of the story. Literature could enhance life, as he wrote in *So Long to Learn*:

> What was I reading? I read and read, whatever I could find to read: mostly prose, borrowed from my shipmates, and much of this of a nautical trend, the novels of Captain Marryat ... and some of Herman Melville. These I came to know pretty well. Then I made acquaintance with Mark Twain and Stevenson, whose books have been lasting joys in my life. I borrowed and read most of the novels of Dickens, and this with a delight difficult to describe. Sherlock Holmes was then a fairly new thing: we did not know his methods: he too delighted me ... I read eagerly any book that I could find on Astronomy and Meteorology. Finding in the library a book of collected Weather-Rhymes and sayings, I copied it out, and for years was able to quote aptly from it. I remember many of the sayings to this day. Apart from these jingles, I was not reading much verse ... My first love, the early poems of Milton, was for the time, set aside.

Mark Twain (1835-1910) and Robert Louis Stevenson (1850-94) will always provide points of reference for critical evaluation of Masefield. Knock-about years before they became famous as writers gave both of them insights denied writers with more conventionally spent lives, but not Jack Masefield who even by his mid-teens had seen modes of living utterly distinct from his own background, challenging it and throwing it into new light. Twain and Stevenson combine an ardent thirst for spirit-testing adventure, as opposed to the stifling mores of the professional/commercial world, with a cynical realisation of the boundless extent of human greed, blindness and callousness. Twain's articulation of the tensions between the two worlds has proved more influential and incisive than Stevenson's, above all in *Huckleberry Finn* (1884), a novel Masefield was to re-read annually throughout his life. Young Huck and the escaped negro, Jim, journey by raft down the Mississippi—on the one hand breaking free of the prison that is their home-town, on the other imperilling themselves further, not least by exposure to society (southwards there are slave-holding states on both river banks)—constitutes the perfect metaphor for both the need for release from convention and the impossibility of ever attaining this. It's a metaphor that will haunt Masefield's life and work. The force of *Huckleberry Finn* derives, to a considerable measure, as both Gertrude Stein and Ernest Hemingway appreciated, from its vigorous, yet cunning, use of vernacular. Masefield learned an all-important lesson here for the composition of *The Everlasting Mercy*. Twain had been a great listener; Masefield was to be this too.

In this respect, as well as in others, he was fortunate in having, in his second year, as Instructor on the *Conway*, Wally Blair, a tremendous story-teller. Jack was to honour him in one of the vividest—and most genuinely tragic—of the *Salt-Water Ballads*, 'One of Wally's Yarns'. In *So Long to Learn* he wrote of him:

> He had been at sea (perhaps for thirty years) in famous ships, at a time of the world when sailors were a race apart, away from land for months at a time, and from home, perhaps, for years. In those days, sailors had to invent their amusements or go without. They either sang, or yarned. As they knew little of life ashore, they yarned usually of life at sea, which they knew thoroughly. In thirty years, Wally had known a good deal and had heard a great deal more, some of it of the nature of folk-lore, most of it stirring event, as told by men who had seen or borne a hand in what was told. The tales were not only interesting, they were amazing ... often and often, some ship

towing or sailing or coming to an anchor near us would light up some memory, and then an extraordinary tale would follow, of things well or ill done, of ships fated or lucky in the fortune of the sea.

To the stories of Wally Blair were added the talk and tales of boys and men encountered in Liverpool, busiest of ports, and from them all he learned about tropical diseases, a subject that was to preoccupy him intellectually and imaginatively for many years, and is the driving interest behind his novel *Multitude and Solitude* (1909). One also sees on what a profound well of rich anecdote Masefield was always to be able to draw. His apprenticeship on the *Conway* ended with his winning the McIver Prize for an English essay, a welcome surprise for him. This restored an inner confidence in himself and his faculties ('You must get this writing-rubbish out of your head,' he was nonetheless told by someone he calls in *So Long to Learn* 'a kind friend, in whose judgement I trusted.') Perhaps, at a deep, and seemingly buried level, this new confidence sustained him in the dark period he was now to enter.

So dark was this that, as late as 1952, in *So Long to Learn*, Masefield cannot bring himself to write about it, promising readers that he will write more openly later. He had, of course, already conveyed the darkness in fiction and poetry; indeed it was a subject of completely compulsive imaginative and emotional interest. For the time being, he says in these vivid recollections by an old man, he wishes to concentrate on his art—restorative of mental and moral health—as he came to practise it. He was, of course, being disingenuous here; self-aware, honest, and far more tortured than he would outwardly admit, he must have known that his imaginative work was indivisible from what happened to him after he'd completed his training on the *Conway* and had embarked on the *Gilcruix*, a fuel-carrying four-master, just the kind of ship he and his chums particularly admired, bound for Chile, for Iquique, a nitrate port and the northernmost port of any consequence on that country's prodigiously long Pacific sea-board.

He knew too that one of his most widely-appreciated works was to all intents a testament of his sufferings on this voyage, *Dauber* (1913). Of this Stephen Spender (1909-1995) says in his *Love-Hate Relations: A Study of Anglo-American Sensibilities* (1974), which contains invaluable insights into the literature of that time:

> John Masefield's *Dauber* shocked contemporaries. ... The shock was still reverberating through my boyhood.

It is a shock readers can still feel today.

☆   ☆   ☆

Publication of that sensational poem lay eighteen years ahead of the voyage which began on April 25th 1894; *Dauber* was first published as *The Story Of A Round-House And Other Poems* in the U.S. in 1912. Here it must simply be registered that an eager-spirited, intelligent boy, just over two months short of his sixteenth birthday, who had come through his training with honour, underwent rites of passage which the *Conway*—and even the old salts he'd listened to in Liverpool—simply had *not* prepared him for. At the time it all must have seemed quite infernal: appaling sea-sickness (something he had not anticipated) hit him from the first, and later there were the storms. The first major ones occurred in the 'roaring forties', but the worst of them accompanied the rounding of Cape Horn; it followed a scarcely less unpleasant 'calm', when the sea-swell was horribly strong, and lasted thirty-two days, a seemingly unending mael-strom of forty-foot waves that battered the ship and commanded the total attention of the crew. Dangerous, exhausting tasks were demanded on which lives depended. There was the constant possibility of death. Anyone who has experienced an ocean storm of magnitude will know that not its least distressing feature is the feeling it imposes of utter suspension from all that is dependable in existence: that sense of severance again. In *Dauber* we read of the protagonist:

> Drenched, frozen, gasping, blinded, dumb,
> High in the night, reeling great blinding arcs
> As the ship rolled, his chappy fingers numb,
> The deck below a narrow blur of marks,
> The sea a welter of whiteness shot with sparks,
> Now snapping up in bursts, now dying away.
> Salting the horizontal snow with spray.
>
> And if he failed in any least degree,
> Or faltered for an instant, or showed slack,
> He might go drown himself within the sea,
> And add a bubble to the clipper's track.
> He had signed his name, there was no turning back,
> No pardon for default - this must be done.
> One iron rule at sea binds everyone.

During the long, long voyage he was impressed by the natural beauties, whales, porpoises, sea-birds including the albatross, sunrises and sunsets on the vastness of water—and stored them in his mind to reproduce later in his art:

> Mournful, and then again mournful, and still
> Out of the night that mighty voice arose;
> The Dauber at his foghorn felt the thrill.
> Who rode that desolate sea? What forms were those?
> Mournful, from things defeated, in the throes
> Of memory of some conquered hunting-ground,
> Out of the night of death arose the sound.

> "Whales!" said the mate. They stayed there all night long
> Answering the horn. Out of the night they spoke,
> Defeated creatures who had suffered wrong,
> But were still noble underneath the stroke.
> They filled the darkness when the Dauber woke;
> The men came peering to the rail to hear,
> And the sea sighed, and the fog rose up sheer.

And once again, he made friends among his contemporaries and elicited kindness from his superiors. But, in addition to the terrors of the elements there must surely have been—this more from the deductions of common sense and from Masefield's imaginative recreations of the voyage than from any printed admissions—discordant, even menacing relations with human associates. And pondering this, one feels justified in entertaining a suspicion that the predominantly amiable manner of *New Chum* disguises bitterer reactions to and reflections on the conduct even of *Conway* trainees that one is asked to acknowledge. Those spiteful practical jokes, those boasts of sordid underhand exploits didn't emanate from any great benevolence of spirit, and Masefield dealt with them most effectively through a certain distancing of himself from others. When the ship at last reached Iquique (the north of Chile is almost as far distant from Cape Horn as, say, Nova Scotia from the westernmost points of the British Isles), Masefield found himself, still only a boy, in an unequivocally rough, debauched and lawless society.

Iquique must surely be the setting for 'Big Jim', one of the most memorable pieces in one of his finest early books, *A Tarpaulin Muster* (1907). It takes place in a 'Western sea-port' behind which stretches a desert-country with silver-mines; we read of 'Chilaneans'. The narrator, finding 'few attractions in the seaport except seamen's dance-houses and drinking-dens' makes his way a little inland, to a point beside a silver-mine from which he has a fine view over the sea:

> It was a beautiful sight, that anchorage, with the ships lying there so lovely, all their troubles at an end. But I knew that aboard each ship there were young men going to the devil, and mature men wasted and old men wrecked; and I wondered at the misery and sin which went to make each ship so perfect an image of beauty.

Close to hand is a tavern which he enters, a large bare drinking bar, full of seamen who have deserted ship (as the author must have dreamed of doing) and then taken to silver-mining. In the corner of the bar is a dead body; beside it a keening woman, a 'quadroon'. Gradually the narrator pieces together what has happened to the dead man, Big Jim: a fight and the woman the cause of it. Educated beyond most sailors, and valued as a worker, 'It was girls done Jim ... "He was a hard case with it ... he never wear more than his oilskins off the Horn. I seen him stand his look-out with only trousers on. I seen it snowing on his chest."'

Jim is buried. Soon afterwards the narrator leaves the country:

> When I sailed from that port I went aloft to see the last of the silver mine. I could see it, in the clear light, quite plainly; and I could see the one evergreen marking the grave. The chance meetings of life are full of mystery, and this chance adventure, with its sadness and beauty, will always move me. The evergreen must be dead by this time, and perhaps the mine will be worked out and the tavern gone. Big Jim will lie quietly, with the surf roaring very far below him, and no man near him at any time save the muleteers, with their bell-mares and songs, going over the pass into the desert.

The dead body in the bar, the grave within earshot of the sea, both connote Masefield's reception of the end of the voyage out. While we will never know the full extent of what he witnessed and went through, what we do know for sure is that in Iquique he suffered a serious breakdown in health of both a physical and mental nature. The Captain of the *Gilcruix* was a humane and sensible man and arranged hospitalisation in Valparaiso. Officially classed as a D.B.S. (Distressed British Seaman) Jack Masefield was discharged from service and arrangements were made for him to go back home to England. Returning home first meant land-travel across north-west South America, and then, boarding a ship at Colon, sea-travel through the Caribbean, through the Spanish Main that was so to exercise his imagination later. *Sard Harker* (1924), *Odtaa* (1926) and the story that lies behind the action of *The Midnight Folk* of 1929 all owe their being to this long homeward journey; their South American country of Santa Barbara cannot but be Colombia. Moreover the regular appearance in his work of dark-haired, dark-eyed 'Spanish' girls, often prostitutes, suggests that his travels were not without sensual appeal.

And then followed an Atlantic crossing, and bad weather again.

It seems an all but risible irony that the author of *Dauber*, and of so many other works which portray and expose the brutality, mortal dangers and fierceness of life at sea should now be best remembered for two early, bland lyrics of sea-nostalgia, 'Sea-Fever' and 'Cargoes'.

There's a conversation between William Golding and Professor John Carey that seems apposite here, in *William Golding: The Man and His Books - A Tribute on his 75th Birthday* (1986):

> JC. It struck me that there might be an analogy between sailing and writing: in that they're both lonely things, and you never quite know what's going to turn up in either of them.
>
> WG (laughing): "All I ask is a tall ship, and a star to steer her by." ('Sea-Fever')
>
> JC. That's all false, isn't it? - Masefield hated the sea, didn't he?
>
> WG. Anybody who knows the sea enough hates it. It's really incredibly hateful and loathsome: beautiful, grand, tremendous— God, it's hateful. You see it's really the cruellest bit of nature. Its cruelty is past believing.

This last sentiment could not be better expressed, and might serve as a motto for some of Masefield's vividest works.

The relief of being classified D.B.S. after such extended sufferings must have been enormous, and we can catch this (in an assumed voice) in the last stanza of 'Cape Horn Gospel II' in *Salt Water Ballads*:

I'm bound for home in the *Oronook*, in a suit of looted duds,
A D.B.S. a learnin' a stake by helpin' peelin' spuds,
An' if ever I fetch to Prince's Stage an' sets my feet ashore,
You bet your hide that there I stay, an' follers the sea no more.

Masefield returned to England, still palpably ill and profoundly shaken, to a Ledbury where his reception was considerably less than sympathetic. It wasn't just that his uncle and aunt were worried about what should now be done with him, their charge who just wouldn't settle down to things, but that Aunt Kate was pleased to jeer and jeer at the boy as one who had ignominiously failed a test. Nothing for it but to go back to sea and prove himself; she seems to have had no doubt about the matter! Jack had had time during the worst of his sickness and during his long homeward journey to ponder his future and knew now deeply and surely that he must be a writer. However, he was in no position to make his own conditions to his guardians, and he appreciated that he had no alternative to temporary surrender to his aunt's decree: that return to sea he must.

Uncle William and Aunt Kate's behaviour was not without literary consequence. They were upright, well-respected pillars of their community, and—the latter especially—had proved not just unimaginative but downright unkind. Their nephew was frequently to show up *bien-pensants* as essentially self-serving and unfeeling, even callous and cruel. For anger at how such respectable folk get away with it see the 'madness' sequence of *The Everlasting Mercy*.

Through the introductions that he asked the Captain of the *Conway* to arrange for him, Masefield got himself a post on an oil-carrier, the *Bidston Hill* then loading in New York. Jack had to sail from Liverpool, on a mail-ship, to join her. While aboard he came to the most dramatic and determining decision of his life: once in New York he would desert. So once he had arrived in the United States he embarked not on a ship, on which a place awaited him, but on a hobo's precarious and health-threatening existence. He was two months short of his seventeenth birthday.

CHAPTER III
Out of the Mill

Shortly after he'd turned seventeen Jack Masefield went into a New York bookshop—Mr Pratt's on Sixth Avenue (near Greenwich Avenue)—and bought himself a cheap edition of Volume One of Sir Thomas Malory's *Morte d'Arthur*. No occurrence in his two-year-long stay in America is more important to his subsequent development than this, and not just because he was to turn repeatedly to Arthurian subjects, devoting in *Midsummer Night and Other Tales in Verse* (1928) a whole volume of verses to them. He wrote in *So Long to Learn*:

> I was at once enchanted by Malory ... In the main, as I supposed, the events or something like them, had happened, and the people, or somebody like them, had lived, in places that were sometimes known: Amesbury, Bamborough, Winchester etc. All the story-telling instinct in me was thrilled as I read. This was a story that gave a great deal of significance to many parts of England. This was (as I supposed) our contribution to epic, and a mine from which poets could take their fables forever. Certainly it was something about which my ignorance had to be lessened. I soon added to my books a complete Malory, and a copy of the *Mabinogion* ...
>
> Two at least of my later Masters thought that all Englishmen ought to reckon the *Morte d'Arthur* as a holy book. Englishmen have not followed them in this, any more than in other directions. Still, the book remains our nearest approach to a holy book, and to any story-maker the holy book should be the source of sources. Of course, most of Malory is translated from the French; but some of the French romance-writers used fables brought to Brittany by refugees from Britain. The foundation of part of the epic must be British. ... To myself, then, it was pure joy: a British tradition, that

43

had passed into the imagination of the world. I will spare the reader
an account of the wild Arthurian tales that were in my imagination
for the next few months.

Malory and the Arthurian legends amounted to a restoration of the England,
of Britain, that had at once nurtured him and, through the unsympathetic
behaviour of Uncle William and Aunt Kate, let him down, especially as
Herefordshire and the Marches were rich in Arthurian associations.

From now on England had a spiritual as well as a physical identity for
him, and Masefield, true to the paradoxes of his nature, greatly needed this.
English realities became more bearable if there were a larger context in
which to place them. Likewise the hardships of New York City could be
better borne if the imagination were an active and creative organ again.
And in its restoration to this the reading of Malory played a major part. So
too must his having acted decisively and unambiguously by deserting.

> I was in New York City in summer-time, when I suddenly found
> that the faculty of mental story-telling had returned to me. I was
> walking in an uptown part of the East Side when a story suddenly
> became bright in my mind, in the way I had known of old, so that I
> could both tell it and enjoy it. In the glaring sun and roaring avenue
> I walked in the old joy, that again, as ever, made all other worries
> nothing.
>
> This resurrection of my inner life was a gladness. New York
> City, in herself, was a gladness, that dazzling, beautiful, exciting
> City, the Queen of all romantic Cities.

Yet his external life was often the very reverse of gladness; it continued
to be very difficult. On the *Conway* and the *Gilcruix* he had at least had
security; in America lack of funds either forced him into a hand-to-mouth
existence or ground him in the economic mill of the factory worker. His
uncle, on learning of Jack's desertion, sent private detectives on his trail,
but later, when asked by a new friend of Jack's to help his nephew with
money, refused: the boy deserved no assistance from him. To begin with,
Jack took to the countryside beyond New York with a chance acquaintance, trying for casual labouring jobs on farms and country holdings,
which they sometimes got and sometimes didn't, just as they sometimes
had enough to eat and sometimes didn't. With summer he came back to
New York City, bumming around Greenwich Village before accepting a

barman's job in an establishment on a slum street. Once again a piece in *A Tarpaulin Muster*, 'A Raines Law Arrest' offers us a glimpse of Jack's life-style and cast of mind. Raines Law forbade drinking on Sundays, the joint that had given Jack employment was determined to get round such proscriptive (and profit-losing) legislation, and co-opted their young English bar-tender, who'd seen and experienced enough bourgeois hypocrisies in his own country to be impatient of them elsewhere:

> When I was working in a New York saloon I saw something of the city police. I was there ... at a time when the city was groaning beneath the yoke of an unaccustomed purity. The old, happy, sinful days, when a man might do as he pleased as long as he kept the police squared, were over ...
>
> It was a curious sight, that silent bar, with its nervous ministrants filling glasses for the greatly venturous. From behind the bar I could see Johnna' (Italian lunch-man) 'sitting in the porch in his black Sunday clothes, with a cigar between his lips and an Italian paper on his knees. Sometimes he would grin across at me as I hulled strawberries or sliced pineapples for cocktails. He would open his mouth and beckon to me; and then, if the boss were not looking, I would fling a berry or a scrap of pine to him. He used to catch them in his mouth with wonderful dexterity, much as a terrier would catch flies. This, and the making of potato salad, were Johnna's two accomplishments. I remember wishing that I possessed some art like this of Johnna's, for I was always stupid at amusing people, and have always envied those with some little trick or skill to cover a natural lack of parts. Then sometimes, as the guests came or went, we heard the alarm. The bottles were rushed under cover. The proprietor and the bar-tenders scattered upstairs to the hotel. The chain clattered as the inner door was shut, and then we heard the challenge from the patrolman on the street and the rattling of Johnna's door as he tried to get in.

Jack worked at this establishment for only two months, however, and in September 1895, left and found himself a job in a carpet-factory in Yonkers, on the periphery of New York City. He was to work there, with increasing responsibilities until July 1897, living in a Yonkers boarding-house. *In the Mill* (1941) presents the hopes with which he embarked on his Yonkers life and the gruelling regimen it imposed in actuality, including deprivation of fresh air and daylight, stuffy, noisy and often very fuggy working conditions. He must frequently have felt lonely, frustrated, mentally under-stretched, and quite cut off from the life into which he had been born, but that same quiet resilience and outward adaptability that had carried him through his training on the *Conway*, served him well at the Alexander Smith and Sons' mill. And on his free days he was able to explore the surrounding landscape, wild here, even though so near one of the greatest cities in the world. 'The romantic boy' of Ledbury had not altogether disappeared. In 'On the Palisades', again in *A Tarpaulin Muster,* he evokes his pleasure in exploring round Yonkers:

> On the west side of the Hudson River there is a cliff, or crag of rock, all carved into queer shapes. It stretches along the riverside for twenty or thirty miles. ... The cliff rises up, as a rule very boldly, to the height of several hundred feet. The top of it (the Jersey shore) appears regular. It is like a well-laid wall along the river, with trees and one or two white wooden houses, instead of broken glass, at the top. This wall-appearance made the settlers call the crag 'The Palisades'.
>
> Where the Palisades are grandest is just as high up as Yonkers. Hereabouts they are very stately, for they are all marshalled along a river a mile or more broad, which runs in a straight line past them, with a great tide. If you take a boat and row across to the Palisades their beauty makes you shiver. In the afternoon, when you are underneath them, the sun is shut away from you; and there you are, in the chill and the gloom, with the great cliff towering up, and the pinnacles and tall trees catching the sunlight at the top. Then it is very still there. You will see no one along that shore. A great eagle will go sailing out, or a hawk will drop and splash after a fish, but you will see no other living thing, except at the landing ... You can lie there in your boat, in the slack water near the crag-foot, and hear nothing but the wind, the suck of the water, or the tinkle of a scrap of stone falling from the cliff-face. It is like being in the wilds, in one of the desolate places, to lie there in a boat watching the eagles.

Though this piece goes on to relate a yarn heard from an old British salt who was a jetty-keeper by the Palisades, once more Masefield portrays himself as a solitary; the intensity of his response to the scene seems inextricably connected with freedom from the demands, and possibly even the proximity of other people.

His American years, building on his experiences of H.M.S. *Conway* and of the fateful voyage to Iquique, intensified Masefield's growing

awareness of humanity as a shapeless, unshapable mass, out of which individuals arise, infinitely important to themselves, infinitely unimportant
when viewed, as they must be, against the tide of the social and economic
forces that throw them up. In the great narrative poems (even though their
settings are not American) he presents figures who, for one reason or
another, detach themselves from the society in which they found themselves, in order to find any fullness of life—religion in *The Everlasting
Mercy*, sexual love in *The Widow in the Bye Street* and *The Daffodil Fields*,
art in *Dauber*. Society is presented as in the American vision—loose-knit,
powerful, amoral—rather than in the stratified or hierarchical form of its
manifestations in English literature. A structured cohesive society is—
principally for psychological and experiential reasons—significantly
missing from much of Masefield's *oeuvre*, and where it exists (as in the
Ned Mansell novels) is found to be every bit as malign as the crowd. Only
in *Reynard the Fox* does he attempt a constructive picture of one, and it is
too shot through with his own ambivalences to be satisfying. The typical
Masefield protagonist sees himself pitted against the world, both elemental
and human, with ultimately only himself as arbitrator and peace-giver.
Even in those works dealing with sexual love, *The Widow in the Bye Street*
and *The Daffodil Fields* the central characters stand alone, their desires
emphasizing the loneliness of their lots (of all our lots). They follow
biological not moral laws; far from being a means of integration in society,
the sexual urge appears as a conductor to alienation. But Masefield's
sojourn in America did enable him to see other people as all, both in isolation and in the mass, as bound on the same, often dangerous journey. He
comes very close in this respect to Walt Whitman's 'Democratic Vistas',
and made possible the cast of mind that produced the famous
'Consecration' to his first volume of poems, *Salt-Water Ballads*. It celebrates a spacial and temporal continuum of human life with concomitant
suffering, which makes the people of the remoter past (of Roman and pre-
Roman Herefordshire, or of Arthurian times) indivisible from those
encountered on any New York, Liverpool or Iquique street or waterfront.
It's hard to imagine the following lines being written by one who had
either stayed in England or had known only the British colonies abroad:

> Not of the princes and prelates with periwigged charioteers
> Riding triumphantly laurelled to lap the fat of the years, -
> Rather the scorned - the rejected - the men hemmed in with the spears;

47

The men of the tattered battalion which fights till it dies,
Dazed with the dust of the battle, the din and the cries,
The men with the broken heads, and the blood running into their eyes. ...

Not the ruler for me, but the ranker, the tramp of the road,
The slave with the sack on his shoulders pricked on with the goad,
The man with too weighty a burden, too weary a load.

For all their young man's rhetoric, the lines have, in addition to the generality of mood, a precision of image that comes from a firmness of conviction. Even more American in its sentiment—especially as one is made aware in the poem of the 'I', of some larger Whitmanesque 'Song of Myself' existing behind its three stanzas—is 'All Ye That Pass By':

On the long dusty ribbon of the long city street,
The pageant of life is passing me on multitudinous feet,
With a word here of the hills, and a song there of the sea,
And - the great movement changes - the pageant passes me.

Faces - passionate faces - of men I may not know,
They haunt me, burn me to the heart, as I turn aside to go;
The king's face and the cur's face, and the face of the stuffed swine,
They are passing, they are passing, their eyes look into mine.

I never can tire of the music of the noise of many feet,
The thrill of the blood pulsing, the tick of the heart's beat,
Of the men many as sands, of the sqaudrons ranked and massed
Who are passing, changing always, and never have changed or passed.

Masefield read 'great quantities' of American fiction, both novels and magazine short-stories, while 'in the mill' at Yonkers (his work-load came to permit him time for extensive reading) as he had also devoured English, French and Russian fiction. But his most intense literary experiences came from English poetry—above all from Chaucer, beginning, perhaps unexpectedly, with *The Parliament of Fowls*. Thus started his relationship with Chaucer which at times can seem a form of artistic identification. Masefield's admiration of him was to grow into a major article of faith with the years, responsible for what was both best and maybe most mistaken in the adult poet. *In The Mill* describes his reading of a 75 cent Chaucer:

> Now I tasted something deeper; I was taken into another world,
> unlike this in its excitement and beauty; it was a new experience. It
> seemed to me, that evening, that very likely there was no limit to the
> world opened by such poetry; it seemed boundless in liberty, inex-
> haustible in riches, deathless in beauty, eternal in delight.

To Chaucer he added Milton (particularly *Paradise Lost*, Books I and
XII), and Dante Gabriel Rossetti whose narrative powers he evidently
thought scarcely less inferior to the two earlier masters. William Morris
was later to supplant Rossetti among Victorian poets in Masefield's admi-
rations, but in *So Long to Learn* he speaks, a trifle cryptically, of the older
poet having created 'unforgettable pieces of deep importance to me'. One
wonders whether he was thinking of *Jenny*, that moving portrait of a pros-
titute, of an urban civilisation's victim; someone who had been so familiar
with New York's underbelly could well have reason to respond to it.
Whatever the personal reasons behind his enthusiasm, Rossetti was for
Masefield 'the last kindling Master who had appeared in England', 'the
love spirit who had changed and enlivened the whole course of art in
[England], who had inspired all who meant most to us, and left the solace
of his protest to those who came too late to know him.' Soon Jack was
adding Shelley and Keats to his reading, though more for their lyrical
powers and ideas than for the stories they told—and Shelley's idealism had
an influence on him: he was converted for a while to vegetarianism.

All these great names are significant; from the first Masefield measured
himself against the mighty, Chaucer and Shakespeare not excluded. In fact
a little more than this; as is perhaps often apt to be the case with auto-
didacts, surrounded by those who don't share their interests, he put himself
into their company—which explains his comparative boldness on his
return to London, when, in a surprisingly short span of time, he was on
terms of almost casual friendliness with many of the most distinguished
literary men of the day. It was during his time in New York that he himself
began to write verses, and though his first attempts do not let his originality of mind come through, they have a certain accomplishment.

In his relationship to his own experiences Jack Masefield showed in his
time in America that doubleness of vision which was always, I think, to be
characteristic of him. He could go through searing experiences of loneliness, discomfort and unease and see into the darkness behind them with
real and brave penetration. He was also capable of living to a far greater

degree than most people in a world of fantasy, often literary in derivation, from which he could bring both ideals and horrors that shed light on the world around him. But the balance between the two was a very uneasy one, and the uneasiness was to come out in his writing, and often vitiate it. Sometimes he saw communities, situations as pervaded by a blackness from which there could be no course but recoil. Sometimes, on the contrary, the chivalrous light of his mind caused too roseate a glow to suffuse grim realities; a kind of honourable falsification could set in. At best the doubleness of the committed Arthurian and the young man who'd cast bourgeois niceties aside for a complex, rougher world was a vision which, translated into literary form, has illuminated much for many.

But in America he was ill, ill with increasing frequency and severity: he was almost certainly suffering from malaria, picked up in the tropics, and from the early stages of tuberculosis. Nobody who had not had severe fevers could have written of them as Masefield was to of Roger Naldrett's in *Multitude and Solitude*, unsurpassed in its vivid sensory details of disease:

> He shivered. His teeth began to chatter. He felt that the cold had stricken to his liver. ... [He] took a strong dose [of quinine]. There was something very strange about the quinine. It seemed to come to his mouth from a hand immensely distant. There was a long, long arm, like a crooked railway, tied to the hand. It seemed to Roger that it could not possibly crook itself sufficiently to let the hand reach his mouth. After the strangeness of the hand had faded, he felt horribly cold. He longed to have fire all round him, and inside him ... He was in for a fever. He got into his bed, and heaped the blankets round him, trembling. Almost at once the real world began to blur and change. It was still the real world, but he was seeing much in it which he had not suspected. Many queer things were happening before his eyes. he lay shuddering, with chattering teeth, listening, as he thought, to the noise made by the world as it revolved. It was a crashing, booming, resolute noise, which droned down and anon piped up high. It went on and on.
>
> In the middle of all the noise he had the strange fancy that his body was not in bed at all, but poised in air. His bed lay somewhere below him. Sitting up he could see part of it, infinitely distant, below his outstretched feet. The ceiling was swelling and swelling just above him. It seemed as vast as heaven. All the time it swelled he seemed to shrink. He was lying chained somewhere, while his body was shrinking to the vanishing-point. He could feel himself

dwindling, while the blackness above grew vaster. ... At last the blackness fell in upon his littleness and blotted it out.

He left New York for England (first Liverpool, then London) in July 1897, physically ill, poor, but tested and ambitious. Just over five years later *Salt-Water Ballads* was published, with far more success than is usual with first volumes of poetry. A number of its poems were to become quite well-known, and one of them, 'Sea-Fever' to be one of the most famous and often-quoted of our century.

To look more closely at *Salt-Water Ballads* is also to discover how Masefield ('Jan' as he now called himself) had developed as a person, his preoccupations and aspirations, and the tensions and stimuli of the culture of which he was now a participant.

2

The confidence of the young poet of *Salt-Water Ballads* (he was a mere twenty-four) is palpable and extraordinary, shown in his at times virtuosic dexterity in rhythm and rhyme, his varieties of form, his ability to write without strain or monotony in sailor's argot and, with no lessening of impact, in his own voice, his movements in mood, sometimes within the same poem (see 'Hell's Pavement' and 'Cape Horn Gospel I'), his insistence on the importance of his subject-matter—the sea and sailors—and his determination to give the rough and inarticulate the benefits of his lively art. The very confidence does not always, in retrospect, work to the volume's advantage, however. Though contemporary readers and critics were (and rightly) impressed by the freshness of Masefield's productions, the more so as he was introducing them to a world largely new to poetry, judges today are likely to see just how apt a student he was of other writers, how skilfully and personally he could vie with them. There's Swinburne here, and R.L. Stevenson and the Hardy of *Wessex Poems* (1898) and *Poems of the Past and Present* (also of 1902). There's W.B. Yeats, though oddly, not in serious evidence in the poem that Masefield himself thought Yeatsian and indeed asked the master's permission to include— 'The West Wind', which reads to me like watered-down Swinburne, with more than a dash of W.E. Henley!

> It's the white road westwards is the road I must tread
> To the green grass, the cool grass and rest for heart and head ...

There's also Kipling. This influence was a sore subject with Masefield who not only detested Kipling's poetry itself but the whole Imperialistic philosophy he felt it served. A comparison was, and is, bound to be made because the title of the volume—his publisher's and not Masefield's own choice—echoes that of Kipling's *Barrack-Room Ballads* (1892) which contains some of its author's most justly famous poems: 'When 'Omer Smote 'is Bloomin' Lyre,' 'Danny Deever,' 'Tommy', 'Fuzzy-Wuzzy', 'Gunga Din', 'Mandalay'. Readers of the day discovering the youthful Masefield can scarcely be blamed for thinking they were being offered a nautical counterpart to those popular *Barrack-Room Ballads* with sailors, rather than soldiers, telling of experiences and feelings in racy accents, when they read verses such as these from 'One of the Bo'sun's Yarns':

> Loafin' around in Sailor Town, a-bluin' o'my advance,
> I met a derelict donkeyman who led me a merry dance,
> Till he landed me 'n' bleached me fair in the bar of a rum-saloon,
> 'N' there he spun me a juice of a yarn to this-yer brat tune.
>
> "It's a solemn gospel, mate," he says, "but a man as ships aboard
> A steamer-tramp, he gets his whack of the wonders of the Lord -
> Such as roaches crawlin' over his bunk, 'n' snakes inside his bread,
> And work by night and work by day enough to strike him dead."

(Compare 'Tommy', though the older poet's production is more incisive and with a deeper emotion behind it:

> I went into a public-'ouse to get a pint of beer,
> The publican 'e up an' sez, "We serve no redcoats here."
> The girls be'ind the bar they laughed an' giggled fit to die,
> I outs into the street again an' to myself sez I:
>   O it's "Tommy this", an' "Tommy that", an' "Tommy, go away";
>   But it's "Thank you, Mister Atkins," when the band begins to play -
>   The band begins to play, my boys, the band begins to play,
>   O it's "Thank you, Mister Atkins," when the band begins to play.)

In fact Kipling not only provides a major point of reference, he stands behind many of the poems, I believe, in that Masefield set out to oppose him. In this respect he was right to resent the linking of their names. The 'Consecration', quoted above to illustrate Masefield's somewhat American democracy of vision directly contrasts with (and refutes) the 'Dedication' Kipling affixed to his *Barrack-Room Ballads*:

Beyond the path of the outmost sun through utter darkness hurled
Farther than ever comet flared or vagrant star-dust swirled -
Live such as fought and sailed and ruled and loved and made our world.

They are purged of pride because they died; they know the worth of their
bays;
They sit at wine with the Maidens Nine and the Gods of the Elder Days -
It is their will to serve or be still as fitteth Our Father's praise.

Kipling's soldiers, however sordid and ignorant their lives, are transfigured by their corporate identity; they have their assured place in History, they serve, and will be seen to have served, a great purpose: the extension and maintenance of the British Empire. There is in Kipling's vision— manifest in its purest form in his stories about animals, the popular *Jungle Books* and *Just So Stories* for children—a pervasive Darwinism, frequently cloaked, as in the lines above, by a sense of a mystic destiny in operation: divine dispensation and the fortunes of the British peculiarly intertwined. There is nothing of this in Masefield (which may make him here a more sympathetic poet, though not a superior one); Darwinism pervades *his* work too, but most often in the Hardyesque form of awareness of the vast wastage of living beings that the struggle for life entails. Masefield's 'Consecration' evokes the nameless, unremembered, unimportant people of history; they were emphatically not transfigured by whatever cause they nominally fought or worked for. The same goes for the sailors of *Salt-Water Ballads*, and it is surely significant that they are not members of the armed forces but merchant seamen with only commercial justification for the hardships of their lives. Masefield's *Salt-Water Ballads* seem to me to be subverting Kipling's, by insisting over and over again on the redundancy of the individual, even to himself and certainly to his bosses—and on the pity of this, something the men tend to disguise from themselves by vaunted callousness of diction.

Masefield's intense, verbally well-judged recapturings of the men's attitudes to themselves and their fellows (pragmatic, decidedly anti-mystic) are the most remarkable feature of his first volume. Examples are many; a complete poem, 'Bill' is as lively a one as any:

He lay dead on the cluttered deck and stared at the cold skies,
With never a friend to mourn for him nor a hand to close his eyes:
"Bill, he's dead," was all they said; "he's dead, 'n' there he lies."

The mate came forrard at seven bells and spat across the rail:
"Just lash him up wi' some holystone in a clout o'rotten sail,
'N', rot ye, get a gait on ye, ye're slower 'n a bloody snail!"

When the rising moon was a copper disc and the sea was a strip of steel,
 We dumped him down to the swaying weeds ten fathom beneath the keel.
"It's rough about Bill," the fo'c'sle said, "we'll have to stand his wheel."

Related to this kind of triumph is Masefield's ability to understand the folkloric aspects of seamen's life; as someone interested from earliest years in legends, superstitions, old sayings, he must have studied the common store of beliefs and fancies from which his mates on the *Conway* and *Gilcruix* regularly drew. Fusing these with the kind of imaginings natural to him produces at best verses which point to his later spectacular ability to render the numinous in a prosaic or even squalid setting (as in Saul Kane's recollection of the bellringer's vision in Ledbury churchyard in *The Everlasting Mercy*). 'Cape Horn Gospel I' is a particularly haunting specimen of this, and again worth quoting entire; the Ariel-like song quality of the third and fourth stanza brings to mind Walter de la Mare whose first volume of poems, *Songs of Childhood* also came out in 1902, and which too, at best, show the author enjoying a relationship to some fathomless reservoir of English lore:

> "I was in a hooker once," said Karlssen,
> "And Bill, as was a seaman, died,
> So we lashed him in an old tarpaulin
> And tumbled him across the side;
> And the fun of it was that all his gear was
> Divided up among the crew
> Before that blushing human error,
> Our crawling little captain, knew.
>
> On the passage home one morning
> (As certain as I prays for grace)
> There was old Bill's shadder a-hauling
> At the weather mizzen-topsail brace.

He was all grown green with sea-weed,
He was all lashed up and shored;
So I says to him, I says, 'Why, Billy!
What's a-bringin' of you back aboard?'

'I'm a-weary of them there mermaids',
Says old Bill's ghost to me;
'It ain't no place for a Christian
Below there - under sea.
For it's all blown sand and shipwrecks,
And old bones eaten bare,
And them cold fishy females
With long green weeds for hair.

And there ain't no dances shuffled,
And no old yarns is spun,
And there ain't no stars but starfish,
And never any moon or sun.
I heard your keel a-passing
And the running rattle of the brace.'
And he says 'Stand by,' says William,
'For a shift towards a better place.'

Well, he sogered about decks till sunrise,
When a rooster in the hen-coop crowed,
And as so much smoke he faded
And as so much smoke he goed;
And I've often wondered since, Jan,
How his old ghost stands to fare
Long o'them cold fishy females
With long green weeds for hair."

If any poem in *Salt-Water Ballads* anticipates the success of *The Everlasting Mercy*, it is this one, even though so much lighter and more restricted in scope. In common with its great successor it works on us above all because of Masefield's assumption of the vernacular voice, which he permits considerable emotional mobility, indicating complexities and depths of response and feeling below the surface. Karlssen sounds a hard enough case as he presents himself in the first stanza, not grieving for Bill at all and seeing his death principally in terms of how he benefited from the illicit division of his possessions. The phrases 'that blushing human error, / Our crawling captain' show Masefield's racy command of idiom; we can just imagine *such* a man in such a position expressing himself thus. But this isn't to say that Karlssen is without feelings; on the contrary, leading the kind of life he does he has to protect himself from feelings; they'd be a troublesome luxury on board his barque. But his very suppression has made him susceptible to the visitation he receives, one which expresses his own fears of death and what awaits us all on its other side. The seaman exists—as Jack Masefield had found out only too thoroughly for himself when rounding the Horn—in constant proximity to the possibility of dying. No wonder the communal seaman's mind has fashioned a Davy Jones Locker for itself. But what if it were true? And what if it weren't? The human reality of the person at once survives and mocks at any notions of his 'translation'. Mustn't men always want to be men again—or men still? As the American folk-song asks: 'What are they *doing* in Heaven today?' Masefield's beautiful poem is another expression of this perennial imaginative problem. Its warmth of human feeling—something by no means always characteristic of him—is evident in the abrupt salutation 'Why, Billy!' in the penultimate line of the second stanza, revealing a fondness (even if only of a matey kind) that the two men had had for each other, and in the completely authentic—and also musical, key-changing—confession by Bill (as to an intimate) of his pining to be back among the living again, words sympathetically received by Karlssen himself:

> "I'm a weary of them there mermaids,"
> Says old Bill's ghost to me; ...

It is also in such a poem as this that Masefield reveals his real (as opposed to fancied) creative debt to that first among his mentors, Yeats, who in some of the best (and now best-loved) poems of *Crossways* (1889), *The Rose* (1893) and *The Wind Among the Reeds* (1899) had presented not just the world but the cosmos through the traditional culture of the Irish peasantry. 'Cape Horn Gospel I' is surely kin to such a piece as 'The Fiddler of Dooney' (in rhythm as well as in ideas); they both show the needs at a time of the hegemony of commercial, official Britain to turn to the perceptions and even confusions of the unsophisticated:

> When I play on my fiddle in Dooney,
> Folk dance like a wave of the sea;
> My cousin is priest in Kilvarnet,
> My brother in Mocharabuiee.

I passed my brother and cousin:
They read in their books of prayer;
I read in my book of songs
I bought at Sligo fair.

When we come at the end of time
To Peter sitting in state,
He will smile on the three old spirits,
But call me first through the gate;

For the good are always the merry,
Save by an evil chance,
And the merry love the fiddle,
And the merry love to dance;

And when the folk there spy me,
They will all come up to me,
With "Here is the fiddler of Dooney!"
And dance like a wave of the sea.

That excellent literary critic, John Lucas, who has made so signal a contribution to the understanding of the relation between English poetry and changing English society, doesn't greatly admire the early Masefield; in *Modern English Poetry from Hardy to Hughes* (1986) he includes him in his chapter on Edwardian and Georgian pre-First World War poetry, entitled, with some irony and aptness, 'The Clerk's Dream of Poetry'. (And Jan Masefield was indeed, for a time, on his return from the United States, just such a clerk — in the Capital and Counties Bank).

'I suggest,' he writes, 'that John Masefield's *Salt-Water Ballads* of 1902/3 is undoubtedly meant to minister to the trapped spirit of the city clerk.'

There is both injustice and justice here. No one knowledgeable of Masefield's early life could deny that he was repeatedly drawing on personal experiences and apprehensions; both here and elsewhere (and pre-eminently in *Dauber*) he is as far from being the weekending sailor as could be; he had been out there, and suffered alongside the characters of his verses. But unfortunately there was another side of Masefield which could — that double-vision! — deliberately and perversely, decide to look at his subjects through the pleasing lens of romance, through other people's day-dreamy fantasizings (and Robert Louis Stevenson's in particular; one sometimes feels it was a pity he ever read *Treasure Island*). He was as accomplished at writing poems in this vein as in the other (indeed his astonishing technical powers rarely let him down throughout his whole career) so that, to offset the genuine mythopoeic qualities of the two 'Cape Horn Gospel' poems or 'Sea-Change', we have such bogus poetic antics as 'The Tarry Buccaneer' and 'A Ballad of John Silver' and, even worse, 'Lyrics from *The Buccaneer*':

> And a merry measure is the dance she'll tread
> (To the clanking of the staysail's hanks)
> When the guns are growling and the blood runs red,
> And the prisoners are walking of the planks.

This is nonsense, and the more regrettable for the fact that Masefield had both a lively knowledge and a lively understanding of the cruelty men were capable of, and was learnèd in the history of the Spanish Main.

The truth is that Masefield was—and remained—a very literary writer as well as a *sui generis* one, and often the literary—which had for so long been his consolation and inspiration in his days of dejection—became dominant, even when dealing with subjects of which he has first-hand knowledge. Furthermore, a certain degree of compensation cannot altogether be discounted; Masefield had been unhappy to the point of breakdown at sea, wished this had not been so, and projected his imagination accordingly. If he had, as some thought, failed in hard reality, then in verses it would be otherwise, his spirits would be high and hearty.

☆ ☆ ☆

There are poems in *Salt-Water Ballads* which do not have the sea as their subject. A number, for instance 'Personal', are informed by the longing for what is not, the nostalgia that came to be associated with the Celtic Twilight and (erroneously) with W.B. Yeats. Something of this mood enters Masefield's tributes to his native countryside, 'On Malvern Hill' (which has a Housmanesque sense of long-ago generations, Celtic and Roman), 'Tewkesbury Road' where the very palpable feeling for plants and animals is undermined by a heartiness of metre and vocabulary derived from Stevenson, Henley and Newbolt, and 'On Eastnor Knoll', perhaps the most successful of the group.

The most interesting of the non-nautical poems is 'The Dead Knight', gentle and elegiac in mood, which achieves a rare concentration on its subject and its imaginative implications, movingly suggesting both the timeless and the ravages of time:

> The cleanly rush of the mountain air,
> And the mumbling, grumbling humble-bees,
> Are the only things that wander there,
> The pitiful bones are laid at ease,
> The grass has grown in his tangled hair,
> And rambling bramble binds his knees.
>
> To shrive his soul from the pangs of hell,
> The only requiem-bells that rang
> were the hare-bell and the heather-bell.
> Hushed he is with the holy spell
> In the gentle hymn the wind sang,
> And he lies quiet, and sleeps well.
> He is bleached and blanched with the summer sun;
> the misty rain and cold dew
> Have altered him from the kingly one
> (That his lady loved and his men knew)
>
> The vetches have twined about his bones,
> The straggling ivy twists and creeps
> In his eye-sockets; the nettle keeps
> Vigil about him while he sleeps.
> Over his body the wind moans
> With a dreary tune throughout the day,
> In a chorus wistful eerie, thin
> As the gull's cry - as the cry in the bay,
> The mournful word the seas say
> When the tides are wandering out or in.

It is hard not to read this as being, on an unconscious level, about the struggle in the poet's mind between his very concrete appreciation of nature and his tendency to soar into the realms of romance, to the detriment of his capacities for observation and action.

3

The transformation in five years of Jack Masefield—of the serious health problems, regular bouts of depression, bad relations with his guardians, no money, and obligations to take uninteresting jobs—into Jan Masefield, a rising literary star, who knew some of the most interesting and influential people of the day, must have been accomplished by formidable determination and application. But from neither Masefield himself nor from those who described him at this time of his life can one hear of these qualities; the success drive he undoubtedly must have possessed seems to have impressed itself on nobody. Dedication, yes—and no one could have written as much as Jan Masefield did without a quite formidable confidence in his powers. But the dedication would seem to have come from the intensity of his inner life, and of his desire to give expression to this in a variety of literary forms (he was also an informed enthusiast of the other arts, especially music and painting, and produced many watercolours) and it is this intensity that his senior contemporaries noted: W.B. Yeats, Laurence Binyon, later John Galsworthy. There seems nothing of ambition, of career-making and the concomitant ability to size up socially and ascertain who would or who would not be useful to him, of the wish to make money or of an interest in business matters. He had a very personal way of talking and loved to let others into confidences about earlier hardships and adventures; he was extremely good-looking, and had not lost the atmosphere of Ledbury's 'romantic boy', and he had an ardour about life, about the development of his own abilities, that comes over even in the autobiography he wrote at seventy-three, *So Long to Learn*.

According to him this ardour was a key quality of the London in which he found himself at nineteen:

> It is not possible to persuade the living that the late Victorian time was in all intellectual ways immeasurably ahead of any time that has succeeded. Those who knew that time know the truth about it, and are the first to admit its defects. Those who did not know the time seem incapable of perceiving anything else. To those who had the happiness to be young in it, the time was one of peace, liberty, abundance, and overwhelming intellectual endeavour. Most of the intellectual endeavour was, of course, directed to setting right what was amiss in the society. Some was very rightly directed to the giving of delight, which, in the main, should be the artist's task at all ages. That delight was then certainly being given, by painters, musicians and writers. It would startle the young of today to know what enormous appetite for thought Victorian London shewed; what dozens of papers fostered delight in writing, what pages of

comment upon thought came daily, what fervour this or that movement caused, what excellence was being achieved.

Some great Victorians still survived. Swinburne could still be
seen by his adorers, at Putney, or in the British Museum. Thomas
Hardy, making a great resolution, had just turned from prose to the
writing of poetry. George Meredith, after long and cruel neglect,
was at last being read. All the reactions seemed to be against the
ruthless and the realist; and against the decadence that had lately
flourished (itself being a reaction).

Most of the countless papers on sale upon the bookstalls
contained work of quality. Books were in enormous abundance and
very cheap. There were more book-shops then than now, and far
more places where, at certain times of the week, the book-lover
might examine book-stalls for treasure, and be pretty sure of finding
some. The out-of-fashion is always cheap, and usually much better
than the fashion has the wit to think.

In this fever and fervour, myself being ill and not expecting nor
expected to live long, I commenced author, with what hesitancy and
uncertainty the young writer will know without my telling.

But the hesitancy and uncertainty, though no doubt painful enough,
were short-lived. 'Nicias Moriturus', a poem about a dying seaman, (there
was surely projection here), was published in *The Outlook* on 3 June 1899
and later included in *Salt-Water Ballads* as 'The Turn of the Tide':

> An' Bill can have my sea-boots, Nigger Jim can have my knife,
>   You can divvy up the dungarees an' bed,
> An' the ship can have my blessing, an' the Lord can have my life,
>   An' sails an' fish my body when I'm dead.

His literary career had begun, and with a highly characteristic piece at that.

His ill-health, his awareness of the possibility of early death, gave a
sharpness to his reception of the life around him—and to his need for his
imaginings to be committed to paper and printed. Yet late Victorian/early
Edwardian England does seem to have been charged with a peculiar
vitality, unsurpassed since, owing to both the prosperity, self-confidence,
and international standing of the society, and to the doubts, guilts and
general review of desiderata that these set in train. Masefield arrived back
in Britain in the Year of Queen Victoria's Diamond Jubilee, when the Tate
Gallery was presented to the nation. Between then and the publication of

his own *Salt-Water Ballads* there appeared works which still contribute to the health of our cultural life: major work by Shaw, James (both Henry and William), Wells, Conrad, Gissing, Kipling, Havelock Ellis, Chesterton, Bennett and Bridges. The movement tends to be either forwards (as in Shaw and Wells, challenging the shibboleths and false assumptions of society and building towards a new society, even a new human being) or inwards, voyaging below the surface level of life, into the depths of the human psyche, as in Henry James and Conrad.

But the poem 'Biography' presents a different picture of the London Masefield experienced from that in his later autobiography. Here he remembers his loneliness and his struggle and the colours are sombre, though not unalleviatedly. He was not a city-dweller by temperament, and he was aware of the stultification and alienated states of so many inhabitants of megalopolis, no matter what cultural activities were in progress:

> Years blank with hardship never speak a word
> Live in the soul to make the being stirred;
> Towns can be prisons, where the spirit dulls
> Away from mates and ocean-wandering hulls,
> Away from all bright water and great hills
> And sheep-walks, where the curlews cry their fills,
> Away in towns, where eyes have nought to see
> But dead museums, and miles of misery,
> And floating life unrooted from man's need,
> And miles of fish-hooks baited to catch greed,
> And life made wretched out of human ken,
> And miles of shopping women served by men.

Then—for 'Biography' seems to have been written in an in-between-time of curious tension—Masefield relents somewhat, giving readers a *chiaroscuro*, with heightened contrasts between the misery apprehended and the spiritual and intellectual excitements experiences at this time, this place—ending the section of the poem with a fine tribute to his chief mentor:

> So, if the penman sums my London days,
> Let him but say that there were holy ways,
> Dull Bloomsbury streets of dull brick mansions old,
> With stinking doors, where women stood to scold,

And drunken waits at Christmas with their horn,
Droning the news, in snow, that Christ was born;
And windy gas-lamps and the wet roads shining,
And that old carol of the midnight whining,
And that old room (above the noisy slum),
Where there was wine and fire and talk with some
Under strange pictures of the wakened soul,
To whom this earth was but a burnt-out coal.

This last is a marvellous image for the imagination of W.B. Yeats. For Masefield, who so fervently admired Dante Gabriel Rossetti and William Morris, Yeats, like them, was a man who had consecrated his entire personality, the range and depth of his mind to his art, so that it partook of religion, and could transform both the individual and society. Masefield first encountered Yeats through *The Wanderings of Oisin* (1889), and its third section intoxicated him with its magical beauty, perhaps too much so, considering his debt to it in later lines of his own, which have Yeats' incantatory quality without the intellectual interest behind it:

And I rode by the plains of the sea's edge, where all is barren and grey,
Grey sand on the green of the grasses and over the dripping trees,
Dripping and doubling landward, as though they would hasten away,
Like an army of old men longing for rest from the moan of the seas.

A convert at once, he read through all Yeats' available books, and then effected a meeting between himself and the poet. Yeats offered him hospitality, they became friends, and the older man advised and encouraged him. Though it is doubtful whether Masefield later really entered into Yeats' wonderful last phase, he never lost his admiration—or affection—for him. These are a tribute to the soundness of his early judgement. One trouble in approaching a period with hindsight is that we see it principally in terms of the famous literary figures who have survived, and forget both the nature of their emergence on the scene, rarely instantaneous, and the nature too of their fellows, of the competition. Though the Edwardian era can indeed be praised for the writers of stature it produced, this is, in point of fact, less true of poetry than of the other branches of literature. The *locus classicus* for a survey of what the reading public of 1910-1914 (and indeed later) were content with, and so were constantly given, is C.K. Stead's masterly *The New Poetic* (1964). Alfred Austin, Henry Newbolt,

William Watson—these were the respected and much-read poets of the day. Masefield had no time for them; his taste for great literature, acquired largely in solitude in America, led him unerringly to one of the supreme and most influential writers of our century. The interesting thing here is that, where Masefield himself achieves a greatness—*The Everlasting Mercy*, *The Widow in the Bye Street*, *Dauber*—it is of a kind utterly dissimilar to Yeats': Masefield has none of his friend's gnomic, arcane powers, and where he is visionary, it is in a far more earth-bound and personalised way.

Yeats showed good judgement himself in his championing of the obscure young man with a knock-about recent past, just as he had done not so long before (in 1896) in his espousal of the also unknown John Millington Synge (1871-1909). Synge is the late close friend Masefield so movingly refers to later in 'Biography'; as with Yeats, he gives him no name. (Synge was by this time two years dead):

> And now I miss that friend who used to walk
> Home to my lodgings with me, deep in talk,
> Wearing the last of night out in still streets
> Trodden by us and policemen on their beats
> And cats, but else deserted. Now I miss
> That lively mind and guttural laugh of his,
> And that strange way he had of making gleam,
> Like something real, the art we used to dream.

Masefield first met Synge on a 'Monday night of January, 1903'. The effect of the Irish dramatist—who, later that year, was to have one masterpiece (*Riders to the Sea*) published and another (*The Shadow of the Glen*) produced—was to be very considerable indeed, and wholly beneficial. *The Everlasting Mercy* and, though to a lesser extent, *The Widow in the Bye Street* could not have been written without Synge's example. The furore that his greatest work, the so-called 'comedy', *The Playboy of the Western World* caused—rioting in Dublin's Abbey Theatre for over a week—anticipates the furore over Masefield's narrative poem (also, in the Shakespearean sense, a 'comedy') and for related reasons. While discussion of the influence of Synge should be deferred until *The Everlasting Mercy* is itself discussed, it is fitting to quote here—in this brief account of Jan Masefield, the writer emergent—from his own essay on his friend, written two years after his death in early 1911 (and thus pre-dating both

The Everlasting Mercy and 'Biography') later published with amendments in *Recent Prose* (1924):

> ... he was guarded, because life had once hurt him, and quiet because he was of low vitality, but in spite of his reserve he gave from the first the impression of a strange personality. He was of a dark type of Irishman, though not black-haired. Something in his air gave one the fancy that his face was dark from gravity. Gravity filled the face and haunted it, as though the man behind were for ever listening to life's case before passing judgement. It was "a dark, grave face, with a great deal in it." ...
>
> His manner was that of a man too much interested in the life about him to wish to be more than a spectator. His interest was in life, not in ideas ...
>
> When I first called upon him, I found him at his type-writer, hard at work ... While I rolled a cigarette he searched for his photographs and at last handed them to me. They were quarter-plate prints in a thick bundle. There must have been fifty of them. They were all of the daily life of Aran; women carrying kelp, men in hookers, old people at their doors, a crowd at the landing-place, men loading horses, people of vivid character, pigs and children playing together, etc. As I looked at them he explained them or commented on them in a way which made all sharp and bright. His talk was best when it was about life or the ways of life. His talk was all about men and women and what they did and what they said when life excited them. His mind was perhaps a little like Shakespeare's. We do not know what Shakespeare thought: I do not know what Synge thought. ...
>
> I met him in the foyer of the theatre just before the first London performance of *The Playboy of the Western World*. I had some talk with him then. During the performance I saw him in his box, "sitting still", as he said, watching with the singular grave intensity with which he watched life. It struck me then that he was the only person there sufficiently simple to be really interested in living people; and that it was this simplicity which gave him charm. He found the life in a man very well worth wonder, even though the man were a fool, or a knave ...

And, before supplying the notes he had been asked for on Synge's life and works, he feels obliged to comment (reiterating the sentiment of his own 'Biography'):

His life, like that of any other artist, was dated not by events but by sensations.

Only partially true, of course, but the point is worth making; it is the inner climate that counts.

Masefield's severance from the England and the class into which he had been born—the compounding of this by his experiences first on the *Gilcruix* and on journey back from Chile as a D.B.S., and then in the United States—is nowhere better demonstrated than in the fact that the two men who influenced him most were Irish, depth-investigators of their country's culture. He was imaginatively inspired by the relationship they had to their provenance. As he says in *So Long to Learn* of his reaction to *Riders to the Sea* and *The Shadow of the Glen*:

> Listening to Synge's plays (both so poignant with his peculiar genius) made me feel what a wealth of fable lay still in the lonely places in England. No-one had touched this wealth, so far as I knew. we had not become alove to its presence: we were dead to it: and much of the theatre of that time was dead in consequence. I had already perceived that Ireland was awake to her own wealth: she was all bright with fervour: hardly a village but saw the light and knew the gladness. The thought occurred to some of us younger Englishmen that some of us might find, in the English country, subjects as moving, fables as lively ...

Masefield is in this passage thinking principally of the contribution the English theatre needed—and in *The Campden Wonder* (first produced in 1907 and printed in 1909) and *The Tragedy of Nan* (first produced in 1908 and printed in 1909) he did his best to supply it, sensitive plays centred on rural tragedies, the latter set by the River Severn (and therefore in his home country) and based on a story told him by his beloved godmother, Miss Flood of Woollas Hall, who had re-entered his life as friend and guide. (The play even contains a detestable hard-hearted aunt.)

But the real fruit of Masefield's appreciation of Synge was to be *The Everlasting Mercy* itself, set nearer his boyhood home even than the banks of the Severn; in Ledbury itself and the woods just above it. He was back among the people he'd listened to with the unerring, wondering yet attentive ear of a 'romantic' boy, and brings to mind Synge's own words in his preface to *The Playboy of the Western World*:

... every speech should be as fully flavoured as a nut or apple, and such speeches cannot be written by anyone who works among people who have shut their lips on poetry. In Ireland, for a few years more, we have a popular imagination that is fiery and magnificent, and tender; so that those of us who wish to write start with a chance that is not given to writers in places where the springtime of the local life has been forgotten, and the harvest is a memory only, and the straw turned into bricks.

4

One of the dedicatees of *Salt-Water Ballads* was a teacher, Constance de la Cherois Crommelin, just over eleven years older than Masefield himself ('slightly older than I am', Masefield was to put it) with whom he was almost certainly already deeply in love. They married in the July of the following year, in the October of which a second volume of poems, *Ballads*, was published. Constance was from the Northern Irish Protestant gentry, had been educated at Newnham College, Cambridge, and taught at the school later to be known as Roedean. When Jan Masefield met her, she shared a flat with Isabel Fry, sister of the distinguished art-critic, Roger Fry. Constance and Isabel's friendship was an intense, perhaps over-intense, one; certainly it was to cause difficulties for both Jan and Constance herself after their marriage. Constance was an intelligent, thoughtful, strong-principled woman; she would seem not always to have had the capacity for putting others at their ease. Accounts of her tend to stress certain difficulties in communication—from those by Masefield's own family (with whom reconciliation had largely occurred, though Masefield never ceased to have good relations with his sisters) to Muriel Spark's extremely vivid and amiable account of her first meeting with the Masefields in December 1950 (which she included in the foreword to the 1992 reprint of her *John Masefield*), though admittedly by this time Constance was almost eighty-four; she died shortly after her ninety-third birthday in February 1960.

'I should think she has been a true companion to him,' remarked Muriel Spark in the notes she made after her visit; the validity of the observation seems beyond dispute. Constance entered into and understood her husband's work, much of which was dedicated to her; visitors commented on the sympathy between them and the courtesy which he unfailingly showed her. On important matters—politics, religion—they were in agreement, also on how they should live their lives. Masefield, moreover, was the most affectionate and devoted of fathers to their children, Judith and Lewis. This is a study of Masefield the writer, and emphatically not a biography; nevertheless certain aspects of his marriage have at this point to be touched on because of their undoubted influence on his *oeuvre*. Constance Babington Smith in her authorised biography of Masefield, *John Masefield: A Life* (1978), which draws on much previously private material, is both subtle and perceptive on the subject of Constance, and on Jan's relation to her—and honest too. She suggests that by 1910, a year Masefield himself confessed to being one of painful difficulties and frustration for him, the marriage had ceased completely to satisfy him. The age differential, and concomitant changes in Constance's appearance were key, and perhaps inadmissible, factors here. This made Masefield susceptible, as he was to be throughout his life, to infatuations, too often of a devouring, demanding kind, with other women, though, curiously, these women did not have to be young. Indeed the first significant friendship after his marriage was with a woman quite a bit older than Constance herself. And even when the loved, the idealised one, was younger, he often behaved and wrote to her as if she weren't.

But no one who reads through Masefield's correspondence with his wife—for example those collected and edited by Peter Vansittart (1984) as *John Masefield's Letters From The Front 1915-17*—can doubt the depth and (frequently) the fervour of Jan's feelings for Constance. 'Your old lover,' is his favourite way of signing himself. 'My darling dear wife,' reads a typical letter of August 1916, thirteen years into their marriage, 'I hope Hampden [their home] won't be sad and tiresome to you. Kiss both the dear Jude and the dear Lewis for me. ... Bless you my sweet Con. Always your old lover, Jan.'

It seems likely that Carrie Masefield's early death, and the total failure of Aunt Kate to be a surrogate of any kind, had left Masefield with an overwhelming need to be mothered, and that this fused to an uncomfortable but not entirely compatible degree with his sexual needs. One is tempted too to think that Carrie/Constance as an embodiment of womanhood (and to this composite should perhaps also be added his mother's best friend, his godmother, Miss Flood) bore a little too much the weight of virtue, was seen too much in term of lodestar and healing rest. Was 'she' to forgive the sexual lapses, the failures in chastity of (in all likelihood) the young Masefield in his New York years, if not before (those many references to Spanish women)? Ports are rather probable places for succumbing to urges of the flesh, and one guesses that the succumbing would present problems for a young man of so romantic and chivalrous a disposition as Jack Masefield. *The Everlasting Mercy* and *The Widow in the Bye Street* are works which treat sexual desire with a quite remarkable frankness, (the franker when closely read), a frankness that in all truth appalled many, but operating in contexts seemingly different from Masefield's own earlier circumstances. But that isn't to say that there isn't a concealed confessional element to them. Indeed, it would seem utterly improbable that there was not, and in that respect the rattled members of the public were probably nearer the truth than such later defenders of Masefield as Alfred Watkins.

One gets a hint, I believe, of what Masefield was asking of the woman, or women, in his life, of the psychological fixation of which he was to some extent a prisoner, in the first story, 'Edward Herries', of the most directly autobiographical of all his early books of prose, the collection, *A Tarpaulin Muster* of 1907. Interestingly, in common with the poems of *Ballads* (1903), subsumed in *Ballads and Poems* (1910) the prose has far more of what has come to be called 'the Nineties' about it, of the *Yellow Book* anthologies and the Celtic Twilight, than the robuster *Salt-Water Ballads*, let alone the work he was to produce after his crisis of self-confidence; it's as if the strong presence of love and his commitment to a life-long relationship had temporarily inhibited his style and made him more reliant on that of others.

'Edward Herries' has idolised a beautiful older woman whom he supposes himself too callow for. 'I am not the man for her. I am too goody-goody. She wants a man with more devil in him.' It's a mistaken assumption, but he goes away for five years to have experience, adventure, and then returns; the house where lives the woman he loves cannot but remind one of Miss Flood's Woollas Hall on the slopes of Bredon. Edward is aware of how much the five years have changed him:

> He had many violent memories, memories of war and of anger, black and savage, to lay by his memories of her beauty. When he thought of her, his thoughts were tinged with these new memories; his mind had been altered by them. ... He could not live the old ordered, secluded life any more. He had been a wild bird, and no cage would ever hold him.

Apprehensively he approaches his mature princesse lointaine, to realise that he had been deceived in his old assessment of what she wanted of him.

> The room was unchanged ... He was disappointed somehow; and the first greeting, so long looked for, so long practised in the spirit, was over before its significance came home to him. He had thought that the touch of her hand would be sacramental, a rapture, a removal of the seals. The fine, delicate hand had merely touched his, and then it was withdrawn. He was conscious of an effort to remember whether he had really touched her. He was disappointed with the greeting. It had been a common thing, after all; after all the dreams. He was disappointed with the face of his old love; his home-coming had been a failure. She was beautiful still; for her beauty was that intellectual beauty which changes little from child-hood to old age. The sweet face had grown, perhaps paler; the eyes, in that light, seemed darker; the expression was changed and calmed; the hair was heaped in a new fashion. He remembered the old, quickly changing, eager look, the flushed cheek, the bright eyes which had moved him so strangely in the past; he was angry that they were no longer there; he was vexed that her voice had lost none of its old laughter. He was conscious that he too had altered. The woman beside him, whose eyes were so dear and yet so strange, was surely aware of that. He, too, had altered. He felt that the woman judged him; and that she, who in the past judged nothing, ate, now only of the golden kernel, drank only of the hidden waters; lived only in an inner temple builded of intellectual beauty. As he spoke to her he thought of his roving in the world, and of the Spanish women he had kissed. It seemed to him that those women sat at his side, with roses in their hair, and their lips still tempting his. It seemed to him that she saw them. It seemed to him that he walked in the temple of her mind for a moment, a smirched and booted figure, and that those women walked with him, laughing, rose-crowned, flushed, spreading defilement. He had thought, of old, that this woman would be won by mastery, by conquest, as it were by storm. He saw now that she could be won only by service, by humbleness, by beautiful sacrifice.

The passage is not the less powerful for being somewhat muddled and essentially unresolved, for it touches on a universal male predicament which Masefield, one infers, knew with peculiar intensity. In order (as Herries here thinks) to be worthy of the woman he so admires, he must be tested, seasoned, a process which will obviously include sexual experience—and experimentation. This achieved, he can return to her with the full maturity of the man as opposed to the boy. But experience, according to the male code (which Masefield will reveal in his greatest works as largely detestable) is in its getting a mostly sordid matter, coarsening the fibre, blunting the sensibility, arousing tastes for what might best not have been appealed to. And then a terrible mocking irony is apparent: when the experienced man is re-united with his woman again, he appreciates that the above is exactly her view too of what has befallen him: that all his rites of passage and their mark on his character are morally distasteful to her. She, in truth, prefers the pure, the dedicatedly innocent, all that he once was, and is no longer. And yet ... Can a man who has been through what the male code asks of him unlearn what he has learned? Does he even want to? Little will have been more urgent or all-consuming in his life than his first knowledge of sex and violence (however interpreted). Can he excise this? Won't he be less than his present self if he so much as tries? Won't boredom and atrophy set in?

This dilemma occurs throughout Masefield's work; his masterpieces are inseparable from discussion of male sexual identity, and this is what gives them their force, their shock of the new. Saul Kane in *The Everlasting Mercy* journeys to the other side of life-by-the-code to find abiding and active peace; Jimmy in *The Widow in the Bye Street* is the victim of overwhelming sexual desire and of the lore of young males that he should let it guide him in the face of all claims from elsewhere; Michael Gray in *The Daffodil Fields* is both hero and villain, master and slave of the male code. It rewards him—if something so basically amoral can be spoken of in such terms—and at the same time is his (and others') ruin.

It is his general inability to deal head on with sexual matters that makes for the ultimately unsatisfying nature of Masefield's many essays in many different literary forms at this time. It was his ability, eventually, to do so that is responsible for the success of the four great narrative poems that preceded the outbreak of the Great War. The climate of the Twenties and Thirties has obscured their achievement, despite the fact that there is demonstrably a good deal in common between the Masefield of these works and the younger D.H. Lawrence (1885-1930). Masefield was an enormous admirer of Hardy's *Jude the Obscure* (1895), speaking to Muriel Spark at their December 1950 meeting of its 'true greatness'. To an important degree he continued the work towards greater literary sexual freedom that *Jude* began, but he was almost thirty years younger than Hardy, and with different temperament and experiences; certain lines of inquiry and methods of presentation were open to him as they couldn't be to the older writer. It is the contemporaneous works of D.H. Lawrence, *The White Peacock* (1911), *The Trespasser* and *Sons and Lovers* (1913) and the short stories, collected in *The Prussian Officer and other Stories* (1914), which essentially travel over the same territory as Masefield's productions. And there is a real connection here: *The English Review* which Ford Madox Hueffer (later Ford Madox Ford), novelist and editor of genius, founded in December 1908, devoted its October 1911 issue to *The Everlasting Mercy*. Lawrence admired *The English Review* enormously—and it was to publish such early masterpieces of his in the short story form as 'A Fragment of Stained Glass', 'Goose Fair', 'Odour of Chrysanthemums', 'The Thorn in the Flesh' and (editorially cut) 'The Prussian Officer'. The deep kinship I perceive between Masefield's and Lawrence's early work thus is also a kinship of publishing venue.

5

Of all the many books that Masefield published in the years between his marriage and *The Everlasting Mercy*—years when he also undertook much journalistic and occasional work, (and must often have felt near to breaking-point)—two seem to me of particular interest in any attempt to come to terms with the knots of his creative personality. The first is from 1909, the second from 1910, and neither is in the least known today. It's also highly unlikely that they could ever recover such reputation as they had, yet they deserve consideration.

While it has serious vitiating faults judged purely as a work of fiction—over-schematisation of design, the characters refused any satisfactory measure of autonomy—*Multitude and Solitude* (1909) is possibly the most alive of Masefield's early prose-works in that it gives us a picture, of some emotional truth, of the author himself and of his moral and artistic plight. Indeed, it could be argued that nowhere else (discounting the too short and too mannered 'Edward Herries') can readers come so close to John Masefield the young writer, and that the very absence of proper fictive distance between him and his protagonist, Roger Naldrett, also a young writer, gives the novel its particular raw fascination. And in this respect what Masefield does not put in, or actually omits, is very nearly as interesting as what he includes or emphasizes.

The novel begins with Roger Naldrett, who 'like Masefield' applies himself with individuality and success to *all* literary forms—fiction, poetry and drama, at the first night of his play, a tragedy called *A Roman Matron*. Its reception has not been warm, and it is to deteriorate during the course of the evening. Only John O'Neill—quite transparently Synge: Irish, aloof, brilliant and mortally ill—can provide the kind of support the worried, disillusioned though ultimately self-confident writer needs. Contemporary readers of the book can forget *So Long to Learn*'s tributes (as quoted above) to the liveliness of pre-Great War London and its cultural life, for the city is here consistently portrayed as self-cripplingly smug, intolerably philistine, stupid to the point of culpability, and Roger—though he certainly expects eventual recognition of the merits he knows himself to possess—is engaged in a running battle with it. Of the audience O'Neill warns Roger:

> "They hate the new mind ... They've been accustomed to folly, persiflage, that abortion the masculine hero, and justifications of their vices. They like caricatures of themselves. They like photographs. They like illuminated texts. they decorate their minds just as they do their homes. You come to them out of the desert, all locusts and wild honey, crying out about beauty. These people won't stand it. They are the people in Frith's 'Derby Day.' Worse. They think they aren't."

His words are soon to be vindicated and in the cameo of the crowd's behaviour 'killing' the play, the crassness of the pub-revellers of *The Everlasting Mercy*, of the gleeful communal unkindness of the crew in *Dauber*, of the jeering louts at market-day in *The Daffodil Fields* are all anticipated:

> A few mild young men, greatly daring, bashfully addressed questions to the stage in self-conscious voices. Whistles sounded suddenly in shrill bursts. Somebody hissed in the stalls. A line reflecting on England's foreign policy, or seeming to do so, for there is nothing topical in good literature, raised shouts of 'Yah!', and 'Pro-Boer,' phrases still shouted at advanced thinkers in moments of popular pride. At the most poignant moment of the tragedy the gallery shouted 'Boo!' in sheer anger. The stalls, excited by the noise, looked round and up, smiling. Songsters began one of the vile songs of the music-halls, debased in its words, its rhythms, and its

tune. Their feet beat time to it. The booing made a monotony as of tom-toms; whistles and cat-calls sounded, like wild-birds flying across the darkness. People got up blunderingly to leave the theatre, treading on other people's toes, stumbling over their knees, with oaths in their hearts and apologies on their lips. The play had come to an end.

But outside the theatre, even outside the company of critics and fellow-writers, Roger encounters nothing that doesn't fuel his Flaubertian feeling of '*La vie est bête*', though he blames much onto the gigantism and commercialism of London itself. His heart is in Ireland, with a woman, a teacher, whom he encountered during his recent, not very satisfactory sojourn there, Ottalie Fawcett, about whom he has a strange dream ('like a Mass in an unknown tongue')—with even stranger bearings on his life. In the dream he understands that Ottalie has gone from him, 'left him to seek for her through the world', while she has a mate in an unknown youth 'with a calm, strong face'. At the end of the dream he receives from her a letter with a Greek postmark, its message 'I have read your last book, it reads like the diary of a lost soul.'

The real Ottalie comes from the Irish landed gentry (quite a bit is made of this; her provenance explains her nobility, her passionate addiction to truth) and spends much time in the company of Agatha, an independent-minded, jealous-temperamented woman (cf Constance and Isabel Fry; the similarity is too close for the relationship as presented in the novel to have the requisite life and credibility). Ottalie and Agatha pass through London on their way back to Northern Ireland, but she and Roger miss each other. This only compounds Roger's dark aggrieved mood. In his despondency he hears the voice of authentic poetry, and it is Baudelaire's:

> La servante au grand coeur dont vous étiez jalouse,
> Et qui dort sans sommeil sous une humble pelouse,
> Nous devrions pourtant lui porter quelques fleurs.
> Les morts, les pauvres morts, ont de grandes douleurs,
> Et quand Octobre souffle, émondeur des vieux arbres,
> Son vent mélancolique à l'entour de leurs marbres,
> Certe, ils doivent trouver les vivants bien ingrats.

These lines are to have an eerie significance for Roger, who has decided that he must follow his loved one to Ulster; by the time he reaches her home Ottalie is of the company of the dead, drowned in a steamer disaster. Agatha and Roger have to make peace with each other in respect of the woman for whom they are grieving, and Roger appreciates both that his dream was prophetic and that he must now consecrate to her memory, her spirit, a quite different life from that he has so frustratedly been living.

In the terrible days that follow his reception of death, both in Ireland and back in England, Roger's attention is brought to the seemingly incongruous subject of tropical disease in general, and sleeping sickness in particular. On his last day in Ireland he picks up a year-old copy of a popular magazine and there reads, expressed in trivial, and in places morally offensive, terms, the following article:

SLEEPING SICKNESS

It is not generally known that this devastating ailment is caused by the presence of a minute micro-organism in the human system. The micro-organism may exist in unsuspected harmlessness for many years in the victim's blood. It is not until it enters what is known to scientists as the cerebro-spinal fluid, or as we should call it, the marrow, that it sets up the peculiar symptoms of the dread disease which has so far baffled the ingenuity of our soi-disant savants. This terrible affliction, which is not by any means confined to those inferior members of the human race, the dusky inhabitants of Uganda, consists of a lethargy accompanied with great variations of temperament. So far the dread complaint is without a remedy.

Various other signs suggest that his destiny and the obtainment of knowledge about/possible cure of this dreadful disease are connected. In particular there's his friendship which begins as chance acquaintance with Lionel Heseltine, a doctor who has devoted some years of his life to studying in East Africa the trypanosomes responsible for sleeping-sickness. Jack Masefield, trainee on the *Conway* in Liverpool, had been fascinated by accounts of tropical disease; in America he had wondered whether he should devote himself to the subject. In their first conversation Lionel says to Roger:

"I could show you some trypanosomes. They're the organisms."
"What are they like?" Roger asked.
"They're like little wriggly flattened membranes. Some of them have tails. They multiply by longitudinal division. They're unlike anything else. They've got a pretty bad name."

"And they cause the disease?"

"Yes. You know, of course, that they are spread by the tsetse fly? The tsetse fly sucks them out of an infected fish or mammal, and develops them, inside his body probably for some time, during which the organism probably changes a good deal. When the tsetse bites a man, the developed trypanosome gets down the proboscis into the blood. About a week after the bite, when the bite itself is cured, the man gets the ordinary trypanosome fever, which makes you pretty wretched, by the way."

"Have you had it?"

"Yes; rather. I have it now. It recurs at intervals."

"And how about sleeping sickness?"

"You get sleeping sickness when the trypanosome enters the cerebro-spinal fluid. You may not get it for six or seven years after the bite. On the other hand, you may get it almost at once."

"Then you may get it?" said Roger, startled, looking at the man with a respect which was half pity.

"I've got it," said Lionel.

"Got it?" said Roger. He stumbled in his speech. "But, forgive my speaking like this," he said, "is there a cure, then?"

"It's not certain that it's a permanent cure," said Lionel. "I've just started it. It's called atoxyl ... Now I'm afraid I'm talking rather about myself."

"No, indeed; I'm intensely interested," said Roger, "Tell me more. Tell me about the sickness in Uganda. Is it really bad?"

"Pretty bad," said Lionel, "I suppose that a couple of hundred thousand men and women have died of it during the last seven years. I don't know how many animals besides. The tsetse will bite pretty nearly every living thing, and everything it bites gets disease of some sort."

This is an extraordinary interchange; the reader cannot miss Roger's nervous excitement, or that a certain call to adventure is, on his part, being harkened to here, or that he has an almost ideological need of Lionel and his medical work. This isn't to diminish his fundamental seriousness, nor to imply that he and Masefield with him do not have a proper objective interest in a subject of importance and gravity. But it still seems legitimate to ask: Why so 'intensely interested'? The disease in the distant African countryside is received as an indication that there are evils from which the western world has averted itself, which it is unlikely to suffer—but which maybe it should. Over the reception of it there hangs surely that whole

malaise about Imperialism and the relation to the colonies that was, somewhere, eating its way into the European mind. There is also the distinct
feeling that the challenge a cure for sleeping sickness posits is to be
welcomed by such as Roger as another type of cure, from the *ennui* of a
spoilt, self-indulgent society. And indeed this is made plain, in both words
and actions later in the novel. Roger accompanies Lionel to Africa, they
investigate and fight the disease in the most practical and distressing way,
and both men suffer from fever and its attendant hallucinations.

Confronting the ravages of sleeping sickness is also to confront an
ineluctable face of reality. It vanquishes the escapes offered by religion
and utopian politics; in part it is the extreme face of Darwinism, given
specific physical expression. Masefield, in common with so many of his
generation, was intensely concerned with the inadequacies of orthodox
religion in the face of expanding scientific knowledge. A conversation
between Lionel and Roger—out in the tropical wilderness—is of real
interest here, in indicating the tortured state of mind that was often
Masefield's at this period—though the novel is to end on an upward movement, with a feeling that temporarily the two men have triumphed:

> "Flies have an uncanny knowledge," said Roger. "How do they
> get their knowledge? Is it mere inherited instinct? I notice that they
> always attack in the least-protected spots? ... And they have appar-
> ently no place in the scheme of the world, except to transplant the
> trypanosome from where he is harmless to where he is deadly."
>
> "Lots of men are like that," said Lionel, "you can see see thou-
> sands of them outside those disgusting pot-houses. Men with no
> place in the scheme of the world, except to transplant intoxicants
> from the casks, where they are harmless, to their insides, where they
> become deadly, both to themselves and to society. Any self-
> respecting State would drown the brutes in their own beer, yet the
> brutes don't get drowned. And as they do not, there must be a scien-
> tific reason. Either the State must be so rotten that the germs are
> neutralised by other germs, or the germs must have some dim sort
> of efficiency for life, just as the tsetses have. They have the tenacity
> of the very low organism. It is one of the mysteries of life to me that
> a man tends to lose that tenacity and efficiency for life as soon as he
> becomes sufficiently subtle and fine to be really worth having in the
> world. I like Shakespeare because he is one of the very few men
> who realize that."

The dark confusion of thought here—which stops short at the conclusion that in the social body there exist many whose sole purpose is the
spread of malign anti-bodies—brings to mind John Carey's study *The
Intellectuals and the Masses* (1992) with its illuminating survey of the
terror of the mob, the wish to control and prune it, of so many of the
thinkers of the Edwardian era. In Masefield's case the view-point
expressed here stems less from ideological conviction and more, I would
suggest, from his boyhood experiences of the herd as something not to be
trusted, whether schoolboys, older 'chums', the flotsam round the Iquique
or New York bars—or the society of a prosperous Herefordshire small
town. That the truly sensitive man is, according to some Darwinist law,
also the weaker one is a necessary corollary of this: Masefield had not been
able to stand the *Gilcruix* and so was branded D.B.S., but he was a subtler
personality than many of those ship-mates who had stood it. Lionel (rather
out of character) even lists the superior Shakespeare figures: Hamlet,
Richard the Second, Brutus, Othello, even Malvolio (the victim of a cruel
practical joke) or Aguecheek (the butt of unkind teasing). But emphatically
not Prince Henry (Henry V) 'that disgusting, beefy brute'.

Masefield was the least self-asserting of writers, even though his
oeuvre corresponds to a covert history of his perceptions of himself and his
place in society. The kind of argument—rather crudely—presented here
was to be subsumed into his properly imaginative studies of the individual
at variance with the herd—such as *Dauber*. *Multitude and Solitude* must
be praised for the ardour of its interest in the sufferings of humanity, particularly a section of it remote from London and English life, testimony to the
generosity of Masefield's sympathies and his refusal to draw the cultural
lines imaginatively necessary (and damaging) to too many of his compa-
triots. The struggles of Roger and Lionel in East Africa are vivid, often
horrifying, coloured by an essential nobility of spirit—and a greatly-to-be-
welcomed change from the hideous wildlife-destroying, 'native'-suspi-
cious Imperialistic adventures of the fictional fellows, whether in Rider
Haggard or (a little later) in John Buchan.

The book ends on a panegyric to man's capacity to extend his powers,
and expressive of a view of Nature as an enemy no longer fashionable, and
rarely associated with Masefield himself, that passionate lover of so many of
its manifestations. In fact (yet another paradox) the ending—neither intellectually nor in fictive terms a success, springs from Masefield's identification with living beings, not from any anthropocentric sense of superiority:

[Said Lionel] "[We] are living in a most wonderful time. The world is just coming to see that science is not a substitute for religion, but religion of a very deep and austere kind. We are seeing only the beginning of it."

They settled a plan of action together.

Roger went out into the garden, and down the hill, thinking of the crusade against the weariness and filth of cities. There was an afterglow upon the hills. It fell with a ruddy glare on the window of his dream. It thrilled him. The light would fall there long after the house had fallen. It had lighted Ottalie. It had burned upon the pane when Ottalie's mother stood there. Nature was enduring; Nature the imperfect; Nature the enemy, which blighted the rose and spread the weed. Thinking of the woman who had waited for him there in his vision, he prayed that her influence in him might help to bring to earth that promised life, in which man, curbing Nature to his use, would assert a new law and rule like a king, where now, even in his strength, he walks sentenced, a prey to all things baser.

It is hard to imagine this passage in any book published after 1918, when man-made poison-gas and all the infernal munitions used to kill millions supplanted the blight and the weed as the enemy of humankind. That doesn't mean that there isn't—even if it demands different vocabulary, a different paradigm—a case here.

The second of these books, *A Book of Discoveries* (1910), dedicated to Masefield's daughter, Judith (though she would surely at six years old have been too young for it), is characterised by the same double attitude to Nature, a tension that, in retrospect, seems characteristic of the age drawing to an end—between Darwinism and a romantic feeling for Nature. The story is a broken-backed one—indeed it scarcely has a backbone—though the central idea behind it is clear enough: that the adventures of the two brothers, Robin and Mac, should not only be escapades of the type Bevis and his friend, Mark, enjoy in Richard Jefferies' classic *Bevis: The Story of a Boy* (1882), but real 'discoveries'—of truths about the history and natural history of their home-country. This last is not Masefield's own, but the Cornwall-Devon countryside, round the River Gara, and the mysterious moor-clad hill, Brown Willy, which he came to know and love through his friendship with Jack Yeats. Furthermore these discoveries are paralleled by the boys' unearthing stories of other discoveries in the past— by travellers, explorers, naturalists, even whole peoples. Not the least interesting feature of the book is that Masefield refuses to take any patronising hierarchical attitude to the peoples of the past, but presents them all as worthy of democratic honour.

Robin and Mac find an adult mentor, the admirable if slightly tedious Mr Hampden, whose noble and sympathetic attitude to the wildlife on his property was quoted at the outset of this study. The brothers are certainly in need of lessons—and once again Masefield's opposition to the whole manly Imperialist cult, familiar to boy-readers from the books of Ballantyne, Henty, Kingston etc. is made refreshingly clear. "'I say," exclaims the armed Robin typically enough, "there's a heron. Shall we whang at her as we go by?'"

They do not seem altogether sorry, however, when Mr Hampden puts a stop to such high-spirited callousness. Indeed they see their lives as being enriched by his example. But the tormented legacy of the Darwinist view-point is present throughout the story—and at times runs close to the Buddhist idea of all living beings existing under the yoke of the travail and pain of existence from which there should be ultimate release into peace:

> It was a fine, hot August day. The English country was at its best. The osiers rustled coolly; the kingfishers darted like flying jewels. There was a murmur aloft of all the multitudinous life which drones and buzzes in the summer air like the world humming as it spins. The world seemed at peace all about the boys as they threshed upstream, but it was not really at peace. Birds, wasps, dragon-flies, and innumerable lesser murderers, darted, and hovered, and killed, as though the fine weather were only sent to make murder easy, when food was a little more plentiful than when the cold struck. Kestrels hovered here and there, poising deliberately, then wheeling away with a sudden swift fluttering and long sweep. Over in the wilderness a weasel was chasing a rabbit. The boys could hear the beast screaming almost like a human being, screaming from fear, not from pain, long before the little red devil leaped upon its back to kill it.

Clearly John Masefield was a man of extraordinarily heightened sensitivity; appreciation of suffering was his daily companion, and this appreciation intensified in this crisis-time, demanding release in work that was stronger and dug deeper than any he'd done before.

A word about Masefield's domestic situation. In 1909 he and Constance were able to take, with Isabel Fry, a farmhouse in the country-side, in Great Hampden, Buckinghamshire, in the beech-wooded chalk hills of the Chilterns. Solace as far as his creative work was concerned was by no means instantaneous, but—as 'Biography' of 1911 is witness—tired, too often despondent, he was whole-heartedly relieved to put urban living basically behind him.

6

It was first in the April, and then in the May of 1911, that Masefield had experiences in which the physical and spiritual were so fused as to amount to intimations of the unitary nature of life, intimations conducive to the creation of major literary work. They constituted break-throughs out of his mental morass, and the second experience led quite directly to the writing of the poem that was to change his reputation—and his life. One cannot do better than quote Masefield's own account of them in *So Long to Learn*, both his depression, and, in the second instance, his ecstasy being conveyed in the very rhythms of the prose just as his protagonist's move-ment from darkness to light was to be in the verse ones of *The Everlasting Mercy* itself.

> On a Sunday morning in that blackness of despair I set out upon a memorable walk in a late April, after a winter of much ill-health and disappointment. Being alone in the country for the weekend I went away through some woodland, in parts that I had never before seen, and have never seen since. It was a sad walk, for my work was not what I had hoped ... The prospect before me seemed black.
>
> Seeing a likely ash-plant in a pile of hedge-trimmings, I took it, and trimmed some five feet of it, with a knife, to be my walking-staff. The day was sunny and fine, but it had been a cold and snowy April. On my walk, I came to a hollow on the northern side of a hedge (it was more than a ditch; it looked like an overgrown shallow quarry). It was still full of dirty unmelted snow-drift, for no sun could reach it and rain had not fallen since the snow. I probed the snow with my staff, and found it to be, roughly, three feet four inches deep; not a bad record for late April; not a cheerful sight, but one well according with my mood.
>
> Presently, on my return, being then on the southern side of that hedge, I found the bank starred with primroses. They were the first I had seen for a year, and in any case would have given me delight;

but as I looked at them a voice within me that I did not know (a man's voice) said clearly: "The Spring is beginning."

I walked home, feeling that the difficulties that beset me in what I was then trying to write would now clear away. I had no doubt of this; a message of hope had been given me.

Throughout Masefield's *oeuvre*, April is a shorthand for renewal and growth of the spirit. Thus, later, in the sonnet that is Poem XXX in *Lollingdon Downs and Other Poems, with Sonnets* (1917) he speaks of 'Beauty herself, the universal mind, / Eternal April wandering alone;' while in Poem LIV he refers to a cycle of 'Aprils of the soul'. In this actual April he found his own divided inner condition mirrored by an unusual trough of unmelted snow and by flowers heralding a brighter and more productive season. Both must have taken him back to the difficult spring-time of his own life, with its problems and its intense (and frequently soli-tary) pleasures, passed in Ledbury, and so turned his mind to his earlier Herefordshire life. But it was a *man*'s voice that seemed to be speaking to him, an indication that creatively he should approach the world of his boyhood not in the immature person of his former self but as an adult, as a fully grown male of the Ledbury countryside who knew the kind of struggle he was himself engaged in now. It is possible that the 'man's voice' could have been, to Masefield's fancy, Chaucer's, for he had opened his *Canterbury Tales* with the most famous of all apostrophes to April, the very name of which is derived from the Latin 'to open', 'to begin afresh'. '... my work was not what I had hoped.' Masefield does not not supply readers with details of what he had hoped. Probably he scarcely knew, was merely aware that a different kind of attentiveness to the world about him and to the motions of his own mind was now needed, to rescue him from depression and sterility. He continues:

> However, the difficulties did not clear away, the work seemed in a tangle, and not to be cleared by any effort of mine. I took it with me into another part of the country, where I stayed alone, working and worrying for a few days, finding no light upon it, yet sure that the promised light would come.
>
> In an evening in May, having written myself weary, I went out for a walk through woodland, then in all the beauty of young leaf and life. I was in a state of great inner joy from a sight that I had seen that morning. [This—which has great bearing on the poem that

was to spring into his head—was of a young ploughman at work.] 'I came home uphill through a wood, feeling that the incredible and impossible were on each side of me. At the wood's edge there was a sort of fence to shut it from the common beyond. The fence was something to step over with the feet, and easily to push through with the body. As I went over and through this division, I said to myself, "Now I will make a poem about a blackguard who becomes converted." Instantly the poem appeared to me in its complete form, with every detail distinct; the opening lines poured out upon the page as fast as I could write them down.

As for the writing itself:

> I had written between fourteen and twenty lines before I reached home. I then lit the lamp and sat down to write, till I had done some sixty odd lines more.
>
> I was alone in the house. It was not a very lonely house: there were two other little houses, one about thirty, the other sixty, yards away. However, it was deep country, nearly midnight, and everybody near me must have been abed and asleep.
>
> Suddenly, as I wrote, the door of the room in which I wrote flung itself noisily wide open.
>
> Do not think that I was scared: no, no; I was terrified, almost out of my wits.
>
> Why the door had opened in that way, I do not know. It had never opened like that before, and never did again. The hint was not lost upon me; I packed up my writing and went to bed.
>
> In three weeks and three days I had finished my tale in verse of the blackguard who was converted.

The physical circumstances of the work's inception and beginning have the clearest psychic connotations: the burgeoning trees announcing the fullness to come, the uphill direction, taking the walker out of the wood towards a common, so leading him towards openness and expanse of vista. The walk is thus in itself like a passing from blackguard-dom (the wood at its densest) to the light of salvation (the commonland gained). By association the poet is back in the country world of his childhood, but, as promised by the previous month's intimation, not as a child but as a mature man. What he was releasing in himself, memory fused with imagination, would take him more extensively and more nakedly through human experience than, in any of his previous work, he had previously dared. Surely the door that so inexplicably opened with such noise in the still of the country night is the opening onto the male psychic world of violence and sexual desire with which his Saul Kane can, until his conversion, only deal with by sottish, and sometimes desperate surrender.

Masefield's uphill walk didn't take him back merely to the generalities of country boyhood, but to somewhere specific, with specific associations and specific histories attached. Asked to write about how he had drawn on places of his earlier years in his work, Masefield replied, in *The Ledbury Scene as I have used it in my Verse*:

> I shall begin (as I feel that I, myself, began as a writer) with the tale in verse called *The Everlasting Mercy*.
>
> The very slight foundation of fact in this tale is as follows. Very many years ago, I heard somehow, somewhere in Ledbury, from someone, I know not now from whom, that many years before that, two poachers had fought at night by moonlight, to decided which of the two should poach in some of the coverts ... I put the scene of the challenge and the fight on the open, somewhat barren pasture above the Coneygree Wood on the field-track leading to Eastnor Knoll and Eastnor.

Without consciously deciding to do so, he had brought himself back to his creatively seminal Herefordshire world, put himself in touch with his emotions, his own and other people's, his knowledge and understanding of which he had buried for too long. And so here is the April, the opening, to the real Masefield canon.

CHAPTER IV
The Canon: *The Everlasting Mercy*

'Fourteen to twenty lines' (by which he must have meant the twenty-four of the first three stanzas, the introduction to the poem proper) had come into Masefield's head before he reached the house at the end of his walk. Subsequent lines (until the coda the work is composed in octosyllabic couplets) 'poured out upon the page as fast as I could write them down.' Their urgency makes them as arresting today as then, as racy, and very nearly as much as shocking, for all the cultural shifts that have taken place since its time. The poet has seemingly become the instrument through which another autonomous individual can speak:

> From '41 to '51
> I was my folk's contrary son;
> I bit my father's hand right through
> And broke my mother's heart in two.
> I sometimes go without my dinner
> Now that I know the times I've gi'n her.

By the brilliant stratagem of giving precise dates in his very first line, Masefield asserts the actuality of the history being recounted: this narrator can demonstrably be assigned to time and to place. Yet the magically pregnant phrase, 'folk's contrary son', with its echo of 'The Prodigal Son', the Biblical tale of another young man lost and then found, suggests this history has a parable-like nature, a suggestion maintained in the couplet that follows on.

The speaker's words about his parents can be taken both literally and metaphorically. As a truculent small boy he may well have attacked his father with his teeth (as Masefield did his governess with a fork) but he also, as the saying has it, 'bit the hand that fed him'. Conversely, while he brought despair and distress to his mother, thus 'breaking her heart', he also could have undermined her physical health with his wild behaviour. The dramatic opening stanza concludes with a significant pointer to what is ahead. Masefield, when conveying the suddenness and intensity of his inspiration, was insistent that 'the poem appeared to me in its complete form, with every detail distinct', and it is as a whole that the long, closely-worked poem must be taken. *'Now that I know'* (my italics)—these words make clear that the narrator occupies a standpoint quite foreign to his past self, and that how he came to this standpoint constitutes the kernel of his story. So readers can take the second and third stanzas accordingly:

> From '51 to '61
> I cut my teeth and took to fun.
> I learned what not to be afraid of
> And what stuff women's lips are made of;
> I learned with what a rosy feeling
> Good ale makes floors seem like the ceiling,
> And how the moon gives shiny light
> To lads as roll home singing by't.
> My blood did leap, my flesh did revel,
> Saul Kane was tokened to the devil.
>
> From '61 to '67
> I lived in disbelief of heaven.
> I drunk, I fought, I poached, I whored,
> I did despite unto the Lord,
> I cursed, 'twould make a man look pale,
> And nineteen times I went to jail.
>   Now, friends, observe and look upon me,
>   Mark how the Lord took pity on me.

The behavioural territory is now established for the greater part of the tale—drunkenness, sexual indulgence, brawling—while the words 'devil', 'disbelief', 'heaven' and 'Lord' are further tokens of his present faith. Saul Kane is about to testify to his own redemption at the age of twenty-six; his ability to see himself as an object-lesson for others is shown by his refer-ring to himself in the third person, and by the didactic final couplet of the third stanza—in which the rhythm ominously changes, with its emphatic substitution of same-syllable endings for rhyme. Saul does not take a subjective view of the experiences and events he is recounting; he believes in an active agency: His 'Mark how the Lord took pity on me' is to be backed up later. Of the challenge to the fight he says:

> Those were the words, that was the place
> By which God brought me into grace.

For Saul it is the Lord's intervention in ordinary life that is the 'everlasting mercy' of the title; the poet himself infers a different interpretation of events. The poem's first readers found it hard to distinguish—indeed often refused to do so—between writer and character. Masefield must *himself* have 'revelled' in the same sordid and violent goings-on as Saul (the scenes in the pub particularly troubled the contemporary public), he must *himself* have undergone a Revivalist-style conversion. While both suppositions were erroneous, the sheer undeniable intensity of the work does point to its having strong personal significance for the author; clearly, in T.S. Eliot's famous phrase, it's an objective correlative for important aspects of Masefield's life.

'Now I will make a poem about a blackguard who becomes converted.' 'Blackguard' is not a word in currency nowadays; this does not mean it should be discounted here. It's essential to a proper understanding of *The Everlasting Mercy* that Saul's badness is not glossed over; otherwise he and the power of his testament are diminished. Almost as soon as he knew the subject of his poem, Masefield was stimulated, by the lie of the land, to remember the field and woods (Coneygree) above Ledbury and the story he'd often heard about a fight between the two poachers. But, as so with true creative imaginations— Henry James and the dinner-table anecdote that was the starting-point for *The Spoils of Poynton*, Federico García Lorca and the newspaper case behind his atavistic tragedy, *Blood Wedding*—Masefield did not stick to the letter of the original story, but changed it for his own purposes. The nature of these changes is illuminating. The fight in Masefield's poem is *not* about who should poach where, though this is how it is later presented to backers and spectators, but arises through Saul's deliberate violation of a longstanding agreement, of a pact between mates. The quarrel between Saul Kane and Billy Myers, as it's given to us—in lines that quickly became famous for their raw colloquialism and are the more powerful for being broken up in angry ejaculations and interjections—makes the former's dishonourable conduct quite clear. The only way he can assert himself and gain a semblance of moral dignity is if the two of them fight it out.

> Now when he saw me set my snare,
> He tells me "Get to hell from there.
> This field is mine," he says, "by right;
> If you poach here, there'll be a fight.
> Out now," he says, "and leave your wire;
> It's mine."
>   "It ain't."
>   "You put."
>   "You liar."
> "You closhy put."
>   "You bloody liar."
> "This is my field."
>   "This is my wire."
> "I'm ruler here."
>   "You ain't."
>   "I am."
> "I'll fight you for it."
>   "Right, by damn.
> Not now, though, I've a-sprained my thumb,
> We'll fight after the harvest hum."

Saul—a further proof of his rejection of morality—will not forget Billy's injury, but will use it to turn the fight to his own advantage. Though just as the fight is about to begin:

> When Bill was stripped down to his bends
> I thought how long we two'd been friends,
> And in my mind, about that wire,
> I thought, "He's right, I am a liar ..."

And, a few lines on, saved Saul recalls unsaved Saul in lines very moving in their shame and retrospective tenderness. Indeed the oscillation between raucousness and reflection, between physical action and quiet waiting, between anger, fear and outrage on the one hand, and stillness and a sense of the spiritual dimension on the other, is most dexterously managed, never calling attention to itself, faithfully capturing each mood of the time, while establishing from the outset the inevitability, intense though the struggle, of the gentle power's victory.

And thinking that way my heart bled so
I almost stept to Bill and said so.
And now Bill's dead I would be glad
If I could only think I had.
But no. I put the thought away
For fear of what my friends would say.
They'd backed me, see? O Lord, the sin
Done for the things there's money in.

Saul has imagination and heart. But his particular form of self-esteem, necessary to his identity, is fuelled by that male code by which he has elected to live, and that code too often calls on blood-lust for its endorsement. The spectators of Saul's and Billy's fight are a vicious lot, wanting to see viciousness done. (The viciousness is a collective affair, however, as later in *Dauber*, as already, more covertly stated, in *Multitude and Solitude*. Salvation will come only with dissociation from the herd.) In a moment of honesty, of rare admission of the truth of his feelings, Saul sees the onlookers and the desires possessing them for what they are, a manifestation of evil:

And thinking that, you'll understand
I thought, "I'll go and take Bill's hand.
I'll up and say the fault was mine,
He shan't make play for these here swine."
And then I thought that that was silly,
They'd think I was afraid of Billy:
They'd think (I thought it, God forgive me)
I funked the hiding Bill could give me.
And that thought made me mad and hot.
"Think that, will they? Well, they shall not ..."

Fear of loss of reputation then goads Saul on, and vanquishes the promptings of goodness. The fight proceeds, and the energy of the couplets describing it is mimetic of that of the action itself. Billy, driven on by his sense of being in the right, is for its greater part the victor, knocking Saul down: the crowd always prefers hitter to hit. Saul realises that if he is to save the day for himself and public opinion of him he must fight foul, and his second, Jimmy, gives him full encouragement. Go for the thumb, he says, and the fight will be 'your own':

Try to imagine if you can
The kind of manhood in the man,
And if you'd like to feel his pain,
You sprain your thumb and hit the sprain,
And hit it hard, with all your power
On something hard for half an hour,
While someone thumps you black and blue,
And then you'll know what Billy knew.
Bill took that pain without a sound
Till half-way through the eighteenth round,
And then I sent him down and out,
And Silas said, "Kane wins the bout."

So Saul emerges triumphant, the spectators of course have already changed their allegiance ('Saul is a wonder and a fly 'un!'). Without this undeserved and false worldly glory, the other kind of glory which he is to know, while leading a humdrum enough life as a Herefordshire agricultural labourer, would have eluded him. Billy refuses to shake Saul's hand, however, and tells him to 'get to hell'. Possibly this injunction scares Saul in the deep recesses of his being, (he knows, after all, just how bad he has been) for in truth his salvation, his deliverance from hell, can be said to begin from this point.

The hour is late, the moon is shining bright in the sky, the church clock strikes twelve, and Saul and the men who have watched him beat Billy make their way to 'The Lion' for an illegal out-of-hours celebration. And now, quite unheralded and therefore quite unexpected, a new constituent of Saul's story enters, an intimation of what the young man himself would not have been able to term the 'numinous' but which belongs to that category nevertheless.

☆　　　　　　☆　　　　　　☆

Masefield on his May-time walk of inspiration and composition was, as his mind kindled to the topic, re-tracing that earlier topographically comparable walk he'd done so many times in his boyhood. In *The Ledbury Scene* he was adamant about the actuality of the route Saul took and the places he passed:

> After the fight, the winner and his friends return through the wood to the Worcester Road, turn left, towards Ledbury, beside what was then a pretty roadside brook under a wall where much toad-flax grew, and then turn right, along what was called Cabbage Lane, to the southern side of the Church.
>
> It was from this point that I, myself, first consciously approached the Church and came to know it. At this moment in my story, my mind

> filled with many childish imaginings of what the Church was and had
> been to many and many, who perhaps still watched and were glad
> there, in a life more full and sweet than any known to us. For some
> lines in the tale, something of this interrupts my story.

It would seem that accompanying Saul Kane as he makes his way from the field of the fight back into Ledbury was a route for Masefield back into the world of his past, with its multitude of ambivalences and half-acknowledged responses and yearnings. It is his involvement with his theme at an unconscious as well as a conscious level that gives *The Everlasting Mercy* its peculiarly unforgettable quality. For even if the story of the poem was fully present in Masefield's head before he actually began to write, its course could not have remained unaffected by pressures from within. The part played by church in his early life would have been simply too strong not to find its way into the narrative now unfolding, and that the church is Ledbury's St Michael and All Angels there can be no disputing: here is the detached steeple belltower, here is the peacock weather-vane. Masefield in later life freely admitted to having been regularly and stupendously bored in church—'Often and often, I used to say [during a service] "it will be over in an hour"'—and at the time of writing *The Everlasting Mercy* he was, in common with Constance, anti-clerical, a position he modified rather than changed with the years. But, ever paradoxical, he could also admit: 'At a very early age, I felt the beauty of [the church's] mystery and its link with eternity.' And such a feeling now overtakes the pub-bound hero of a dishonourable fight.

Saul, as he walks past the churchyard, recalls how bell-ringer Dawe and his two sons saw on Christmas Eve a host of the long dead; they rose from the churchyard, pressed against the church-windows, and entered the church itself, glowing with fire-like light, a sort of mass transfiguration, signifying the life everlasting and unquenchable. For Saul, as he thinks of the curious witness of the bell-ringer and his boys, as for dreamy young Jack Masefield (who spent the crucial years of his boyhood in a house next-door to the old churchyard in which he so loved to wander and browse) it is the notion of communion with the many generations of the countless dead that is important, comforting even though awesome (though the converted Saul also looks back on bell-ringer Dawe's host as an earnest of redemption and the Christian afterlife). The whole passage is quick with a strange beauty, making it clear that Saul is a far more complex and spiritually responsive individual than could have been deduced from his conduct so far. (And so, beneath their hard exteriors, may each one of his abetters also be):

Ringer Dawe aloft could mark
Faces at the window dark
Crowding, crowding, row on row
Till all the church began to glow.
The chapel glowed, the nave, the choir,
All the faces became fire
Below the eastern window high
To see Christ's star come up the sky,
Then they lifted hands and turned,
And all their lifted fingers burned,
Burned like the golden altar tallows,
Burned like a troop of God's own Hallows,
Bringing to mind the burning time
When all the bells will rock and chime
And burning saints on burning horses
Will sweep the planets from their courses
And loose the stars to burn up night.
Lord, give us eyes to bear the light.

These lines bring irresistibly to mind paintings by Stanley Spencer. In point of fact, Spencer (born 1891) would, in 1911, have been only twenty and still a student at the Slade. But in this very year he was to paint *John Donne arriving in Heaven* and, over the next three years, to execute paintings which unite his vision of the supernatural with an intimate vision of his own Cookham. Masefield and the thirteen-years-younger Spencer were not so much travelling in the same imaginative direction, as entering into the long, if sometimes fractured, English spiritual tradition: Herbert, Vaughan, Traherne, Crashaw, Blake and the Ancients, especially Calvert and Linnell, Samuel Palmer, and in music the Vaughan Williams of the *Fantasia on a Theme by Thomas Tallis* (1910) and *Five Mystical Songs*: settings of poems by George Herbert (1911).

So though Saul Kane's contemplation of the Advent visitations may be a seeming 'interruption', just as his later telling of a fairy-tale to little Jimmy Jaggard has appeared to some critics (Muriel Spark, for example), it is in fact an organic interruption, quite indispensable to realisation of the poem's purpose. 'On reaching the southern side of Church,' continues Masefield in *The Ledbury Scene*, and truly, as a summary of the poem as well as a geographical commentary on it, his words could not be bettered:

my hero and his friends turn to the left, cross the great Western front of the Church to the parvise known as The Scallenge, go down Church Lane, and, at the end of the Lane enter an imaginary tavern, supposed to be in the Homend, directly north of the Market-House building. Here they drink, and here a few moments of bitter reflection make my violent hero outrageous. From this supposed inn near the Market House, he is near the town Fire-Bell, that in his day, and later, in mine, hung near St Katherine's Chapel, just below the Feathers Hotel. With this bell, he rouses the town, and proceeds to run riot; that, after brief rest, is repeated the next day. In the evening of this day, somewhat saddened and sickened, he goes up the Worcester Road for a little distance, and drinks at a lovely spring, that in those days gushed from the road's southern wall. Wild weather is rapidly coming on; the turmoil is also in himself; and as the storm breaks, so something of his past shatters within himself; and he experiences illumination with all the violence of his nature.

One senses concealed autobiography here. Not autobiography of a literal kind (one remembers the admonitions of 'Biography' that Masefield felt compelled to write so soon after *The Everlasting Mercy*) but of what might be termed the quintessential kind, acknowledging the inner world of drives and longings as well as the outer one of actions and relationships. What the poet and critic Edwin Muir (1887-1959) said about the art of autobiography, in *The Story and the Fable* (1940) seems pertinent here:

> In themselves, our conscious lives may not be particularly interesting. But what we are and can never be, our fable, seems to me inconceivably interesting.

In *The Everlasting Mercy* Masefield was discovering his fable, and the next sequence provides a particularly potent instance of this. The pub-scenes (in the deliberately fictitious 'Lion') gave particular offence to many of the poem's first readers. As late as 1931, in *The Masefield Country*, Alfred Watkins, who knew the Ledbury pubs as a young man from having sold them beer from his father's brewery, said of Masefield's portrayal here: 'I know that it is a true picture', and then found it, a little comically, necessary to assure readers:

> I have been in and out of [Masefield's] birth-town when he was rising to fame, and long before and after, and naturally have talked with townsfolk about him.

Two facts emerge; all speak with the utmost respect of the lad; not one (and I knew those who had opportunities of judging), gave the slightest hint of Masefield having taken any part in the life he depicts in this book (*The Everlasting Mercy*). Had he been not gentle we should know more of him.

What was it/is it that so distressed contemporaries in Saul's account of the celebrations in 'The Lion'. The insistence on the dirty talk and jokes, the singing of filthy songs? The time-hallowed, almost *de rigueur* harass-ment of the barmaids (Saul has previously availed himself of Doxy Jane, and is perfectly aware of what is often the lot of such women when no longer in favour with the men):

> Jane brought the bowl of stewing gin,
> And poured the egg and lemon in,
> And whisked it up and served it out
> While bawdy questions went about.
> Jack chucked her chin, and Jim accost her
> With bits out of the "Maid of Gloster."
> And fifteen arms went round her waist.
> (And then men ask, Are Barmaids chaste?)

It shocked, to a good measure, I believe, because it assaulted the partic-ular male code, which, often sentimentalised and distorted into a semblance of respectability, had been celebrated in a diversity of cultural forms throughout the Victorian and Edwardian eras without proper recog-nition of what its constituents truly involved—violence bordering on sadism, sexual greed that disregarded its objects, an allegiance to the destructive rather than the constructive principle. Synge's *Playboy of the Western World*, which so appalled its first audiences that, insulted, they rioted, was, it seems to me, a great example here in its unflinching treat-ment of the code—as it operated in a seemingly remote society, in truth far nearer to home than people cared to admit. The shebeen that is the play's setting—complete with the requisite hearty 'mine host' and beautiful, sharp-tongued bar-maid—is, we soon realise, an utterly amoral place, prepared at first to welcome a newcomer because he has performed the doubtfully heroic act of killing his father. And yet the reception has a precarious quality about it: this is a fickle society which will prefer the consolations of fantasy (vicious, lethal) to the complicated and morally difficulties of reality. So in 'The Lion' in this transparent version of Ledbury the drunken party gives no thought to the unfairly worsted Billy now in such pain and amuses itself with selfish flights of fancy:

> If I'd my rights I'm Squire's heir.
> By rights I'd be a millionaire.

After some dalliance with Doxy Jane which ends with her, like 'all the drunken others' in the room, falling asleep, Saul goes to the window, leans out into the coolness of the benighted market-place and hears the church-clock strike three, ('Holy, holy, holy,' he thinks.) As earlier when recalling bell-ringer Dawes' vision he has an awareness of all the countless generations before him, the uncountable dead of whose vast number we all sooner or later will be. This unites with a sense (present also in Synge's masterpiece, and in Hardy and Yeats) that the present has debased the past, squandered its inheritance. While it wouldn't be quite true, given Masefield's idiosyncratically non-doctrinaire agnosticism, to say that he pines, like so many of his generation, for an age of faith, that sentiment is not altogether absent—even though it is the cultural and social consequences of faith of which he is most mindful:

> And then I thought, "I wish I'd seen
> The many towns this town has been;
> I wish I knew if they'd a-got
> A kind of summat we've a-not,
> If them as built the church so fair
> Were half the chaps folk say they were;
> For they'd the skill to draw their plan,
> And skill's a joy to any man;
> And they'd the strength, not skill alone,
> To build it beautiful in stone;
> And strength and skill together thus ...
> O, they were happier men than us."

St Michael and All Angels can inspire such reflections even today. Masefield seems in fact to have been largely hostile to Roman Catholicism, to serve which this particular pre-Reformation edifice 'beautiful in stone' would have been built. But the desire for an organic society bound by metaphysic as well as by social and economic interdependencies was also strong in him, one of the reasons for his abiding devotion to Chaucer, and Saul's lines articulate, in non-intellectual form, this desire. Nevertheless this is a profoundly Protestant poem, its religion an individual's affair.

To the male code under attack, to the herd mentality, another set of values, another way of living are to be opposed—utilising all the masculine qualities, gentle but ultimately tougher, more resilient, and, introduced to the protagonist by—of all people—a do-gooding virginal elderly woman, 'tall, pale ... grey, bent.'

2

Saul Kane presents himself, and the thirty-six hours leading to his redemption, *sub specie aeternitatis* (under the mirror of eternity). This is what gives the whole poem its distinctive blend of urgency and moral beauty (for all its not infrequent raunchiness of style and scene) and its sense of a fraught, eventful journey through a strictly measured chunk of time towards the timeless. Normally this point of vision is adopted by a narrator who is not a protagonist in the action but an omniscient surveyor of it, as in much of Hardy. What is so remarkable about *The Everlasting Mercy* is that the change of heart which is its culmination is the beginning of a new life for the speaker *and is still continuing without likelihood of cessation.* The Saul addressing us knows even now the quiet, satisfying, useful, beautiful life of a ploughman to which the epiphany of the climax led him. That autumn dawn—after he'd passed the brook and the gipsies—he found the 'everlasting' in the quotidian. How he lives now is a foretaste of God's eternity itself:

> All earthly things that blessèd morning
> Were everlasting joy and warning.

He is addressing us now because he wants us to follow him, to have the reformed Saul Kane as model:

> And in men's hearts in many lands
> A spiritual ploughman stands
> For ever waiting, waiting now,
> The heart's "Put in, man, zook the plough."

It's hard to think of another work, so rooted in topographical and human actuality, which moves towards an ending at once so definitive (for Saul will never retract or backslide) and yet open (Saul's life will go on and on, characterised by many satisfactions and rewards). A possible parallel is with the end of Hardy's *The Return of the Native* (1880), and it's clear from his later remarks in *The Ledbury Scene* that Hardy, the writer who had made out of a particularised locality a universal territory, was very much in Masefield's mind as he worked on his narratives of Marches life.

> Who, now, of the post-war generations, can know how the young of fifty years ago thought of the late Thomas Hardy, and his achievement in creating "Wessex" ... [I] often wished Thomas Hardy had lived ... somewhere west of the Severn, between the Avon and the Wye. Then some familiar fields and hills would have been within his great system, and parts of Imagination.

The Return of the Native concludes with Clym Yeobright, the 'native', who has been through so much, having become an itinerant preacher. The novel has shown the conflict between Clym the gentle believer in a Stoic's philosophy of resignation and Clym the reluctant man of passion. His eventual mode of life is a vindication of his wiser self and—like Saul Kane's—seems set to last him to the end of his days.

> Yeobright had, in fact, found his vocation in the career ...; and from this day he laboured incessantly in that office, speaking not only in simple language on Rainbarrow and in the hamlets round, but in a more cultivated strain elsewhere ... in the neighbouring Wessex towns and villages. He left alone creeds and systems of philosophy, finding enough and more than enough to occupy his tongue in the opinions and actions common to all good men. Some believed him and some believed not; some said his words were commonplace, others complained of his want of theological doctrine; while others again remarked that it was well enough for a man to take to preaching who could not see to do anything else. But everywhere he was kindly received, for the story of his life had become generally known.

The all-important difference between Hardy's novel and Masefield's poem in this respect is that, whereas Clym's post-conversion is no more than a coda (if a moving one, which reaches out), Saul's occupies the last sixth of the long poem. This not only contains some of its finest lines, characterised by an extraordinary exultant lyricism, but casts beams of light back into the darkness of the preceding narrative. Now, with hindsight, what has gone before illustrates and emphasizes the spiritual necessity of Saul's being brought to grace.

Can a moral framework be found for the story independent of Saul's own Revivalist/Salvationist one? I believe so. *The Everlasting Mercy* portrays an ordinary enough man's realisation of the limitations and essentially self-destructive nature of the code by which he has been living. (Not for nothing is he called Saul—who also had to unlearn a harsh and exclusive code, in order to become 'God's messenger', Paul!) This realisation is of such moment there can be no return from it. A deeper self has been discovered, with other needs beyond the crude Darwinian ones with which Saul—with all his toughness and amoral strength—has been concerned. His wrong-doing to Billy and his subsequent guilt are the catalysts for reappraisal of his life-style and abandonment of it, making it indeed something of a *felix culpa*. Contemporary readers and critics were in a literal sense mistaken in supposing that Masefield had undergone a religious conversion himself, but—especially in the light of the tormented passages in both *Multitude and Solitude* and *A Book of Discoveries*—he most certainly had come to a crisis in his outlook on life, his whole *Weltanschauung*, one which—largely unconsciously, and through the excitement of creating a new work of art—he resolved. The starker Darwinian interpretation of existence was not enough for him, however strong and undeniable its basic tenets. The human being *is* able to rise to pity, sympathy, altruism, a sense of the mystery and beauty of living things, all of which are at variance with survival of the fittest as the key to existence. That is the real conversion behind the poem.

Nor is it only human beings who have these transcending capacities. There is little more touching in all Masefield's poetry than Saul's memory of his old dog. In his great peroration against the unkindness of the towns-people, he interrupts himself on behalf of:

> "Those poor lonely ones who find
> Dogs more mild than human kind.
> For dogs," I said, "are nobles born
> To most of you, you cockled corn.
> I've known dogs to leave their dinner,
> Nosing a kind heart in a sinner.
> Poor old Crafty wagged his tail
> The day I first came home from jail,
> When all my folk, so primly clad,
> Glowered black and thought me mad,
> And muttered how they'd been respected,

> While I was what they'd all expected.
> (I've thought of that old dog for years,
> And of how near I come to tears.)"

And similarly in the tale which the exhausted Saul tells little Jimmy Jaggard waiting for his mother outside the shop, in which he pays tribute to the secret lives of cats.

Essentially then *The Everlasting Mercy* is the story of an individual's passage from a life in which contest and conquest are all—the snaring of birds and animals, the fight with a mate over territory, wenching (sex without love or tenderness)—to one in which these are no longer of any account: where rejoicing in the abundance of the earth and assisting its yield determine the day—and the attendant state of mind. And this passage derives from Masefield's walk that day in May 1911, and to the mental walk it solicited round Ledbury, from Coneygree Hill to within sight of May Hill, crested by that ploughman-like copse. The journey ends in peace, a peace related to New Testament parables recalling the seasons, and the spiritual forces apprehendable behind it.

Before he attains that peace, however, Saul has to make a kind of pilgrim's progress, stages of which are dangerous to himself and to others, some internal, some external, the two fusing in his confrontation with Mrs Jaggard. (It's worth pointing out that the society which produced Saul was one soaked in Bunyan's book, its quest and tests, *The Pilgrim's Progress* being the staple reading in many a rural household during the 18th and 19th centuries, surpassed only by the Bible itself.)

After opening the bar-windows of 'The Lion' so that fresh air can dispel the oppressive fug, and hearing the church-bells chime three, Saul, thinking of all the generations that have preceded him, even here in Ledbury, is sobered (literally) into sombre reflection:

> O they were happier men than us.
>
> But if they were, they had to die
> The same as every one and I.
> And no one lives again, but dies,
> And all the bright goes out of eyes,
> And all the skill goes out of hands,
> And all the wise brain understands,
> And all the beauty, all the power
> Is cut down like a withered flower.

> In all the dumb show from birth to rest
> I give the poor dumb cattle best.

As far as his own spirits are concerned, this is the lowest point of his trajectory to salvation. He has realised how hollow his victory over Billy was, how very little in his life he has to be proud of. A seductive inner voice, which he ascribes to the Devil, suggests he kill himself: "'Saul / Why should you want to live at all?'" He resists the temptation, however, and the words in which he does so are themselves of significance to the poem's overall design:

> "I've not had all the world can give.
> Death by and by, but first I'll live."

The code which Saul has inherited is an inadequate measuring-rod for the immense variety and richness of life, which should elicit reverence and tenderness from us. Deciding to live is a tacit appreciation of this, and, though it may, to the onlooker, appear otherwise, from now on Saul begins his ascent to self-knowledge and deliverance.

If he is to achieve the release for which in his inmost being he craves, he must undergo another kind of release—of all that has been pent up in him during his short life, all that is responsible for him having been the baleful, uncreative fellow 'Ledbury' has known. And the release will take the form of acts of mayhem, cathartic if also destructive. The first of the three 'madnesses'—Masefield's term both inside and outside the poem—now begins, *The Everlasting Mercy* repeating Christianity's three-fold patterns. I believe that they are all, but perhaps most of all this first bout, in part inspired by Christy Malone's behaviour in Synge's *Playboy of the Western World*.

The first 'madness' concerns his personal relations to his society, the second society itself, the third his own inner (imaginative) life. When, after the third, judgement on him by another is given, then he is ready for the conversion, though how it occurs will take him by surprise (as is surely usually the case).

Out of the pub window he shouts out imprecations not only with Biblical parallels (he compares himself to 'Lijah') but more probably than not what 'romantic' young Jack Masefield must have longed to declaim to the burghers of Ledbury—who paid him so little attention, gave him such little love, and, in the persons of his uncle and aunt were sneeringly and self-righteously anxious to send him back to what had made him unhappy and ill to the point of collapse:

> "I'll tell this sanctimonious crowd,
> This town of window-peeping, prying,
> Malinging, peering, hinting, lying,
> Male and female human blots
> Who would, but daren't be, whores and sots,
> That they're so steeped in petty vice
> That they're less excellent than lice,
> That they're so soaked in petty virtue
> That touching one of them will dirt you ...

Saul's attack on the *bien-pensants* accuses them both of the meannesses they actually commit (begrudging and denying charity; doing one another down in business; pettifogging litigation) and, more importantly, those greater ones they would like to commit but daren't (such as, Saul echoing the Christ of *St John*, Chapter 7 here, the adultery which, in their pharisaic way, they'll be the first to condemn). Inspired by his own words, Saul tears his clothes off, becoming naked 'unaccommodated man', and rushing out into the street, exclaiming "'I'm Satan, newly come from hell,'" he seizes the town's fire-bell, and, ringing it, shatters the calm of that night. And in doing so he serves his own soul.

Saul is Satan only in the Blakean sense: in the small hours of this autumn morning he addresses and challenges the dark desires, doubts, hopes and fears that convention has made the townsfolk suppress—or at any rate deny. The dullness of their lives is a convenience to them, and a burden too. Saul would have them see that fear is by no means only a negative force. The prospect of fire—a hoax on this occasion—can be a liberation; sometimes only when devastation's at hand can the blinkered be in touch with the beautiful precariousness of being alive, and the inexhaustible demands and interest of our condition:

> I'm fire of hell come up this minute
> To burn this town, and all that's in it.
> To burn you dead and burn you clean,
> You cogwheels in a stopped machine,
> You hearts of snakes, and brains of pigeons,
> You dead devout of dead religions,
> You offspring of the hen and ass,
> By Pilate ruled, and Caiaphas.

Saul is not to stay with this punitive purgative attitude long: this is a 'madness' after all, but during it he makes points of great seriousness. Caiaphas and Pilate, the Christ-condemning High Priest and Roman Governor, are evoked by him (like so many country-people of his time and upbringing, he has a mind amply stocked with Bible-references) because Christ with his inclusive, forgiving spirit, is indeed being put daily to death by the stultifying mores of the community. Already he seems no stranger to the idea of the Christ within by which Miss Bourne, the Quakeress, will save him. And shortly he will tell the parson:

> "The English Church both is and was
> A subsidy of Caiaphas."

Saul goes on his way through the town in a dark dionysiac frenzy, knocking at and shouting through the doors of, among others, the triumvirate who rule the Ledbury citizenry: parson, lawyer and squire. (He deals more kindly with the parson than with the others, because he'd been kind to Saul as a child.) Finally he exhausts himself; this first madness burns itself out:

> Left me worn out and sick and cold,
> Aching as though I'd all grown old;

But it has brought about a revelation nonetheless.

Rescued by Si and Doxy Jane of 'The Lion', who later also rescue his scattered clothes, he is carried back to the pub, where, sleeping his wildness off, he remains until half past two in the afternoon. (The clock of *The Everlasting Mercy* has been most carefully attended to; as with the topography its exactness lifts the work from the level of parable to that of a credible history of the operation of grace in the workaday world.)

Saul replenishes himself with food and more drink, and then at four o'clock lets a second 'madness' seize him. Back into the streets of Ledbury he rushes for what he calls The Second Trump, another hurling of 'Judgment' at his home-town, only this time he aims it at the government of the community rather than those who make up 'the dead devout of dead religions'(to use his own derogatory words). He encounters by a happy chance the parson himself, 'old puffing parson' with 'turkey gills ... red as wrath', and delivers to him, in lines of barbed Popean bitterness, an attack not just on the Church of England itself but on the social system it both represents and upholds. It's impossible not to feel Masefield's emotional endorsement here. At this time of his life he was no kind of friend to the Anglican orders, (and, for that matter, as late as 1935, in *The Box of Delights*, he was prepared creatively to subvert them):

> "You mumble through a formal code
> To get which martyrs burned and glowed.
> I look on martyrs as mistakes,
> But still they burned for it at stakes;
> Your only fire's the jolly fire
> Where you can guzzle port with Squire,
> And back and praise his damned opinions
> About his temporal dominions.
> You let him give the man who digs,
> A filthy hut unfit for pigs,
> Without a well, without a drain,
> With mossy thatch that lets in rain,
> Without a 'lotment, 'less he rent it,
> And never meat, unless he scent it,
> But weekly doles of 'leven shilling
> To make a grown man strong and willing
> To do the hardest work on earth
> And feed his wife when she gives birth ...
> With all your main and all your might,
> You back what is against what's right.

Unfair? The parson is not an unkind or a bad-living individual, and hasn't assisted in the impoverishment of any men or women. But he has (think Saul Kane and John Masefield) given moral approval, if not assent, to a caste ladder the bottom rung of which is misery and resentment:

> "You teach the ground-down starving man
> That Squire's greed's Jehovah's plan.
> You get his learning circumvented
> Lest it should make him discontented
> (Better a brutal, starving nation
> Than men with thoughts above their station),
> You let him neither read nor think,
> You goad his wretched soul to drink
> And then to jail, the drunken boor;

O sad intemperance of the poor.
You starve his soul till it's rapscallion,
Then blame his flesh for being stallion."

The frenetic drunken binges, the whoring, the fighting—should these all be viewed as expressions of frustration consequent on a self-serving inflexible social hierarchy? Yes and no! No, because, as the parson is to reply, evil deeds cannot be attributed solely to economic deprivation or class humiliation. Even in Saul's own low-life circle we can see moral discrepancies between people: for example, Billy has been good where Saul has not. Again, to find a sociological explanation sufficient is to ignore the very real appetite for destruction these deeds—and others like them—gratify. But while Masefield thinks Saul's condemnations a partial truth only, he undoubtedly thinks they are a truth. Even if one accepts a qualified wisdom in the parson's retort to Saul (given in convincing, not unsympathetic, rational language:

"You think the Squire and I are kings
Who made the existing state of things,
And made it ill. I answer, No,
States are not made, nor patched; they grow.)

one has to add that collusion with perpetuation of injustice will serve to make those at the wrong end of it cynical, grasping, self-centred, resorters to brute force (Saul can be described in all these terms) and this in itself is to be condemned. One's way of living should, as much as possible, promote benevolence. Furthermore, the upholding of a rankly unfair and stratified system must entail the stifling of pity, something again always to be deplored. One remembers how distressed the boy Masefield was by the poverty in Ledbury, and how in after-years he wrote, refusing to lament any 'good old days', in *Wonderings*:

I saw filthy alleys, close and dark,
Where few could read or write, but made their mark,
Where men and women lived and died in tetter,
So little human that the dogs were better.

So as in the case of the first madness, Saul in his second bout both broke out of his mental chains by saying what up till then was unsayable, and forced others (one hopes to their own benefit) to face a disagreeable home-truth.

The third 'madness' occurs almost three hours later—after Saul has had time to be by himself and has already received, without quite knowing it, intimations of the revelation to descend on him. He has begun to see himself, if not exactly part of a greater plan, then as a member of a world in which great plans could be at work. The carelessness of his life comes home to him, and the means of its doing so is a dramatic change in the weather.

He lingers for a while by the brook on the Hereford Road:

> And dowsed my face, and drank at spring,
> And watched two wild duck on the wing.
> The moon come pale, the wind come cool,
> A big pike leapt in Lower Pool,
> The peacock screamed, the clouds were straking,
> My cut cheek felt the weather breaking;
> An orange sunset waned and thinned
> Foretelling rain and western wind,
> And while I watched I heard distinct
> The metals on the railway clinked.
> The blood-edged clouds were all in tatters,
> The sky and earth seemed mad as hatters;
> They had a death look, wild and odd,
> Of something dark foretold by God.

In his earlier two 'madnesses' Saul was driven by the violence within him to make war on the external world when it was seemingly at peace— asleep in the still of the night, quietly busy in the middle of the afternoon. But in his third 'madness' Saul, paradoxically, is driven by a gathering violence without, the onset of a rainstorm, to journey inward, where he finds a still centre, a creative, mythopoeic self, which expresses itself in the fairy-tale he spins for little Jimmy Jaggard. And in a further paradox, whereas his first two 'madnesses' elicit basically kindly reactions from other people, from Si and Jane, and from the tolerant old parson, the third brings him a sustained telling-off, an angry cataloguing of his misde- meanours from Jimmy's mother. Because what she says is largely just, Saul takes note of her in a way he had not of Si, Jane or the parson.

> I slunk away into the night
> Knowing deep down that she was right.
> I'd often heard religious ranters,
> And put them down as windy canters,
> But this old mother made me see
> The harm I done by being me,
> Being both strong and given to sin
> I 'tracted weaker vessels in.

What Saul's third 'madness' consists of is stopping outside a shop in the market-place and entertaining little Jimmy Jaggard with a tale about cats and their antics at night, one that anticipates delightful episodes in *The Midnight Folk* (to be published sixteen years later) with its feline trio of Blackmalkin, Greymalkin and Nibbins ('who is the nicest cat there is'). The tale certainly pleases Jimmy, but his mother emerges from her shopping, irate. How dare the boy keep company with such as Saul? Saul—in a meeker, more supplicant voice than any we have heard from him before—begs her not to punish the child, the fault was his. For the first time, therefore, and for a child's, an innocent's sake, he is prepared to be honest (as he was not in the case of Billy) and face up to blame or punishment. Mrs Jaggard rounds on him:

> "Oh! And how dare you, then?" says she,
> "How dare you tempt my boy from me?
> How dare you do't, you drunken swine,
> Is he your child or is he mine?
> A drunken sot they've had the beak to,
> Has got his dirty whores to speak to,
> His dirty mates with whom he drink,
> Not little children, one would think."

Her words echo Christ's about the corruption of children being the supreme sin, but they also have a very particular significance for Saul. Mrs Jaggard, unlike the Ledbury burghers whom he aroused with the fire-bell, unlike the parson who hobnobs with the Squire, comes from the same stratum as himself; he knows the hardships she's had to put up with, he has even known personally her children of whose sorry stories she reminds him as she upbraids him. He helped to drag her son, Dick down; probably he'll do the same for Jimmy.

> "... And now I see
> That just as Dick was, Jim will be,
> And all my life will have been vain.
> I might have spared myself the pain ..."

In refusing to live a life that can be exemplary for the children of his own sort, a bright beacon for their future, Saul has committed a betrayal graver even than that he perpetrated on Billy. It is a betrayal he has given no thought to until now, and—after all he has been through the past night and day—it is to be the last stage in his progress to goodness, the happy point of no return.

Not that Mrs Jaggard's religion will be what descends on him on his own Road to Damascus, though hers partakes far more of the Revivalist tradition usually evoked when this poem is mentioned. The story Masefield is telling is one of movement from temporal combat to the ever-lasting mercy proclaimed in the title. That couldn't be attained by the doctrine she expounds to him:

> "Whatever seems, God doth not slumber,
> Though he lets pass times without number
> He'll come with trump to call His own,
> And this world's way'll be overthrown.
> He'll come with glory and with fire
> To cast great darkness on the liar,
> To burn the drunkard and the treacher,
> And do His judgment on the lecher
> To glorify the spirits' faces
> Of those whose ways were stony places,
> Who chose with Ruth the better part;
> O Lord, I see Thee as Thou art,
> O God, the fiery four-edged sword,
> The thunder of the wrath outpoured,
> The fiery four-faced creatures burning,
> And all the four-faced wheels all turning,
> Coming with trump and fiery saint.
> Jim, take me home, I'm turning faint."

Whatever its scriptural derivations, all this is not for Masefield—nor for his hero either. The punishments heaped on the sinner's head belong to essentially the same barbarous tradition as the fighting, drinking, whoring it opposes. For

Masefield, the story of *The Everlasting Mercy* is not just about Saul's salvation, but that of England—what in the country's culture can redeem it from the greed, aggression, social divisions and cruelties that beset it?

Masefield's answer is quietism, and Christian quietism, even though he himself was not a believing Christian. This is what Saul Kane must embrace to become, for his creator and his readers alike, a pattern.

After seeing Mrs Jaggard, Saul is to make one last resistance—and his resistance is to lead him to his healer, his saviour. He goes back to the pub to get drunk. At ten o'clock, as is her habit, Miss Bourne comes in, a Quaker who commands respect even where she's resented as a do-gooding busybody. Saul decides to stand up to her; never will he be so cockily recalcitrant again:

> She wore a Friend's clothes, and women smiled,
> But she'd a heart just like a child.
> She come to us near closing time
> When we were at some smutty rhyme,
> And I was mad and ripe for fun;
> I wouldn't a minded what I done,
> So when she come so prim and grey
> I pound the bar and sing "Hooray,
> Here's a Quaker come to bless and kiss us,
> Come, have a gin and bitters, missus.
> Or maybe Quaker girls so prim
> Would rather start a bloody hymn.
> Now, Dick, oblige. A hymn, you swine,
> Pipe up the "Officer of the Line,"
> A song to make one's belly ache,
> Or "Nell and Roger at the Wake,"
> Or that sweet song, the talk in town,
> "The lady fair and Abel Brown."
> "O, who's that knocking at the door.
> Miss Bourne'll play the music score."
> The men stood dumb as cattle are,
> They grinned but thought I'd gone too far,
> There come a hush and no one break it,
> They wondered how Miss Bourne would take it.
> She up to me with black eyes wide;
> She looked at me as though her spirit cried;
> She took my tumbler from the bar
> Beside where all the matches are

And poured it out upon the floor dust,
Among the fag-ends, spit and sawdust.

"Saul Kane," she said, "when next you drink,
Do me the gentleness to think
That every drop of drink accursed
Makes Christ within die of thirst,
That every dirty word you say,
Is one more flint upon his way,
Another thorn about His head,
Another mock by where he tread,
Another nail, another cross,
All that you are is that Christ's loss."
The clock run down and struck a chime
And Mrs Si said, "Closing time."

Truly it is closing time for the old Saul Kane. Outside the rain is tumbling down. Rain is perhaps the most persistent symbol of creativity, the divine-sent shower of fertilising sperm. With eloquent simplicity Saul admits 'something broke inside my brain.' His redemption has come, the mercy is about to engulf him, to drench him like the autumnal downpour itself. Masefield obviously was not the first poet to use rain as a consciously realised metaphor for a person's spiritual refreshment; George Meredith (1828-1909), whom Masefield greatly revered, had done so in his poem, 'Earth and a Wedded Woman', where to the lonely Susan the rain brings creative solace:

Through night, with bedroom window wide for air,
Lay Susan tranced to hear all heaven descend:
And gurgling voices came of Earth, and rare,
Past flowerful, breathings, deeper than life's end,
From her heaved breast of sacred common mould;
Whereby this lone-laid wife was moved to feel
    Unworded things and old
    To her pained heart appeal.
Rain! O the glad refresher of the grain!
And down in deluges of blessed rain.

Miss Bourne's action and her defeat of Saul—which will be converted into victory, the victory of his better and profounder self—mark the beginning of the end of the poem. But they also constitute an end, after which the true Saul can begin—and this beginning will have no ending.

3

Quakers acknowledge no hierarchy, either within themselves or beyond; they have no creed or dogma, their services lack any set pattern. Their concern is with the Inner light, the Christ within, which every human being possesses. A Quaker Meeting gathers in silence, a collective and unifying silence often as palpable and potent as the music it lacks; from time to time someone may feel moved by the spirit to stand up and give witness, and his or her words may evoke responses in others. The belief in quietness and simplicity is carried over into ordinary life; indeed, eschewing religious sacraments, they regard the whole of life as sacramental. Following Christ's example, they make their Yea their Yea, their Nay their Nay, and therefore will not take oaths; they will not take arms let alone kill another person (who must also be a receptacle for Christ), not for the sake of their country, not even—in a sublime paradox—for the sake of Christ himself. Though, to circumvent any politics of envy, they do not object to inequality of wealth, they are deeply concerned with human fellowship, with a society at one with itself. Whether acting on personal initiative, like Miss Bourne in the poem, or as a body, they have contributed enormously to the penetration of justice and compassion in British life and institutions—in the treatment of those with mental illness, in the conditions within prisons, in the care for the war-wounded and for animals, in the establishment of amenities for workers, and in (as here) the encouragement of temperance as more consonant with a life of harmony than one dependant on stimulants. And they have been influential through example as well as through the activities of the Society itself.

Much of what Saul proceeds to feel and which makes for his new and continuing life can be seen in Quaker terms. His awareness of Christ welling up thirst-quenchingly inside him and of this corresponding to the benign cyclical operations of the natural world couldn't be more unlike the elect-and-damned, the fire-obsessed religion of Mrs Jaggard. When Saul speaks of burning, it too turns out to have been a gentle and natural process:

> I did not think, I did not strive,
> The deep peace burnt by me alive;
> The bolted door had broken in,
> I know that I had done with sin.

110

I knew that Christ had given me birth
To brother all the souls on earth,
And every bird and every beast
Should share the crumbs broke at the feast.

O glory of the lighted mind,
How dead I'd been, how dumb, how blind.
The station brook, to my new eyes,
Was babbling out of Paradise;
The waters rushing from the rain
Were singing Christ has risen again.
I thought all earthly creatures knelt
From the rapture of this joy I felt.

When Saul says of his walk that dawn, which will grant him the double epiphany of the ploughman (old farmer Callow and the 'natural' figure of one in the form of the copse atop May Hill), 'Along the road Christ led me forth,' he's speaking in the language of the Society of Friends' Founder, George Fox, as he was also doing when he insisted that he did not 'think' or 'strive' but let himself be consumed by peace. And so too is he speaking when he tells how he saw Christ partaking in the operation of early morning ploughing:

I kneeled there in the muddy fallow,
I knew that Christ was there with Callow,
That Christ was standing there with me,
That Christ had taught me what to be,
That I should plough, and as I ploughed
My Saviour Christ would sing aloud,
And as I drove the clods apart
Christ would be ploughing in my heart,
Through rest-harrow and bitter roots,
Through all my bad life's rotten fruits.

(The metaphor here, incidentally, is characteristically exact. Horsedrawn harrows were often stopped in their tracks by the plants known as restharrow because of its long, thick, tough rhizones. Sometimes ploughmen would dig these up and chew them; they tasted like liquorice, so were 'bitterfruits' indeed. Ploughing went better without them.)

But there is another English spiritual tradition than Quakerism to which Masefield is surely appealing here, indeed throughout the wonderful last sixth of his poem; its finest flowering was roughly contemporaneous with Fox and his first followers, and though Neo-Platonist, hermetic, mystical maybe its raptures are not so very different from the transports that made the Friends quake. Its two great exponents in poetry, Henry Vaughan and Thomas Traherne (1637-74) were both from the Marches, Traherne indeed from Hereford itself, where he was born, brought up (by their relation, Philip Traherne, inn-keeper and mayor) and educated, and to which city he left in his will five houses in trust for the poor. Curiously, Traherne was literary news in Masefield's youth and early maturity, and corresponding as his work does with both a general and a personal quest for fructifying elements in pre-industrial, pre-Imperial England must have impressed him. In 1896, a notebook containing Traherne's prose-work subsequently called *Centuries of Meditations* and some poems was bought for a matter of pence on a London bookstall; Traherne's *Poetical Works* (edited by Bertram Dobell) was published in 1903, and in 1910, (the year preceding *The Everlasting Mercy*) the *Centuries*—which C.S. Lewis called 'almost the most beautiful thing in English literature' and Ronald Blythe 'very near to being the happiest thing in English Christianity'. The marvellous sense of rapture, the words promoting a wordless state of being and oneness, to which no sensitive readers whatever their religious beliefs or lack of them could fail to respond, seems, with cultural hindsight, to be part of an English line on which stand Wordsworth, Coleridge, Clare, Samuel Palmer, Richard Jefferies, Gerard Manley Hopkins, Elgar, Vaughan Williams (whose tribute to English spirituality, *Fantasia on a Theme of Thomas Tallis* was written in 1910, the year of *The Centuries'* publication)—and Masefield himself.

Here is Masefield giving us Saul Kane's ecstasy over the corn for the sake of which he will be working as a ploughman:

> O Christ who holds the open gate,
> O Christ who drives the furrow straight,
> O Christ the plough, O Christ, the laughter
> Of holy white birds flying after,
> Lo, all my heart's field red and torn,
> And thou wilt bring the young green corn
> The young green corn divinely springing,

The young green corn for ever singing;
And when the field is fresh and fair
Thy blessèd feet shall glitter there.
And we will walk the weeded field,
And tell the golden harvest's yield
The corn that makes the holy bread
By which the soul of man is fed,
The holy bread, the food unpriced,
Thy everlasting mercy, Christ.

And here is Traherne, in *Centuries*, who is recreating his infant's vision of a deathless world where the corn will always be ripe:

> The corn was orient and immortal wheat which never should be reaped nor was ever sown. I thought it had stood from everlasting to everlasting. The dust and stones of the street were as precious as gold; the gates were at first the end of the world. The green trees when I saw them first through one of the gates transported and ravished me; their sweetness and unusual beauty made my heart to leap, and almost mad with ecstasy, they were such strange and wonderful things. The men! O what venerable and reverend creatures did the aged seem! Immortal cherubims! And young men glittering and sparkling angels, and maids strange seraphic pieces of life and beauty! Boys and girls tumbling in the street were moving jewels: I knew not that they were born or should die. But all things abided eternally as they were in their proper places.

Saul Kane reveals himself as having been mindful from his earliest years of the beauties of the natural world, of the flowers at his feet, and surely the same could be said for all (or, at any rate, almost all) his mates in wildness. There's a Christ within. In his ecstasy all seasons and their blessings are present to him, and, still possessed by it, he makes the leap into his new life—a correlative surely for Masefield's own when he embarked on these narrative poems so different from his previous work:

I jumped the ditch and crossed the fallow,
I took the hales from farmer Callow.

The new Saul Kane has come into being just as (with the completion of this work) a new Masefield has, who decides to end his poem with mysterious, almost incantatory lines, (reducing the number of syllables from eight to six). The lines emphasize the ending of another cycle and the promise of renewal. What makes *The Everlasting Mercy* a great work of art is its perfect matching-up of two fidelities: fidelity to the external world (which means on one hand the ways of country people, their speech, their mores, the lustiness of an aggressive but normal enough young man, and on the other, to the plants and animals of the Herefordshire countryside, at all stages of their lives) and fidelity to the workings of the inner spirit. An ineffably beautiful but truthful calm pervades the coda to this most inspiriting and quietly revolutionary poem (since it proclaims that each of us can achieve revolution if we are both bold and patient):

> How swift the summer goes,
> Forget-me-not, pink, rose,
> The young grass when I started
> And now the hay is carted,
> And now my song is ended,
> And all the summer spended;
> The blackbird's second brood
> Routs beech-leaves in the wood,
> The pink and rose have speeded,
> Forget-me-not has seeded.
> Only the winds that blew,
> The rain that makes things new,
> The earth that hides things old,
> And blessings manifold.

> O lovely lily clean,
> O lily springing green,
> O lily bursting white,
> Dear lily of delight,
> Spring in my heart agen
> That I may flower to men.

The lily is the flower of Christian devotion, said to have sprung up from tears Eve shed in her repentance when she left the Garden of Eden, and later associated with the Annunciation to the Virgin. Such recourse to mythology isn't necessary. The 'green' lily can be thought of as Solomon's Seal with its luminous greenish pendant flowers, the 'white' as the lilies-of-the-valley in Herefordshire woods. They have, in the true sense, spiritual significance simply because of the intense radiance of the poet's art,

The Knapp, built by Edward Masefield, where John was born

The view from the Knapp that Masefield would have seen from his bedroom, looking out towards Marcle Hill

*The view that most people associate with Ledbury, that of Church Lane.
To its south at the top lay The Priory, where Masefield moved when he
was eight*

The Brewery Inn, Bye Street, and the rear of the Bye Street Shop Row c.1890. At the top end of the street stood a tannery, demolished in 1895 to make way for the Barrett Browning Memorial Institute and Clock Tower (HCL/WMC/558)

Bye Street c.1900, showing the front of the shop row on the left. A new cattle market lies to the right of the picture (HCL/WMC/559)

The Homend in the late 1800s, with hurdles erected ready for penning stock for market (HCRO/AB48/B10)

Dog Hill. The ancient route from Hereford to Worcester crossed over this hill (HCL/WMC/554)

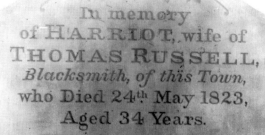

In memory
of HARRIOT, wife of
THOMAS RUSSELL,
Blacksmith, of this Town,
who Died 24th May 1823,
Aged 34 Years.
Also THOMAS RUSSELL,
who Died 24th May 1838,
Aged 46 Years.
My Sledge and Hammer lie reclined,
My Bellows too have lost their wind.
My Fire's extinct my Forge decayed,
And in the dust my Vice is laid.
My Coal is spent, my Iron gone,
My Nails are drove, my work is done.
My fire-dried Corpse now lies at rest,
My Soul smoke-like is soaring to be blest.

HILL & SONS.
LEDY

*'The carved heads in the church looked down
On Russell, Blacksmith of the Town.'*
The Everlasting Mercy

*The Ledbury Canal, photographed by Alfred Watkins during a two day
canoe trip along its entire length in 1880 or 1881*

Log sawing during the Great war (Watkins)

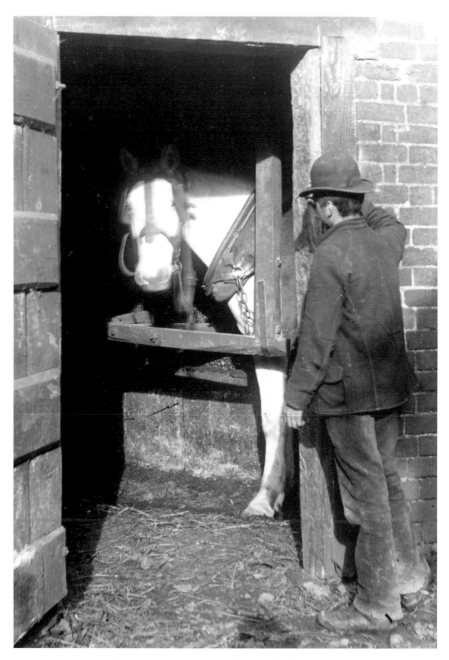

Horse hitched to a cider mill (Watkins)

Portable cider press at Bartestree, on the Ledbury to Hereford road

'The Great Lion Show'. Masefield was drawn to the travelling fairs

Hop poles stacked in a field near Ledbury in 1934 (Watkins)

Sharpening and creosoting hop poles in a heated furnace

Welshwoman hop picking with a crib (Watkins)

'The Poacher' (Watkins)

The haymaker sharpening his scythe (Watkins)

Butter churning (Watkins)

The Great Eastern, Conway *and* Akbar, c.*1886*

Liverpool Docks at about the time Masefield was undertaking his training on the Conway

*The plaque erected by the John Masefield Society at Preston Church,
where John Masefield was baptised after his parents had fallen out with
the vicar of Ledbury*

who, after having lost himself for too long in the exhausting struggles of an emergent writer, had found his true creativity at last.

In his poetry collection of 1936, *A Letter from Pontus and Other Verse*, Masefield returns to the subject of corn in a poem of singular and exultant loveliness, 'Joseph Hodges, or The Corn'. As one reads, once again Traherne comes to mind, in a literal respect more aptly, since Masefield envisions the corn here in specifically Christian terms. The first part consists of seven stanzas of six lines painting a picture of a ploughman and reaper who could be Saul Kane in old age. Masefield, himself nearing sixty, asks whether Joseph, like Saul, is aware of the metaphoric stature of his work, and whether it is true consolation for him, and decides that he must be and that it is:

> What harvest did his inner eyes behold
> From his spent Summer, now that Winter came?
> The women who had cherished him of old?
> The friends whom ninety Autumns had made tame?
> The ploughteams pondering out, on shaggy hoofs,
> At dawn, from farms with pigeons on their roofs?
>
> These; and perhaps, some feeling of the link
> Of Destiny, that bound him to the Corn,
> Beauty and bounty of man's meat and drink,
> That greens, and browns, and then is waggon-borne,
> And then is food, and strength, and then is Joy,
> Seed-corn of crops that nothing can destroy.
>
> For, as a man declines toward the tomb
> The symbols of his life, that ruled his way
> Before his spirit quickened in the womb,
> Gather to cheer him through his hut's decay,
> So haply here, as darkness gathered dim,
> Immortal cornland shone, and nourished him.
>
> Till, as he gazed into the past, the sound,
> The scene and colour of his life's delight,
> The crop in April, green upon the ground,
> The crop in rank, in bristle, sickle-white,
> The crop in barn, in bread, all merged and made
> A Word that led him deathwards unafraid.

The poem's second section moves into blank verse and traces the life of a field throughout a year with an extraordinary intimacy of detail, more intent perhaps than anything in Masefield's earlier work. He shows the bare soil on which the seed is 'flung' ('It is like meat, it shines'), its spring emergence, the falling on it of the May rain, the 'harvest-mice / Weaving their ball of joy above bright stems', and ends at Harvest Festival time, when the poem moves into its third and concluding part. Here the Corn is raised, Traherne-like, to its full mystical stature:

> By Corn we eat the radiance of high heaven
> And inmost blood and marrow of the earth;
> All that the easter chills and wester fosters;
> All that the will of life within the seed
> Can suck of plumpness from the clay; of greenness
> Out of the air, the rain, or resolved atom;
> Of ripeness from the turning of the wheel.

Masefield, turning to the church's absorption of corn into its sacramental and communal life, finds in this an apotheosis of its natural properties and glorious appearance.

Therefore the poem ends:

> Out of this Corn, that is such joy, men build
> Their churches, where they act day after day
> With singing, music, dancing, lights and colour,
> The death and resurrection of glad man,
> Till the eared corn of man becomes a flame
> No longer Earth, but burning from the Sun,
> No longer multitudinous but one,
> No longer bread of sacrifice but Joy.

But fine though these lines are, and adventurous in thought, seeking a transcendent reconciliation of Masefield's own vision of man and the natural world with that of Christian orthodoxy, I find the conclusion to *The Everlasting Mercy* more successful, more moving indeed. It has grown out of the poet's empathy with an individual who scarce understands the intellectual foundations of the faith he's so gratefully embraced but is passionate and devout nonetheless. His passion and devotion irradiate everything else.

CHAPTER V
The Canon:
The Widow in the Bye Street and *The Daffodil Fields*

If *The Everlasting Mercy* is a successful search for an English philosophy of all-embracing gentleness, Masefield's next narrative poem, *The Widow in the Bye Street* (of 1912) and its companion, *The Daffodil Fields* the following year are examinations of disruption—disruption of a seemingly cohesive rural community, disruption of the individual, disruption of any view of life that emphasizes harmony. And if *The Everlasting Mercy* partakes of a pilgrim's progress, *The Widow* and *The Daffodil Fields* concern themselves with the inter-action of lives. What one person does, will, indeed must, affect what happens to others.

The story of Saul Kane showed the necessity and the rewards of rising above a Darwinian interpretation of existence. By contrast, *The Widow* and *The Daffodil Fields*, for the greater part of their course, reverse this process; they demonstrate the indomitable assertion of a natural force irrespective of opposing personal attributes or cultural expectations and wishes. That force is sex. Masefield's purposeful concentration on sexual desire makes him as frank and unflinching in the tracing of its course as that fellow-contributor of his to *The English Review*, D.H. Lawrence. Jimmy Gurney, male protagonist of *The Widow in the Bye Street*, standing outside his two-timing loved one's cottage, senses what's going on inside:

> ... in the dim the lovers went upstairs,
> Her eyes fast closed, the shepherd's burning stark,
> His lips entangled in her straying hairs,
> Breath coming short as in a convert's prayers,
> Her stealthy face all drowsy in the dim
> And full of shudders as she yearned to him.

While, in *The Daffodil Fields*, more Lawrentian still is the account of Mary Keir's surrender to Michael Gray, the beauty of which makes her afterwards view herself as sexually and emotionally his wife, though she is not:

> No word profaned the peace of that glad giving,
> But the warm dimness of the night stood still,
> Drawing all beauty to the point of living,
> There in the beech-tree's shadow on the hill.
> Spirit to spirit murmured; mingling will
> Made them one being; Time's decaying thought
> Fell from them like a rag; it was the soul they sought.

Sex at once is and therefore must be given consideration in its own terms, yet is also the determining, shaping force in human destinies, responsible for new lives, and a destroyer.

In *The Widow in the Bye Street,* Mrs Gurney, a widow old beyond her years through hard work and poverty, has jealously guarded her only son from women, which makes his eventual succumbing to one—to Welsh Anna, also a widow—the more painfully consuming. Anna is having a relationship with a married man, Shepherd Ern, whose search for libidinous gratification is, however, by no means confined to her alone. It suits Anna to string the (by now) obsessed Jimmy along, but he comes to realise what she's been doing, and his jealousy is devouring. In turn this acts as a kind of sexual stimulant to Anna, though she is never in doubt about her preference. Maddened by his thwarted feelings, and taunted beyond endurance by Ern, Jimmy attacks and kills him. Anna becomes distraught, though she is never honestly to acknowledge her own responsibility for the crime. Jimmy is arrested, tried, sentenced to death and hanged. His mother mourning him preserves him in a virtue and a constancy of devotion, to her superior to what he evinced when alive.

The Daffodil Fields, too, deals with the passions a woman arouses in two men—though they are as different in both character and social background from Jimmy and Ern, as the woman Mary is from the 'fast' Anna. Mary has from girlhood loved Michael for the very qualities that make him incapable of commitment to her, and impel him (even after their betrothal and delayed but ecstatic love-making) to leave the neighbourhood and try his luck at farming in the Argentine. The tumultuous nature of Mary's love blocks the possibility of her responding to the feelings for her of her other friend and neighbour from earliest years, Lion Occleve. Circumstances arise, however, in Michael's prolonged absence, which make her marrying Lion seem the wisest course of action. She does so, but Michael arrives back, and Mary realises at once the physical and emotional incompatibility of herself and Lion, and leaves him to live with Michael. Lion, devastated by her abandonment of him, meets Michael in a spot by the famous daffodil fields, and picks a fight with him. The two young men, in the fierce intensity of combat, kill one another. But, as in *The Widow*, the end is informed by a tragic irony. Lion hears before his death and from Michael's lips that Mary, out of conscience, was returning to him; Michael had been on his way to tell him this news. When Mary discovers both men dead, however, she is in no doubt (again recalling The Widow) which one is her preference, which she grieves over the deeper: Michael to whom she first gave herself. The shock of what has happened kills her, and she is buried beside Michael.

☆ ☆ ☆

The Everlasting Mercy was a journey, a movement forward from sin into grace, and for this the swiftly, gracefully moving rhyming couplet was an ideal vehicle. But for these tales of affective relationships, where now one character, now another would dominate—and in *The Daffodil Fields* Masefield is particularly assiduous in his division of attentions—quite another medium was needed, one suited, moreover, to an omniscient narrator. The rhyming couplet had in fact been used by Chaucer not only for his 'Prologue' to *The Canterbury Tales* (the setting-out on a journey) but for many of the best-known and strongest of the tales themselves— 'The Knight's Tale' and 'The Miller's Tale'. But to do justice to the themes of *The Widow in The Bye Street* and *The Daffodil Fields* Masefield's mind turned to Chaucer's most sustained narrative poem, *Troilus and Criseyde* (1382-6/7), the subject of which is sexual desire, the emotions it releases, and the tragedy of its frustration and betrayal. Furthermore, Chaucer's central character is the adherent of a hegemonic cultural code where relations to the opposite sex are concerned, at once binding on the male, and constrictive on the woman (cf Jimmy with Anna; Michael and Lion with Mary). The Courtly Love code that permeates Chaucer's poem shows the male maintaining his devotion by constant act, rites, and professions that are at once a secularisation of religion and an elevation of the carnal to the psychic heights usually appropriated by religion. Masefield's interests in his character's behaviour differed in no way from Chaucer, though his interpretation was made in accordance with his own troubled re-reading of Darwinist determinism. And in *The Widow in the Bye Street* and *The Daffodil Fields* Masefield continues his concern with the relationship of the individual male to the culture of malehood—though there is to be no salvation from it as in *The Everlasting Mercy*. Those lines in *Troilus* in which Chaucer describes the willing enslavement of the young man to desire for Criseyde can be regarded as 'arguments' for the histories of Jimmy and Lion, but particularly the former:

> Within the temple he went him forth pleyingé,
> This Troilus, of every wight abouté,
> On this lady and now on that lookingé,
> Whereso she were of town or withouté;
> And upon case befell that through a routé
> His eyé piercèd, and so deep it wenté
> Till on Criseyde it smote, and there it stenté.
>
> And suddenly he wex therewith astonèd
> And gan her bet behold in thrifty wysé.
> 'O mercy, God,'; thought he, 'where hast thou wonèd,
> That art so fair and goodly to devysé?'
> Therewith his herté gan to spread and rysé,
> And softé sighèd, lest men might him hearé,
> And caught again his firsté pleying cheré.

These stanzas are composed in Rhyme Royal, ABABBCC, each line being an iambic pentameter. This stanza-form Masefield decided on not just for *The Widow in the Bye Street* and *The Daffodil Fields*, with their closely related subject-matter, but for *Dauber* and *King Cole* too. On the one hand its very constraints give the discipline suitable for the poet's unfolding of his multi-stranded story; on the other hand, within the rigidity there is a measure of flexibility, for the last couplet can sometimes be enjambed and therefore contribute to the flow of the narrative, can at other times, in closed form, act as a (mostly ironical) comment on what has gone before—and even herald a change of mood. Masefield was a writer who relished, to use his friend W.B. Yeats' words, 'The Fascination of What's Difficult'. Mostly, of course, the rhymes are masculine ones, and a stanza's final couplet benefits from the sonority of this, as here, telling of the Widow herself:

> Life can be bitter to the very bone
> When one is poor, and woman, and alone.

Or this, Chaucerian almost to the point of pastiche, telling of Anna who has tried to leave her reputation for 'looseness' behind:

> Passing for pure a hundred miles, I guess,
> From where her little son wore workhouse dress.

But, every so often, the use of feminine endings can be extremely effective, as in that reporting the local gossips' uncertainty abut what what will happen to Jimmy now he has killed Shepherd Ern:

> "He's just a kid. She trapped him." "No, she didden."
> "He'll be reprieved." "He mid be and he midden."

It should be said that not only *Troilus* but the poem which, in his American years, first made Masefield fall in love with—and even model himself on—Chaucer, *The Parliament of Fowls*, is written in Rhyme Royal, as are some of *The Canterbury Tales*, the great Scottish poem attributed to James I of Scotland, *The Kingis Quair* (hence the form's name), and Shakespeare's *The Rape of Lucrece*. In addition Masefield's 'master', William Morris, revived it for his *Earthly Paradise* (1868-70), surely significant in appraising Masefield's own revival of the form, and subsequent devotion to it. Nonetheless, I believe *Troilus and Criseyde* to be the main point of reference, and the relation between Chaucer's and Masefield's scrutiny of sexual desire in operation and of the conventions attendant on it, is surely abundantly apparent in such passages as that in *The Widow* in which Jimmy first falls for Anna. From these laden moments everything follows.

Jimmy has been victor at the ram-wrestling contests which constitute a major attraction of the October Fair. Anna, having arrived at the fair late, realises she's been let down by her lover, Ern, and finds herself drawn to the young strong-man (if only temporarily):

None but the lucky man deserves the fair,
For lucky men have money and success,
Things that a whore is very glad to share,
Or dip, at least, a finger in the mess.
Anne, with her raddled cheeks and Sunday dress,
Smiled upon Jimmy, seeing him succeed,
As though to say, "You're a man, indeed."

All the great things of life are swiftly done,
Creation, death and love the double gate.
However much we dawdle in the sun
We have to hurry at the touch of Fate;
When Life knocks at the door no one can wait,
When death makes his arrest we have to go.
And so with Love, and Jimmy found it so.

Love, the sharp spear, went pricking to the bone,
In that one look, desire and bitter aching,
Longing to have that woman all alone
For her dear beauty's sake all else forsaking;
And sudden agony that set him shaking
Lest she, whose beauty made his heart's blood cruddle,
Should be another man's to kiss and cuddle.

She was beside him when he left the ring,
Her soft dress brushed against him as he passed her;
He thought her penny scent a sweeter thing
Than precious ointment out of alabaster;
Love, the mild servant, makes a drunken master.
She smiled, half sadly, out of thoughtful eyes,
And all the strong young man was easy prize.

Masefield presents 'love'—the name we often give to sexual attraction—as being as swift and unbrookable as birth and death. Here he unites the Chaucerian Courtly Love with his own debate about biological programming. Both these narrative poems show love as a kind of alternative government which imposes its own laws, obligations and penalties on those in fealty to it, a government often at necessary variance with the other authorities of life—religious, familial, civic—yet exercising incalculable influence on these, and, more often than not, when spent or brought to impasse, yielding its power to them. At its strongest, sexual love is omnipotent if only briefly; in its decay it cannot sustain itself or only if shored by other emotions.

One thing we cannot expect from the government of love is justice. Jimmy's desire for Anna is not just stronger than hers for him, which is transient and vitiated by her desire for another man, it is of a completely different order. This begets its own compulsions. As the third of the above stanzas makes clear, jealousy is of the essence of the descent of love; even to think of the past of the love-object arouses it, yet it has its own fascination, its own pleasures, because it is a physical as much as a mental or emotional condition:

> So she had loved. Another man had had her;
> She had been his with passion in the night;
> An agony of envy made him sadder,
> Yet stabbed a pang of bitter-sweet delight -

In the grip of obsession Jimmy will jettison most of his principles. Up till now, doted on by his mother, he has been decent enough as a son, if also pretty selfish and apt to take her ministrations for granted. Under love's spell he keeps back the portion of his pay-packet he made over to the widow to spend on knick-knacks for Anna; he is utterly cavalier about his hours and his duties. Worse still, weakening his moral constitution, he betrays his mother in both his mind and his heart, Masefield never showing himself a keener psychologist, a finer delineator of the workings of the inner self, than in these stanzas following his mother's rebuke that he has 'a whore for friend':

> Jimmy said nothing in reply, but thought
> That mother was an old, hard jealous thing.
> "I'll love my girl through good and ill report,
> I shall be true whatever grief it bring."
> And in his heart he heard the death-bell ring
> For mother's death, and thought what it would be
> To bury her in churchyard and be free.

> He saw the narrow grave under the wall,
> Home without mother nagging at his dear,
> And Anna there with him at evenfall,
> Bidding him dry his eyes and be of cheer.
> "The death that took poor mother brings me near,
> Nearer than we have ever been before,
> Near as the dead one came, but dearer, more."

123

(Note the translation of his adoring mother into 'thing', a common enough turn of phrase, and completely convincing in the circumstances, fore-warning us of Jimmy's capacity to de-humanise, realised later in the murder he commits.)

☆   ☆   ☆

Injustice is, if anything, an even stronger feature of *The Daffodil Fields* where Michael possesses a greatly more magnetic sexuality than his boyhood companion, Lion—generally, and particularly, for Mary Keir. Nothing can be done in the face of this fact, for a fact of life it is, if a tragic one—like an earth-quake fault-line, or a congenital deformity. Michael's make-up, however, is such that desire and ability to attract are not accompanied by inclination for relationships, other than of convenience (such as that he enjoys out in the Argentine with the 'dark Spanish woman') until he is in danger of losing his childhood sweetheart's love for good. Until then the following interchange with his friend, Lion, sums up his attitude well enough:

> "Well, Lion," Michael said, "men make mistakes,
> And then regret them; and an early flame
> Is frequently the worst mistake man makes.
> I did not seek this passion, but it came.
> Love so happens in life. Well? Who's to blame.
> You'll say I've broken Mary's heart; the heart
> Is not the whole of life, but an inferior part."

This is far from the sentiment of the good, grave Lion, who persuades Mary to marry him in the face of the seeming certainty that Michael won't ever come back to England. Yet when he does, it is he who is 'rewarded', simply for his nature, his chemistry, not for any deeds or sentiments. Overcome with emotion at seeing Michael after the years of separation, she knows immediately that she must leave her husband who has shown her nothing but consideration and kindness:

> Lion was by the window when she came,
> Old Occleve and his wife were by the fire;
> Big shadows leapt the ceiling from the flame.
> She fronted the three figures and came nigher.
> "Lion," she whispered, "I return my hire."
> She dropped her marriage-ring upon the table.
> Then, in a louder voice, "I bore what I was able,

> And Time and marriage might have worn me down,
> Perhaps to be a good wife and a blest,
> With little children clinging to my gown,
> And this place would have been a place of rest
> For you and me; we could have come to know
> The depth; but that is over; I have to go.
>
> He has come back, and I have got to go.
> Our marriage ends."

Lion himself isn't immune from the moral havoc that sexual feelings can work. He too, like Jimmy Gurney, like Michael, will abandon central tenets of the code by which he has lived, of fair scrupulous conduct. When out in the Argentine, having tracked the errant Michael down, he showed his capacity for altruism by trying (in vain) to persuade Michael to return to Mary. However, after his later fight with Michael, only minutes before his own death, he tricks his boyhood comrade into helping him so that he can plunge his knife into his back.

What *The Widow in the Bye Street* and *The Daffodil Fields* both stress—again bringing our minds back to the tormented dialogues between artist Roger and scientist Lionel in *Multitude and Solitude*—is that the sex drive, in addition to being a means of procreation, is also a way of eliminating the (apparently) superfluous, of achieving the wastage which Nature would seem to require to survive. Jimmy, Shepherd Ern, Michael, Lion and Mary are all destroyed as a result of their sexuality. It is a gloomy, indeed a terrifying interpretation of life, of self-destruction masking as self-fulfilment.

2

As with *The Everlasting Mercy*, topography played a key part in both the inception and the writing of *The Widow in the Bye Street*:

> Down Bye Street, in a little Shropshire town,
> There lived a widow with her only son:

So begins the poem, but the somewhat disingenuous attempt at geographical detachment has deceived no one. For one thing Masefield retained the curious and resonant Ledbury street-name—Bye Street is a corruption of 'Bishop Street'—for the home of his two main protagonists.

The town of the narrative cannot be other than Masefield's native one as he knew it in early childhood, the years when, as he describes with such feeling and detail of memory in *Grace Before Ploughing*, the canal was being converted into a railway line. At an important level *The Widow* is an elegy for the countryside before its industrial violation, as Masefield saw it, (though obviously the particular railway under construction was being built a good fifty years after the main incursions into the England landscape—which in so way invalidates the point being made). Jimmy Gurney, the young man at the centre of the drama, is employed as a navvy:

> He got a job at working on the line
> Tipping the earth down, trolley after truck,
> From daylight till the evening, wet or fine,
> With arms all red from wallowing in the muck,
> And spitting, as the trolly tipped, for luck,
> And singing "Binger" as he swung the pick
> Because the red blood ran in him so quick.

The replacement of canal by rail, the human exertions this costs, these also connote the destructive, intrusive force of Jimmy's sexual feelings for Anna—which is to bring literal death to himself, and a living death to his mother. (They also could be said in part to cause them.) After he has been hanged for murder, the widow is so overwhelmed by grief that she loses a proper sense of time and place. By this time the railway has been long completed, is a permanent fixture in the land, but old Mrs Gurney walks along the footpath beside it, strewn with black cinders, as if it were indeed the old canal tow-path and life was what it was before the gangs of navvies wrought the changes:

> Over her head the Chester wires hum,
> Under the bridge the rocking engines flash.
> "He's very late this evening, but he'll come
> And bring his little packet full of cash
> (Always he does) and supper's cracker hash,
> That is his favourite food excepting bacon.
> They say my boy was hanged; but they're mistaken."

> And sometimes she will walk the cindery mile,
> Singing, as she and Jimmy used to do,
> Singing, "The parson's dog lep over a stile,"
> Along the path where the water lilies grew,

> The stars are placid on the evening's blue,
> Burning like eyes so calm, so unafraid,
> On all that God has given and man has made.

Yet this last line, with its echo of William Cowper's 'God made the country, and man made the town', is also bitterly ironic, since the God worshiped as the Creator of nature, of all things visible and invisible, also made the sex instinct. There certainly is a sense throughout the poem of a corruption of values having occurred—the mining community of Mountain Ash where Anna comes from would at this stage have tended to be harsh, rootless, self-preservative; the Union workhouse takes her children who should have grown up with support of a less impersonal kind; as in *The Everlasting Mercy* officialdom in the form of the law and the church are revealed, in the very distressing stanzas dealing with Jimmy's hanging, as useless humbugs out of touch with ordinary feelings and people. But against this must be set the unpleasantness of Shepherd Ern, who practises a rural skill with Biblical antecedents, and is shown up as a filthy-minded, treacherous, vicious boor, whose death cannot greatly be regretted.

It is of the greatest importance that Jimmy is a navvy (short for 'navigator'), navvies representing a Darwinian truth as well as being an inseparable feature of Victorian England from its beginning to virtually its close, and of John Masefield's own Ledbury childhood. Navvies were notorious for their heavy drinking, (quarts of beer at one sitting, such as Jimmy himself consumes before he goes to Anna's cottage and murders Ern), for their wenching, their fighting, their general lawlessness which would involve poaching, thievery and terrorising of the district, and 'randies' or wild binges after pay-day. Jimmy, unlike many of his mates, lives at home; the others would probably have been quartered in temporary, over-crowded, squalid huts in spectacularly insanitary conditions. An ordinary manual labourer didn't become a navvy overnight. In his authoritative study, *The Railway Navvies*, Terry Coleman says:

> It took a year's solid work to turn an agricultural labourer into a navvy. When he first came to the railway he was likely to be an indifferent specimen of a labourer. At about three in the afternoon he would down tools and be too exhausted to go on, and would not be worth more than two shillings a day. But he gradually got better, his wages rose, he could buy better food, and in twelve months he was about as strong as he ever would be.

Which was very strong indeed (as Jimmy tragically proves when he goes for Ern: "'I only give him one like, with the bat.'" "'I only meant / To hit him with a clip, like, nothing more.'" ..."'Not kill, the clip I give him, couldn't do.'") Jimmy, once he's passed the test, is a member of perhaps the most powerful underclass of Victoria's Britain. And not only powerful physically and numerically; its success couldn't have been achieved without them. To quote Terry Coleman again:

> In the eighty years from 1822 onwards, millions of navvies made 20,000 miles of railways in Britain ... The nineteenth century is not only the railway age but also the age of the navvy. The railway brought cheap, fast travel, encouraged commerce and ideas, and did a lot to create Britain's national prosperity and international ascendancy. But the railway was made by navvies, not by machines. A piece of engineering like the Great Western Railway from London to Bristol ... was built with picks, shovels and gunpowder.

And yet this indispensable body of men were largely social pariahs, considered, often justifiably, so wild, reckless and dissolute, as to be beyond redemption, let alone accommodation. Their welfare was rarely thought of, and by the bulk of the population never, bosses often didn't know how many navvies they employed and didn't take tallies of those (many) killed in the course of their work. Though sexual infatuation is Jimmy's ruin, he is also a casualty of the navvy system: heavy drinking and culture-backed lack of physical restraint, enable him to commit the crime for which he will die.

Throughout the poem Jimmy's navvy status is stressed:

> Anna was singing at her kitchen fire,
> She was surprised, and not well pleased to see
> A sweating navvy, red with heat and mire,
> Come to her door, whoever he might be.

His killing of Shepherd Ern not only is a demonstration of the rude ungovernable strength that characterises those of his employment, it also symbolises the death of an older rustic occupation at the hands of a member of, so to speak, a new race. And Jimmy's own death—dealt out to him by 'certain Justice with the pitiless knife' with the blessing of 'the white sick chaplain'—illustrates the expendability of that race not thought good enough for even rudimentary death-records, illustrates the Darwinian waste throughout the vast kingdom of living beings in order that the few and fit should inherit.

Jimmy's story had, again like *The Everlasting Mercy*, its origins in the Ledbury lore Masefield had heard as a boy. Yet there was a certain design in his seizing about the particular piece of lore he did. He had, with an urgency that surprised him, completed *The Everlasting Mercy* with the psychological release described in the last chapter, and now, only some weeks afterwards, on holiday with friends in a rainy Snowdonia, he realised that the creativity which had, as it seemed, seized him with Spring's own suddenness and power, had by no means relinquished its grip. There was more, as he recollects in *So Long to Learn*:

> I said to myself that I had written about a violent man who had been made happy for no apparent reason, but that that was only half of the picture: the opposite case must also be stated; I must show a quiet woman made heart-broken for no apparent reason. Instantly, as before, the fable came into my mind, complete, distinct in all its details: I had only to pull it down, as it were, from where it stood, on to the paper. ... The tale of the woman I cannot date, even approximately. I was playing or reading in a room in which two old men were discussing ancient murders; next to ghosts and Red Indians, murder was my favourite subject. The old men agreed that a certain murderer was rightly hanged for his crime, but one of the two (who had seemed the less merciful of the two) said: "The Judge ought to have let the young fellow go: the woman was the one to blame there. I was sorry for that poor fellow."

It is with the widow that the poem opens and—hauntingly—closes. Masefield says above that he wished to depict 'a quiet woman made heart-broken *for no reason*' (my italics). By this he does not mean, obviously, for no cause: Jimmy's taking up with Anna and his neglect of his mother would have been cause enough in itself, but there followed the murder, the trial— which could have gone either way and went the worse—and the execution. The widow can only bear all this by losing her wits, by retreat into a world where the real and the fancied are muddled. What happens to Mrs Gurney is further proof of life's amoralism, and Masefield suggests that, with certain 'givens', things could not have been otherwise, that they serve some overall plan which not only incorporates but counts on destroyed lives.

Part One of *The Widow in The Bye Street* would be termed its 'proem', a sequence of introductory, enunciatory stanzas, had it occurred in a work contemporary with *Troilus and Criseyde*. Everything is set out here, the characters, their circumstances, their situations which have logical developments, logic indeed demanding recognition that only one development was possible. Mrs Gurney is truly to suffer 'without a reason', but that doesn't mean that she hasn't made her own contribution to the tragedy. Her predicament has understandably resulted in an obsessional fear of Jimmy's finding a woman, and though obsession has heightened her powers of observation, it has reduced her natural psychological wisdom. Masefield's closed couplet on her behaviour has a poignant acidity:

> She took great care to keep the girls away,
> And all her trouble made him easier prey.

The 'proem', telling us of Jimmy's working as a navvy, speaks of his 'red blood', and we know that red blood will not stay dammed. Besides, the enormous physical demands of a navvy's labours, though often punishingly exhausting, also tended to strengthen his body for purposes other than the construction of embankments, cuttings and tunnels.

As for Anna, Masefield is anxious to establish her as destructive and deceitful before readers are presented with her. So he gives her history (and its harshness of tone does not preclude sympathy for her past):

> There was a woman out at Plaister's End,
> Light of body, fifty to the pound,
> A copper coin for any man to spend,
> Lovely to look on when the wits were drowned.
> Her husband's skeleton was never found,
> It lay among the rocks at Glydyr Mor,
> Where he drank poison, finding her a whore.

As for Shepherd Ern he is damningly enough described as 'A moody, treacherous man of bawdy mind'. Not for the first or last time in Masefield is male coarseness presented as a palatable surface covering something essentially cruel. This was, after all, a major theme of *The Everlasting Mercy*.

Masefield concludes his 'proem' with a stanza perhaps a little too imitative of Hardy (and a little too pat in its imitation) to be altogether successful—except for its darkly beautiful last lines which have a

Jacobean note that Masefield can sound through strength of his own personality:

> So the four souls are ranged, the chess-board set,
> The dark, invisible hand of secret Fate
> Brought it to come to being that they met
> After so many years of lying in wait.
> When we least think it he prepares his Mate.
> Mate, and the King's pawn played, it never ceases
> Though all the earth is dust of taken pieces.

The chess analogy brings home the lack of freedom at the heart of the poem.

Part Two opens the drama proper. It takes readers to Ledbury's October Fair, which Masefield brings to life with a youthful zest entirely consonant with his male protagonist's own enthusiasm for it, and showing in both detail and affecting atmosphere the writer's novelistic powers, as his fiction all too rarely displays them. (*Dead Ned* will have similar scenes to offer.) Jimmy, there with his mother ('Dressed in her finest with a Monmouth shawl') encounters Anna. Anna has arrived late at the fair because of a mishap with a cart, and Ern, whom she is to meet, bored with waiting for her, dives into a nearby pub where he's quite happy to be distracted by the gipsy, Bessie:

> A bold-eyed strapping harlot with black hair,
> One of the tribe which camped at Shepherd's Bois.
> She lured him out of inn into the noise
> Of the steam-organ where the horses spun,
> And so the end of all things was begun.

Again the Hardyesque/determinist note is sounded.

If for Anna Jimmy is a means of diverting herself in Ern's deceitful absence, for Jimmy it's a case of what Chaucer, describing his Courtly Lover in 'The Knight's Tale' expressed so memorably:

> And therewithal he bleynte and cried 'A'!
> As though he stongen were unto the herte.

His mother has lost—and Jimmy has surrendered the better part of himself. He believes however that his hard tedious existence has been miraculously transfigured:

"No. Wait a moment. May I call you Anna?"
"Perhaps. There must be nearness 'twixt us two."
Love in her face hung out his bloody banner,
And all love's clanging trumpets shocked and blew.
"When we got up today we never knew."
"I'm sure I didn't think, nor you did." "Never."
"And now this friendship's come to us for ever."

Jimmy is truly to show himself both callous and vicious, but all his innocence is revealed in this stanza, as well as his raw emotional yearning, an explosive combination. Whatever the readers' moral view of him, their sympathies are now engaged—accompanied by a feeling that these cannot prevail against what has to run its terrible—and bloody—Darwinian course.

Jimmy leaves the fair a-flame with feeling for Anna who merely takes herself to the pub for a drink. Mrs Gurney realises from her son's demeanour the serious nature of his enslavement. What she has long dreaded is about to take place. From that moment on the course is, from one point of vision, entirely clear, even straight-forward (though each stage takes the people by surprise and calls out for subtlety on behalf of the narrator): the inability of Jimmy to concentrate on anything but his love; Anna's two-timing; Shepherd Ern's need to take back the woman he thinks of as his own; Jimmy's neglect of his mother and his work; Anna's opting for Ern; Jimmy's crime and punishment—and the widow heart-broken, lonely and out of her mind as in Masefield's initial conception:

Singing her crazy song the mother goes
Singing as though her heart were full of peace,
Moths knock the petals from the dropping rose,
Stars make the glimmering pool a golden fleece,
The moon drops west, but still she does not cease,
The little mice peep out to hear her sing,
Until the inn-man's cockerel shakes his wing.

3

In 1951, in *The Ledbury Scene* Masefield wrote:

The Daffodil Fields were usually known in my childhood as "the Hall House Meadows". When I last saw these meadows, some seventeen years ago, they still bore the abundant daffodils that gave them such beauty every Spring.

> The brook that runs through these meadows rises under the east of Coneygree Wood near the place called Cheltmoor Cottage. It flows, as I describe, "crusting the leaves with lime", past Dunbridge Farm, and then by way of High Bridge Coppice to the River Leadon. I do not know its lower reaches. Its passage through the Hall House Meadows gave me at all times the liveliest delight. When I came upon the story of *The Daffodil Fields* in a foot-note to an old book on Iceland, I resolved to tell the tale in verse, as happening in three more or less imaginary farms along the course of the brook. It is many years since I looked at the tale; but when I last looked upon the scene of the imagined quarrel, I understood with what power the quiet scene had wrought upon me.

In the 'proem' to *The Daffodil Fields* (which does not occupy the entirety of Part One) Masefield evokes the scene which is to hold and, to some measure, to condition the drama. 'Human fate brought tragic things to pass,' he tells us; there is the same sense of inevitability and inescapability here as in *The Widow*. Much emphasis is placed on the brook itself which at once waters the lands of the three adjoining farms, and stands for the unstoppable course of life which flows on, whatever tragedies its human constituents have to endure. So it has always been 'Babbling the self-same song that it has sung through time.'

Most lives contain seasons of beauty and a kind of palpable promise, usually attendant on discovery of sexual capacities. The beauty is real enough, the promise more often than not an inappropriate projection of desire onto the external world:

> Then, on its left, some short-grassed fields begin,
> Red-clayed and pleasant, which the young spring fills
> With the never-quiet joy of dancing daffodils.

As was the case with the railway in *The Widow*, the part of the daffodils is sociologically correct. The country round Newent, Dymock and Ledbury is so profuse in daffodils of such quality that it has become known as 'The Golden Triangle'. (There were at one time 'Daffodil Special'"trains, and now there's a 10-mile Daffodil Way.) The flowers here—which Richard Mabey in his definitive *Flora Britannica* (1996) praises as having a quite remarkable 'lightness and vivacity', 'dazzle and daintiness'—also brought income to the fields' owners, of whom Lion is one of the sons and heirs, and who benefit particularly from the lavish crop, something which makes Lion's ultimate fate the more poignant.

For, in *The Daffodil Fields*, Masefield has left the low-life of the preceding two narrative poems of the Marches; he takes us to three adjacent farms—Ryemeadows, The Roughs and Foxholes, belonging to the Gray, Occleve and Keir families respectively. He is therefore in a social world more akin to his own; Michael, Lion and Mary are articulate people, well able to analyse and express their own feelings, if not to withstand them. For, if anything, they are less prepared for the impact of the physical on their emotional and external lives than Saul Kane and Jimmy Gurney, whose existences made them far more in touch with their physical impulses.

Michael, Lion and Mary have to conduct themselves on two levels—that of their personas, shaped by others' perceptions of them (Lion, who will die having just committed murder, is a gentle boy 'always at his book') and that of the demands of their sexual beings, which regardless assert themselves.

Two episodes in this intense, closely-worked and critically neglected poem call for attention. Both must be seen in context; the very considerable lyricism of the work—which surely owes something in the *kind* of work it is to George Meredith's long and revolutionary poem-sequence of 1862, *Modern Love*—is always at the service of the characters and their inter-actions, and never deserts the governing theme. Michael Gray has left behind his undisciplined life in France, where he is meant to be studying agriculture, in time for his father's death-bed. Old Nick Gray has left his affairs in a terrible mess, and Michael has to rely on the kindness of the neighbouring families, particularly the Keirs with whom he stays for a while. Michael has decided that, for an adventurous soul such as himself, 'The River Plate's the country!'; he will be a cattle-raiser there. His guardians assent, and, ironically, it is Mary's father, Keir who is the more approving of the scheme, for having the boy around is costing him money. (Ultimately his assent will cost him his daughter, though he can hardly be blamed for not realising this.) Mary has never wavered in her love of Michael, but it is only now, when he knows he will be spending three whole years in South America, that he, for his part, feels drawn to Mary, appreciates what it is to have her heart:

> ... a night time came
> When the two walking down the water learned
> That life till then had only been a name;
> Love had unsealed their spirits: they discerned.
> Mutely, at moth time there, their spirits yearned.

"I shall be gone three years, dear soul," he said.
"Dear, will you wait for me?" "I will," replied the maid.

They become betrothed, summer arrives, and Michael must soon be leaving. At last his final night in his home-country comes round. The ensuing stanzas not only exhibit Masefield's art at its richest and most mature, they are crucial to the meaning of the poem—of the discrepancy, the tensions between Nature's justice and other kinds of justice:

Dim red the sunset burned. He bade her come
Into the wood with him; they went, the night came dumb.
Still as high June, the very water's noise
Seemed but a breathing of the earth; the flowers
Stood in the dim like souls without a voice.
The wood's conspiracy of occult powers
Drew all about them, and for hours on hours
No murmur shook the oaks, the stars did house
Their lights like lamps upon those never-moving boughs.

Under their feet the woodland sloped away
Down to the valley, where the farmhouse lights
Were sparks in the expanse the moon made gray.
June's very breast was bare this night of nights.
Moths blundered up against them, grays and whites
Moved on the darkness where the moths were out,
Nosing for stickysweet with trembling uncurled snout.

But all this beauty was but music played,
While the high pageant of their hearts prepared.
A spirit thrilled between them, man to maid,
Mind flowed in mind, the inner heart was bared,
They needed not to tell how much each cared;
All the soul's strength was at the other's soul.
Flesh was away awhile, a glory made them whole.

Nothing was said by them; they understood,
They searched each other's eyes without a sound,
Alone with moonlight in the heart of the wood,
Knowing the stars and all the soul of the ground.
"Mary," he murmured. "Come." His arms went round,
A white moth glimmered by, the woods were hushed;
The rose at Mary's bosom dropped its petals, crushed.

After a while:

> The moonlight found an opening in the boughs;
> It entered in, it filled that sacred place
> With consecration on the throbbing brows;
> It came with benediction and with grace.
> A whispering came from face to yearning face:
> "Beloved, will you wait for me?" "My own."
> "I shall be gone three years, you will be left alone."

Even remembering Meredith and Hardy, I find it hard to think of another writer before D.H. Lawrence who could have achieved the rapture and the solemnity of this passage, or drawn the same conclusions from what it describes. Consummation is consecration, and the reverberations are to be profound and extensive. But while it may embody a deeper truth than the kind of consecration given by church or registry office, it also can act as no guarantee of security. Nature is cruel and fickle as well as revealing and magnificent. Despite these moments of ecstasy, when two become one, and that one is absorbed into a larger unity still, Michael is unfaithful to and heedless of Mary in his absence, and sets in train the complications that are to end with three deaths.

The second episode occurs in Part Four, when all but four months of the three years Michael is to spend in the Argentine have passed—with no word from him. The Occleves breed a bull-calf, which cattle-raisers from South America see and pay 'a mighty price' for. Lion decides that he will take the animal himself to the River Plate country, where he will seek out Michael. Once again comparisons with Lawrence spring to mind. The transported bull is kin to the horses of *The Rainbow* (1916), *Women in Love* (1920) and— even more nearly—*St Mawr* (1925), but all post-date *The Daffodil Fields*. The bull is not just male sexuality but the male principle:

> He sailed in Lion's charge, south, to the Plate's red tide.
>
> There Lion landed with the bull and there
> The great beast raised his head and bellowed loud,
> Challenging that expanse and that new air;
> Trembling, but full of wrath and thunder-browed,
> Far from the daffodil fields and friends, but proud,
> His wild eye kindled at the great expanse.
> Two scraps of Shropshire life they stood there; their advance

136

> Was slow along the well-grassed cattle land,
> But at the last an end was made; the brute
> Ate his last bread crust from his master's hand,
> And snuffed the foreign herd and stamped his foot;
> Steers on the swelling ranges gave salute.

The qualities the bull possesses are those that Michael, the emigrant, rather than Lion, bound to his native county, possesses: energy, aggression, excitement at new territory opening out before him, courage, independence—and also pride in winning a mate. Lion, in bringing the animal over from England, has both literally and metaphorically become the author of his own doom. In the face of young bulls like Michael, graver, more introverted individuals like Lion—his name suggesting the essential nobility of his cast of mind, a nobility he is to betray—tend to go under. This is not a judgement, it's a statement.

Certainly, Lion's magnanimity is never better shown than in his dealings with Michael whom he now tracks down, living with a Spanish woman on the pampas. In their dialogue two different ways of life, two halves of the male psyche are being articulated:

> ... Lion spoke:
> "Do you remember riding past the haunted oak
>
> That Christmas Eve, when all the bells were ringing,
> So that we picked out seven churches' bells,
> Ringing the night, and people carol-singing?
> It hummed and died away and rose in swells
> Like a sea breaking. We have been through hells
> Since then, we two, and now this being here
> Brings all that Christmas back, and makes it strangely near."

Michael's own brand of truthfulness, to his own reactions and impulses, commands a kind of admiration:

> "Yes," Michael answered, "they were happy times,
> Riding beyond there; but a man needs change;
> I know what they connote, those Christmas chimes,
> Fudge in the heart, and pudding in the grange.
> It stifles me all that; I need the range,
> Like this before us, open to the sky;
> There every wing is clipped, but here a man can fly.

137

We are hearing, if you like, in these verbally felicitous stanzas, the voice of the settled English yeoman vying with that of the English colonialist, the opener-up of territory, soldier or sailor. Both voices are to be stilled, both men to go under, lost to no purpose—for the woman they both love dies too.

At the close of *Troilus and Criseyde* Troilus was able to look back from the 'eighth sphere' and survey human activity so much of the tragedy of which springs from blind desire. Masefield doesn't attempt this—he lacked the framework of metaphysical belief to do so—but he does place his stories in the wider context of the natural world. The agricultural workers watch Mrs Gurney going about her crazy business:

> Dully they watch her, then they turn to go
> To that high Shropshire upland of late hay;
> Her singing lingers with them as they mow,
> And many times they try it, now grave, now gay,
> Till, with full throat, over the hills away,
> They lift it clear; oh, very clear it towers
> Mixed with the swish of many falling flowers.

At the end of *The Daffodil Fields* Masefield returns his readers, mourning the deaths of all the protagonists, to the brook. In a coda, as beautiful as it is unexpected, he follows the water-course out to sea, where sailors are to be found singing the story of the poem:

> Slowly it loitered past the shivering reeds
> Into a mightier water; thence its course
> Becomes a pasture where the salmon feeds,
> Wherein no bubble tells its humble source;
> But the great waves go rolling, and the horse
> Snorts at the bursting waves and will not drink,
> And the great ships go outward, bubbling to the brink.
>
> Outward with men upon them, stretched in line,
> Handling the halliards to the ocean's gates,
> Where flicking windflaws fill the air with brine,
> And all the ocean opens. Then the mates
> Cry, and the sunburnt crew no longer waits,
> But sings triumphant, and the topsail fills
> To this old tale of woe among the daffodils.

CHAPTER SIX
The Canon: *Dauber*

In the notes she made after her visit to Masefield on December 6th 1950, (first published in her introduction to the 1991 reprint of her book *John Masefield*), Muriel Spark wrote—for December 9th:

> Masefield also remarked on the true greatness of *Jude the Obscure*. I have remembered, too, that Masefield said that the theme of *Dauber* was that the artist is compelled to obey the law of his own being, no matter if death or disaster ensues.

Dauber, which, in the poet's *oeuvre*, has enjoyed a success only rivalled by *The Everlasting Mercy* and *Reynard the Fox*, hasn't always been read as if this were its theme; indeed Muriel Spark herself isn't quite certain whether it should be so read. In her chapter on the poem, full of insights and keen appreciations though it is, she says:

> Judging simply by the text of the poem, I do not see Dauber as an artist involved in single-minded devotion to an inner law; but as a young man with a leaning towards painting, who has not yet earned the designation of "artist" and who, in obedience to his obligations as a ship's hand, proves his prowess not as an artist but as a member of the crew.

And further on:

> ... [Masefield] does not show the Dauber emerging triumphant from the situation with a foot in both worlds, a sailor-artist or an artist-sailor. For dramatic and realistic purposes the Dauber must be artist or seaman.

Perhaps taking his cue from Muriel Spark, critic and poet G.S. Fraser, contributing to *The Penguin Companion to Literature: Britain and the Commonwealth* (1971), says the poem is:

> remarkable both for its realistic life at sea and its acute probing into the psychology of the frustrated artist, with the true urge, but without the technical gift.

The Oxford Companion to Twentieth Century Literature in English (1996), with less aptness or accuracy, calls it

> a psychologically compelling treatment of a sailor with artistic instincts.

Examination of the true nature of the artist, or a study in conflict? A psychological study of artist as young sailor, or of a young sailor who partakes of the artist? Whatever interpretation is put on it, one thing about *Dauber* is undeniable—and the more undeniable it is the more we know of Masefield's own life: in this narrative poem he draws on his own experiences, in both their external and their internal aspects, to an extent that puts it at once in a different category from any of his other imaginative works. They were experiences, moreover, he very obviously did not wish to present or analyse directly. Later on, in *So Long to Learn*, he was virtually to admit as much. But in view of the fidelity to both outward events and inward states throughout the poem, there seems every good reason to believe that Masefield was thinking about himself, and indeed about the whole question of identity, of selfhood, while at work on this darkest and most tormented of his four pre-Great War masterpieces. Which isn't to say that its protagonist, the Dauber himself, and his predicament, don't have life of their own, aren't given autonomy through the poet's art.

☆   ☆   ☆

The story itself of *Dauber* is simple and linear, in this respect closer to *The Everlasting Mercy* with its concentration on one person's destiny than to its two fellows in Rhyme Royal; indeed it relies on no interactions, no pressure from other human agencies, for its development. For all that, I believe it to be, in an interesting respect, the least deterministic work of the four. Though its course is the fraught but forward-striving one of the ship's voyage, it does include one seeming detour, an excursion into the protagonist's past, in the form of the account of his early life and of what brought him to sea that he gives to one of the few crew-members friendly to him: 'reefer' (apprentice) Si. Muriel Spark dislikes this piece of personal history; to her it's an inartistic digression. For me it contains the key to the whole work, and to the questions it poses. And artistically it has a certain Dutch masters' quality that provides a needed contrast with life on the ship, both claustrophobic and as beset by the elements.

The Dauber—his real name is Joe—was, he tells Si, born and grew up on a farm.

"I come from out past Gloucester," Dauber said;
"Not far from Pauntley if you know those parts."

The farm is tenanted but tenancy passes from father to son, and it is his father's intention that Joe will take it over from him. But it's not a very productive enterprise, and can be kept going only with backbreaking work:

"Yet still he couldn't bear to see it pass
To strangers, or to think a time would come
When other men than us would mow the grass,
And other names than ours have the home.
Some sorrows come from evil thought, but some
Comes when two men are near, and both are blind
To what is generous in the other's mind.

"I was the only boy, and father thought
I'd farm the Spital after he was dead,
And many a time he took me out and taught
About manures and seed-corn white and red,
And soils and hops, but I'd an empty head;
Harvest or seed, I would not do a turn -
I loathed the farm, I didn't want to learn."

After their mother's death, Joe's sister Jane keeps house for her him and their father. Jane nags and nags at her brother to take a proper interest in his inheritance, and succeeds in rousing his father's anger against him. Both know that the lad's real interests are water and ships, together with art, this last enthusiasm dating from his discovery of some drawings done by his late, unhappy mother. His artistic ambitions meet with nothing but scorn; Jane sneers at him:

"... It's not as though
You are a genius, or could ever be."

this apparently being the only circumstances in which pursuit of the medium could ever be justifiable.

With commendable honesty Joe tries to present his case:

"Father would see it, if he were not blind.
I was not built to farm, as he would find.
O Jane, it's bitter hard to stand alone
And spoil my father's life or spoil my own."

"Spoil both," she said, "the way you're shaping now.
You're only a boy not knowing your own good.
Where will you go, suppose you leave here? How
Do you propose to earn your daily food?
Draw? Daub the pavements? There's a feckless brood
Goes to the devil daily, Joe, in cities
Only from thinking how divine their wit is.

Clouds are they, without water, carried away.
And you'll be one of them, the way you're going,
Daubing at silly pictures all the day,
And praised by silly fools who're always blowing.
And you chose this when you might go a-sowing,
Casting the good corn into chosen mould
That shall in time bring forth a hundredfold."

So we went on, but in the end it ended.
I felt I'd done a murder; I felt sick.
There's much in human minds cannot be mended,
And that, not I, played dad a cruel trick.

Joe discovers in himself the courage to leave home, but does so weighed down with guilt; he feels he has in effect committed parricide. He gets work as a house-painter near the banks of the lower Severn, and then, catching sight of a clipper, knows where his destiny lies—both as an individual and as an artist.

Then on a day she sailed; but when she went
My mind was clear on what I had to try:

To see the sea and ships, and what they meant,
That was the thing I longed to do; so I
Drew and worked hard, and studied and put by,
And thought of nothing else but that one end,
But let all else go hang - love, money, friend.

He sets about getting a position for himself on a similar ship, a lowly position at that, as an 'idler', best described in Masefield's own glossary to the work: 'The members of the round-house mess, generally consisting of the carpenter, cook, sailmaker, boatswain, painter etc.' They exist in humble distinction even to the young reefers; in fact Si is to be severely reprimanded for talking to idler Dauber, and is forbidden to do so again. But nonetheless, on board ship, which is where he wants to be, Dauber can practise his art, can fuse his two passions: he will be a painter of sea-scapes.

The distance between the Dauber's past (the necessary prelude to the story proper, even if presented in flash-back) and Masefield's own is not especially wide. Jack Masefield was jeered at by his elders for his literary interests (which he liked to think he had inherited from his mother, Carrie, who had made up stories and enjoyed poetry); his Aunt Kate, who'd disliked her sister-in-law, thought her nephew's absorption in writing and reading unhealthy and useless, and it will be remembered how one of his elders and betters, 'a kind friend', as *So Long to Learn* sarcastically styles him, told the boy just after he'd won the McIver Prize for an English Essay: 'You must not let this be fatal to you. You must get this writing-rubbish out of your head.' Jack, too, was burdened with the knowledge that only if he were a genius would he be permitted, let alone encouraged, to follow his vocation, and Constance Babington Smith quotes in her *John Masefield: A Life* a letter he wrote to his brother-in-law after the publication of *Salt-Water Ballads*, in which he found it necessary to say:

> Genius I'm not, but I'm pretty sure that I've kept my talents unrusted under pretty tough circumstances, and, by God's gilt-edged clouds, I'll have another smack at the shams and humbugs of this wicked world before I've done.

Like Dauber he had faith in himself—and the faith had had to come entirely from within; he had no champion, no active recogniser. Like his hero he'd invested life at sea with imaginative hopes and dreams of self-realisation which were to be shattered (though in his case his family had wanted him to be on board ship). Like him too he had to resist pressures and denigration in order to be himself and pursue what most interested him. And like him again he knew constant feelings of guilt and self-inadequacy occasioned by his relations with his family; these conditioned both his inner life and his dealings with his ship-mates and the tasks they expected him to discharge.

And now the questions arise:

Is Dauber gifted (as Masefield was)? Does he believe himself to be so? Is he even a 'genius'? Or is he (the commonest view of the poem) talent-less, a pathetic example of someone who's prepared to sacrifice himself for art but hasn't the desirable originality or the requisite capacity needed, and goes to his early death as result of his delusions? And the only answer the poem itself allows us to make is -

We do not know. More—we *cannot* know.

Dauber is to die before there can be any proof whatever, even to himself, of the quality of his painting. And there is no objective judge on whose opinion we can rely. He meets his end as sailor rather than painter, it's true, but the role is imposed on him entirely by the demands of external circumstances. All we can be sure of is that for him his intention of becoming a painter and his feeling for the sea—it amounts virtually to a *participation mystique* with it—are indivisible and incontrovertible.

The voyage that *Dauber* describes—ending in Valparaiso, where Jack Masefield himself was hospitalised—can be taken, with hindsight, as the voyage the author made in his unhappy youth *before he was able to show the world that poet was what he was*. Life with a sense of vocation before the vocation can be vindicated—that is *Dauber*'s real subject. In order for the discussion of this to be complete, Dauber must not, as Jack did, fall ill, be medically treated, be registered as D.B.S., but die. Paradoxically, it is the Dauber's death that makes the work so strongly an autobiographical one, since by means of concluding his story with it, Masefield is able to concentrate on his youthful self and what befell him without the impediments of later experiences and self-vindications. Of course, the behaviour of the crew-members, and the Dauber's reactions to these and to the terrors of the sea-storm will change in complexion according to whether the young man turns out the painter he dreamed of being, or a failure. His dying eliminates both possibilities, and makes us see him and his fate more existentially. In a curious way his death—so horribly final, and brought hauntingly home to us by the unforgettable descriptions of the youthful corpse, and of the ship's arrival in port without him—makes *Dauber* as thought-provokingly open-ended as *The Everlasting Mercy*.

And so to what happens on the voyage itself—to situations, emotions, and experiences—Masefield could apparently present only through the vehicle of art, the poem's ultimate concern. Dauber's sufferings, it must be insisted, are not only appaling, they're quite unmerited. They receive no resolution, he never attains the perspectives that would make sense of them, nor any state of release.

First, his sufferings at the hands of his shipmates. These, I feel certain, relate to indignities and cruelties Masefield himself endured on the *Gilcruix*, foreshadowed in the pranks he had to put up with on the *Conway* and which he later recounted with somewhat self-conscious resigned good humour in *New Chum*. This is not a possible response for those which form the crucial episodes in *Dauber*, and indeed Masefield conveys Dauber's distress and resentment at them with a nerve-rasping vividness unsurpassed in his work.

Dauber's very presence is an irritant to the reefers and other idlers, because, one suspects, he is too self-contained—his preoccupations are of an independent nature, concerned as he is with marrying his interior world to the exterior one of the ship at sea. His absorption in his paintings they view as insulting to themselves; the sobriquet 'dauber' was not given in any spirit of affection:

> "Now," said the reefer, "up! Come, Sam; come, Si,
> Dauber's been hiding something." Up they slid.
> Treading on naked tiptoe stealthily
> To grope for treasure at the long-boat skid.
> "Drawings!" said Sam. "Is that what Dauber hid?
> Lord! I expected pudding, not this rot.
> Still, come, we'll have some fun with what we've got."
>
> They smeared the paint with turpentine until
> They could remove with mess-clouts every trace
> Of quick perception caught by patient skill,
> And lines that had brought blood into his face.
> They wiped the pigments off, and did erase,
> With knives, all sticking clots. When they had done,
> Under the boat they hid them every one.

All he had drawn since first he came to sea,
His six weeks' leisure's fruits, they laid them there.
They chuckled then to think how mad he'd be
Finding his paintings vanished into air.

The destruction is an act of unmitigated sadism; Dauber has done nothing to deserve it, has never shirked work or been unfriendly or unco-operative. But the sadism has not spent itself. When he discovers the damage done to his work, his ship-mates deny all knowledge of what's happened, while mocking Dauber for his anguish. Sam, who started the 'fun', in brilliantly rendered dialogue, even feigns sympathy and eggs him on to complain to their Captain:

A sigh came from the assembled seamen there.
Would he be such a fool for their delight
As go to tell the Captain? Would he dare?

Dauber does. For all his gentleness he is not lacking in daring; his very presence on the ship and his very concentration while aboard on his art attest to that. But before he can put his case to the Captain he has to deal with the Mate, a man more on the side of the men than on that of Dauber (also the position of the all too distant Captain). Dauber's complaint, in which he only too obviously lives up to Masefield's initial description of him as 'young for his years', is one of the high spots of the work as a real-istic poem; it exhibits the writer's technical skills at their most virtuosic and their most aurally attentive:

"Please, sir, they spoiled my drawings." "Who did?" "They."
"Who's they?" "I don't quite know, sir."
"Don't quite know, sir?
Then why are you aft to talk about it, hey?
Whom do you complain of?" "No one." "No one?"
"No, sir."
"Well, then, go forward till you've found them. Go, sir,
If you complain of someone, then I'll see.
Now get to hell! and don't come bothering me."

Later the Mate is pleased, mockingly, to give Dauber a lesson in painting, and all those present agree that what he produces is far better than

the young man's pretentious effort. Dauber defends himself with a rare—
and very touching—dignity:

> "You've said enough," he said, "now let it end.
> Who cares how bad my painting may be? I
> Mean to go on, and if I fail, to try.
> However much I miss of my intent,
> If I have done my best I'll be content."

There is, if on a modest scale, a mystic's raptness in Dauber's application—both to seeing and to the rendering of what he sees. He achieves
with unknown results a fusion of eye and hand, and with this fusion comes
peace, which banishes—for a while completely—the evil around him.

> There the great skyline made her perfect round,
> Notched now and then by the sea's deeper blue;
> A smoke-smutch marked a steamer homeward bound,
> The haze wrought all things to intenser hue.
> In tingling impotence the Dauber drew
> As all men draw, keen to the shaken soul
> To give a hint that might suggest the whole.
>
> A naked seaman washing a red shirt
> Sat at a tub whistling between his teeth;
> Complaining blocks quavered like something hurt.
> A sailor cut an old boot for a sheath,
> The ship bowed to her shadow-ship beneath,
> And little slaps of spray came at the roll
> On to the deck-planks from the scupper-hole.
>
> He watched it, painting patiently, as paints
> With eyes that pierce behind the blue sky's veil,
> The Benedictine in a Book of Saints
> Watching the passing of the Holy Grail;
> The green dish dripping blood, the trump, the hail,
> The spears that pass, the memory, and the passion,
> The beauty moving under the world's fashion.

How appropriate is Masefield's likening of the Dauber's relationship to
both his material and his medium to a religious votary's! He has the same

awed humility towards the mystery that is the world, the same desire to put whatever abilities he possesses to the service of its glorification. So, if in one way his (and Masefield's) idea of the artist is a Romantic one ('We were the last romantics,' declared his friend, Yeats, after all), in another it is that of a medieval 'maker'; the Dauber's mentality is that of the reverent stone-carvers of the great cathedrals, or the painters of their rood-screens.

Whilst the cruelty of his fellow-men cannot be avoided, indeed can rarely be defeated, the determined, those faithful to their own inner vision, of which Dauber is one, can rise above it through the creative strengths of their own natures. With Nature's cruel elements, however, which are able, if for only the duration of their extreme ferocity, to unite divided men—it is quite another matter. Survival is at stake, and in struggling for this all other considerations have to yield. And yet ...

Any contemporary readers familiar with the voyage of the *Gilcruix* would not have had any difficulty in recognising the stages of the journey on which the Dauber is bound: when first met, his ship is in the South Atlantic. Had they read *A Tarpaulin Muster*, they would have appreciated what the richness of detail, and the almost unbearable atmosphere of physical tension, proclaim: that the poet is drawing very closely on what he personally underwent. With Valparaiso its first port of call, the Dauber's ship will have to round the Horn in late June, the very height of the Southern Hemisphere's winter. Even before the Horn there is the 'wester' at the mouth of the River Plate, where the weather poses problems, demands concentration and even elicits fear. But the ship is able to hold her own, and the men, the Dauber himself not wholly excluded, are accordingly composed:

> The wester came as steady as the Trades;
> Brightly it blew, and still the ship did shoulder
> The brilliance of the water's white cockades
> Into the milky green of smoky smoulder.
> The sky grew bluer and the air grew colder.
> Southward she thundered while the westers held,
> Proud, with taut bridles, pawing, but compelled.
>
> And still the Dauber strove, though all men mocked,
> To draw the splendour of the passing thing,
> And deep inside his heart a something locked.
> Long pricking in him, now began to sting -

A fear of the disasters storm might bring;
His rank as painter would be ended then -
He would keep watch and watch like other men.

Already a point pivotal to an understanding of *Dauber* has been made. It is not that Dauber has to make a choice between artist and seaman—or that anybody else in his situation has to make such a choice. (For I do not believe this to be primarily a psychological poem, with a particular personality as the focus of interest.) The point is the far more disturbing one that human-beings can have their decisions made them by forces utterly beyond their control.

Masefield, to judge by *A Tarpaulin Muster*, appears to have been exhilarated by the River Plate 'squalls', and not to have suffered the Dauber's worries and forebodings. In place of the poem's comparison of ship with caparisoned horse, there is an analogy with a leaping stag; instead of the 'long pricking', an 'ecstasy':

> For that one wonderful day we staggered and swooped, and bounded in wild leaps, and burrowed down and shivered, and anon rose up shaking ... We tore through the seas in great jumps—there is no other word for it. She seemed to leap clear from one green roaring ridge to come smashing down upon the next ...We were possessed of the spirits of the wind. We could have danced and killed each other. We were in an ecstasy. We were possessed. We half believed that the ship would leap from the waters and hurl herself into the heavens, like a winged god.

In reality Masefield probably knew some of his Dauber's uneasiness; it is only too possible, especially in unfamiliar conditions, for ecstasy and *angst* to alternate, even to coexist. Not that the Dauber himself doesn't experience something of the former emotion, even if it's primarily vicarious, gained by observation of the fearless crew, and no sooner entertained than translated into further hopes for his art:

                    ... a thought occurred
Within the painter's brain like a bright bird:

That this, and so much like it, of man's toil,
Compassed by naked manhood in strange places,

Was all heroic, but outside the coil
Within which modern art gleams or grimaces;
That if he drew that line of sailors' faces
Sweating the sail, the passionate play and change,
It would be new, and wonderful, and strange.

That that was what his work meant; it would be
A training in new vision - a revealing
Of passionate men in battle with the sea,
High on an unseen stage, shaking and reeling;
And men through him would understand their feeling,
Their might, their misery, their tragic power,
And all by suffering pain a little hour;

'New, and wonderful, and strange'; 'new vision'; 'a revealing'—who can doubt that these were Masefield's own desiderata for art, in particular the poetry he was engaged in writing, which, in truth, was like nobody else's.

Certainly his technical control is nowhere better or more memorably exhibited than in the conclusion to Part V, which is in effect the conclusion to that part of the poem when Dauber is still under the impression that he can come to decisions and make choices. The ship has been journeying ever southwards towards what everyone, old sea-lag and novice alike, cannot but dread, the weather temporarily belying the nature of the season:

That night the snow fell between six and seven,
A little feathery fall so light, so dry -
An aimless dust out of a confused heaven,
Upon an air no steadier than a sigh;
The powder dusted down and wandered by
So purposeless, so many, and so cold,
Then died, and the wind ceased and the ship rolled.

Rolled till she clanged - rolled till the brain was tired,
Marking the acme of the heaves, the pause
While the sea-beauty rested and respired,
Drinking great draughts of roller at her hawse.
Flutters of snow came aimless upon flaws.
"Lock up your paints," the mate said, speaking light;
"This is the Horn; you'll join my watch tonight."

The closed couplet as stanza ending can never have been used to more telling effect; it has an ominous quality that what is to come abundantly vindicates. It is subtle as well as ominous, for in their strongest parts these narrative poems unite the perceptions of Masefield the novelist with those of Masefield the poet. From his tone alone we understand that the Mate, hitherto an unsympathetic figure, knows what he's talking about, can read the weather signals as Dauber, and we with him, cannot. *He* realises what *we* haven't yet, that the 'sea-beauty's' 'rest' and 'respiration' are but a predictable prelude to something very different. And so we are prepared to forgive him his crude insensitivity, his mockery of a high-minded young man, just as, in the face of Nature at her most implacable, all men tend to forgive each other, as they strive together to get through alive. "This is the Horn."

I have called the narrative course of Dauber simple and linear; if that suggests a work approximating to the parable (like *The Everlasting Mercy*) or the ballad/folk-tale (a major constituent of *The Widow in the Bye Street* and *The Daffodil Fields*), then it is inappropriate. *Dauber*'s originality is shown in the fact that the simplicity of the concentration on one individual and his aspirations, the linear purity of the poet's tracing of his South Atlantic voyage, do not really pertain in the last two parts (VI and VII), once the ship has begun the rounding of the Horn. If, on one level, all the men, and the Dauber with them, are now furiously, tirelessly active, in another they are, every one of them, passive—the elements, the combat with death, take all assertion of individual life away from them. True, Dauber has very much his own reactions and feelings, and even has to make up his mind as to how best to cope with the appaling conditions, but the deliberating, self-dedicating young man of the earlier parts of the poem has vanished, and could not have done otherwise. And with him the narrating voice telling his story has given place to one intent on rendering a scene where human beings are dwarfed and conventional notions of character and incident have to be jettisoned. (Not only humans are thus reduced, other forms of life are too; here occurs that wonderful passage quoted earlier about the whales, who speak out of the night, 'defeated creatures who had suffered wrong, / But were still noble underneath the stroke.')

> An hour more went by; the Dauber lost
> All sense of hands and feet, all sense of all
> But of a wind that cut him to the ghost,
> And of a frozen fold he had to haul,

Of heavens that fell and never ceased to fall,
And ran in smoky snatches along the sea,
Leaping from crest to wave-crest, yelling. He

Lost sense of time; no bells went, but he felt
Ages go over him. At last, at last
They frapped the cringled crojick's icy pelt;
In frozen bulge and bunt they made it fast.
Then, scarcely live, they laid in to the mast.
The Captain's speaking-trumpet gave a blare,
"Make fast the topsail, Mister, while you're there."

The poet is obliged now to describe the indescribable. Only orders given
with as much authority as seasoned man can muster and the assent to them
have any meaning, significance or consequence in a world with all norms
taken away.

Masefield on board the *Gilcruix* met a relentless and fiercesomely cold
storm of thirty-two days' duration, with waves forty feet in height and ice
everywhere.

"Is it cold on deck?" said Dauber. "Is it cold?
We're sheeted up, I tell you, inches thick!
The fo'c's'le's like a wedding-cake, I'm told."

He too must have contemplated an end to all the dreams, longings, plans
of his lonely short life, and derived some comfort from his long-delayed
incorporation into the communal life of the ship, from the oneness of
which he was temporarily now a part:

"Thank you," the Dauber said; the seaman grinned.
"This your first foul weather?" "Yes." "I thought
Up on the yard you hadn't seen much wind.
Them's rotten sea-boots, Dauber, that you brought.
Now I must cut on deck before I'm caught."
He went; the lamp-flame smoked; he slammed the door;
A film of water loitered across the floor.

The Dauber watched it come and watched it go;
He had had revelation of the lies
Cloaking the truth men never choose to know;

He could bear witness now and cleanse their eyes.
He had beheld in suffering; he was wise;
This was the sea, this searcher of the soul -
This never-dying shriek fresh from the Pole.

Whether the possessor of artistic talents or not, whether a guilty misfit or not, Dauber has been given a new common humanity by the inhuman, the anti-human:

Faces recurred, fierce memories of the yard,
The frozen sail, the savage eyes, the jests,
The oaths of one great seaman syphilis-scarred,
The tug of leeches jammed beneath their chests,
The buntlines bellying bunts out into breasts.
The deck so desolate-grey, the sky so wild,
He fell asleep, and slept like a young child.

(The younger Masefield springs to mind here who wrote: 'Faces— passionate faces—of men I may not know / They haunt me, burn me to the heart as I turn aside to go.')

During the storm's terrible duration Dauber reviews his life and personality and finds himself wanting. This procedure is, I think, seen in generic rather than particular terms. Nobody would fail to do likewise.

And then the thought came: "I'm a failure. All
My life has been a failure. They were right.
It will not matter if I go and fall;
I should be free then from this hell's delight.
I'll never paint. Best let it end to-night.
I'll slip over the side. I've tried and failed."
So in the ice-cold in the night he quailed.

Death would be better, death, than this long hell
Of mockery and surrender and dismay -
This long defeat of doing nothing well,
Playing the part too high for him to play.
"O Death! who hides the sorry thing away,
Take me; I've failed. I cannot play these cards."
There came a thundering from the topsail yards.

And then he bit his lips, clenching his mind,
And staggered out to muster, beating back
The coward frozen self of him that whined.
Come what cards might he meant to play the pack.
"Ai!" screamed the wind; the topsail sheets went clack;
Ice filled the air with spikes; the grey-backs burst.
"Here's Dauber," said the Mate, "on deck the first.

"Why, holy sailor, Dauber, you're a man."

He has passed an initiation test such as few have to take, but of the kind from which that species of rite ultimately derives. Psychologically Masefield is, I believe, here avenging himself on sneering, dismissive Aunt Kate, and on the Ledbury bourgeoisie generally, who did not know what he had had to face up to, how he had gained his manhood, but tormented him as if he had been indeed the 'failure' Dauber has been imagining himself.

What he went through we *know* took an enormous toll of young Jack Masefield; one part of him never recovered. The man he grew into did not permit his stand-in to survive the voyage. Not for Dauber Valparaiso, a breakdown, hospital treatment. He is to meet his death *after* the storm but *before* the ship reaches the Chilean coast.

2

I have said that I consider *Dauber* the least deterministic of Masefield's four great narrative poems; I do so precisely because of the nature of its protagonist's death, the account of which, in my view, constitutes Masefield's greatest poetic attainment.

In *The Widow* and *The Daffodil Fields* we see the *dramatis personae*, the Widow, Jimmy, Ern and Anna in the first, Michael, Lion and Mary in the second, programmed to their tragic fates by genetic inheritance and familial and societal circumstances over which they have no control, and specific stanzas in which the author comments on characters and action make this point of view plain enough. *The Everlasting Mercy*, which ostensibly deals with the descent of Christian grace on a sinner through the agency of an elderly Quaker lady, is sufficiently attentive to both the psychological and the sociological aspects of Saul Kane's situation to make us appreciate the reasons why this ne'erdowell should turn to Jesus, ploughing and a life of harmony, aged only twenty-six.

But in *Dauber* neither the young man's character nor his circumstances have any bearing on his actual death. None of the problems his wanting to be an artist raised either in himself or in others is proved or disproved by it. Nature and chance are instead responsible. The Dauber is indeed the victim of accident, in the fuller meaning of that word, of the blind and, from a human perspective, incomprehensible workings of natural forces.

The ship has, much battered with an exhausted crew, come out of the storm and can head for port. 'Clear rang the songs. "Hurrah! Cape Horn is bet!"' 'Hurray!/For three more weeks to Valparaiso Bay!' give out the almost incredulous and grateful sailors. '"She smells old Vallipo,"' the Bosun cries. The atmosphere on the ship is more inclusive now as far as the Dauber is concerned, warmer even, though, says the Mate:

> "And now you'll stow that folly, trying to paint.
> You've had your lesson; you're a sailor now ...
> With all your colours on the paint-box lid.
> I blushed for you ... and then the daubs you hid.
> My God! you'll have more sense now, eh? You've quit?"
> "No, sir." "You've not." "No, sir." "God give you wit."

However, the Dauber, young, tired, and hopeful, is looking as eagerly forward to being in port as any of the crew. Before being either an artist or a seaman, he's a human being in need of shelter and fructifying rest, even a little fun. And then (again a couplet of great economy and ominous suggestion):

> The mate gazed hard to windward, eyed his sail,
> And said the Horn was going to flick her tail.

She does; the wind gets up, increases, is laden with snow, and threatens the topsails which must, says the Captain, be taken down. Significantly — considering that 'what if' autobiographical element in *Dauber*, its pondering of how Jack Masefield's life would have appeared as a totality had he not survived the voyage to become a writer — the action that brings about the Dauber's death is one he himself had carried out on instructions and described in *A Tarpaulin Muster*:

155

There was the sail I had come to furl. And a wonder of a sight it was. It was blowing and bellying in the wind, and leaping around like "a drunken colt", and flying over the yard, thrashing and flogging. It was roaring like a bull with its slatting and thrashing. The royal mast was bending to the strain of it ... The wind pinned me flat against the yard, and seemed to be blowing all my clothes to shreds. I felt like a king, like an emperor. I shouted aloud with the joy of that "rastle" with the sail. Forward of me was the main mast, with another lad fighting another royal; and beyond him was yet another, whose sail seemed tied in knots. Below me was the ship, a leaping mad thing, with little silly figures, all heads and shoulders, pulling silly strings along the deck. There was the sea, sheer under me, and it looked grey and grim, and streaked with the white of our smother.

Then, with a lashing swish, the rain squall caught us. It beat down the sea. It blotted out the view.I could see nothing more but grey, driving rain, grey spouts of rain, grey clouds which burst rain, grey heavens which opened and poured rain. Cold rain. Icy-cold rain.

But what if that greyness had been the last he'd seen of this world? Dauber is first up the mast, as nimble and bold as Masefield himself had been, but the weather is not the Plate squalls but the aftermath of those dreadful thirty-two days. One has the curious and disconcerting sense in the stanzas following that Masefield is re-creating an event he had often in his mind experienced as his own:

> There came a gust, the sail leaped from his hands,

> So that he saw it high above him, grey,
> And there his mate was falling; quick he clutched
> An arm in oilskins swiftly snatched away.
> A voice said "Christ!" a quick shape stooped and touched,
> Chain struck his hands, ropes shot, the sky was smutched
> With vast black fires that ran, that fell, that furled
> And then he saw the mast, the small snow hurled,

> The fore-topgallant yard far, far aloft,
> And blankness settling on him and great pain;
> And snow beneath his fingers wet and soft
> And topsail-sheet-blocks shaking at the chain.
> He knew it was he who had fallen; then his brain
> Swirled in a circle while he watched the sky.
> Infinite multitudes of snow blew by.

"I thought it was Tom who fell," his brain's voice said.
"Down on the bloody deck!" the Captain screamed.
The multitudinous little snow-flakes sped,
His pain was real enough, but all else seemed.
Si with a bucket ran, the water gleamed
Tilting upon him; others came, the mate ...
They knelt with eager eyes like things that wait

For other things to come. He saw them there.
"It will go on," he murmured, watching Si.
Colours and sounds seemed mixing in the air,
The pain was stunning him, and the wind went by.
"More water," said the Mate. "Here, Bosun, try.
Ask if he's got a message. Hell, he's gone!
Here, Dauber, paints." He said, "It will go on."

Not knowing his meaning rightly, but he spoke
With the intentness of a fading soul
Whose share of Nature's fire turns to smoke,
Whose hand on Nature's wheel loses control.
The eager faces glowered red like coal.
They glowed, the great storm glowed, the sails, the mast.
"It will go on," he cried aloud, and passed.

It is surely a stroke of genius to make Dauber in his last minutes
imagine that one of his mates and not himself has fallen, as if the lad dropping off the mast is his own receding humanity. And the devastating realisation of the truth which is also the realisation that he's on the point of
death is given thereby an added tragic dimension—the undeniability of the
body's demise set in *chiaroscuro* against an inner brighter world of hopes
and fantasies.

'It will go on,' the Dauber says. But what? We shall misread the poem,
I think, if we take this to be anything except a statement of the infinite
continuation of suffering and pain. 'It' can't be life; the stanzas describing
Dauber's body under the sail-cloth on the table emphasize his reduction to
a slab of cold meaningless flesh; 'it' can't be his art either; he has left
nothing behind, not even confidences about his projects to a trusting
friend, and 'it' can't be the love his personality has engendered: he's been
cast out by his family who cared nothing for him, and, within days of his
commitment to the sea his mates have either forgotten him, or, greeting the

changed weather and the Chilean coast, are dismissing him as a possible 'Jonah'.

The concluding stanzas—with their evocation of Valparaiso as seen from the approaching ship—were, when the poem was popular, much praised, though I wonder if their bleakness, their spiritual desolation were ever acknowledged in their fullness. Even Muriel Spark, commenting on their beauty, stops in her citation two stanzas before the end, as if drawing back from the final grimness of the work's conclusion: that no meaning can be found for Dauber in life or death:

> Then in the sunset's flush they went aloft,
> And unbent sails in that most lovely hour
> When the light gentles and the wind is soft,
> And beauty in the heart breaks like a flower.
> Working aloft they saw the mountain tower,
> Snow to the peak; they heard the launchmen shout;
> And bright along the bay the lights came out.
>
> And then the night fell dark, and all night long
> The pointed mountain at the stars,
> Frozen, alert, austere; the eagle's song
> Screamed from her desolate screes and splintered scars.
> On her intense crags where the air is sparse
> The stars looked down; their many golden eyes
> Watched her and burned, burned out, and came to rise.
>
> Silent the finger of the summit stood,
> Icy in pure, thin air, glittering with snows.
> Then the sun's coming turned the peak to blood,
> And in the rest-house the muleteers arose.
> And all day long, where only the eagle goes,
> Stones, loosened by the sun, fall; the stones falling
> Fill empty gorge on gorge with echoes calling.

To re-enforce the previous images of Dauber's lifeless body and its disposal, and of the ship, carrying, so to speak, the young man's absence, come (the poet's parting gift to us) these of heights and spaces—beautiful, magnificent, and totally, gigantically, devoid of life, impervious to and incapable of any forms of sensation as we know it: the crags, the snow-covered mountain cones, the layers of atmosphere before Space is reached, the mind-defying inter-stellar distances, the stars which themselves begin and are extinguished. What special treatment for our individual selves could we sanely expect from a universe of such vast hostile extent?

The final couplet with its feminine endings — which like the sound they evoke go on echoing in the chambers of the mind — impresses on us the ceaseless falling of (apparently) inanimate stones. And who can say that the existence of any or all of us has greater importance than these, dislodged from their places by uncontrollable forces and making themselves known only by the brief ever-fading echoes of their unstoppable downward tumble?

☆　　　　　☆　　　　　☆

Wastage — that is what, above all else, *Dauber* addresses, and it doesn't matter whether the eponymous hero was another Turner or completely talentless. Dauber contained in himself a whole universe of emotions, thoughts, dreams; the greater universe puts these at nought. He has been given no more part to play in it, for all the intensity with which he lived, for all the striving of his attempt to find his true identity, than one of those countless stones flying down the Chilean mountain-chasm. He sent out echoes before he finally came to a stop — Masefield had heard a story about such a young man on board a ship — but they will fade quickly enough into utter silence.

It may have been coincidence that in her note for December 9th 1950, Muriel Spark jotted down Masefield's admiration for *Jude the Obscure* (1895) before recording his comments on *Dauber*. For though the central character of that masterpiece is indeed destroyed by weaknesses deep in his personality, as well as by certain logical consequences of his social position in an unjust, anti-egalitarian world, *Jude the Obscure* is a novel above all of waste. All Jude's aspirations, his plans for learning and a more fulfiling life for all, come to nothing, his is a premature, squalid and sad death. It is symbolically prefigured in the famous pig-killing scene in which Jude has reluctantly to assist his wife, Arabella, in the slaughter of an animal whom he has reared by hand.

> The animal's note changed its quality. It was not now rage, but the cry of despair; long-drawn, slow and hopeless ...
> The dying animal's cry assumed its third and final tone, the shriek of agony; his glazing eyes riveting themselves on Arabella with the eloquently keen reproach of a creature recognising at last the treachery of those who had seemed his only friends.

The killing is a metaphor not only for how we treat each other and our fellow living-creatures, but for the way we are treated by the universe itself, which, at times seeming our mother and friend, inflicts unbearable pain on us and does not relent until the death we all fear has overtaken us. Did the pig come into the world just to have his throat slowly cut? Did Jude have a sensitive, promising boyhood just so he could grow up into a drunken failure dead before thirty? What was the point of all the Dauber's struggles and inner debates if he were to be killed at twenty-two because the Horn flicked its terrible tail?

If one looks at *Dauber*'s companion narrative poems, one sees that wastage is, in truth, the dominant theme in them. This is so even in *The Everlasting Mercy* which might seem the most hopeful of the works, a creation of spiritual radiance. Take the other people of the poem. Billy, the mate whom Saul betrayed, died young and in obscurity, and yet, during the years when they were friends, was the better person, the one who kept honourably to his promise and fought clean. Nell, the girl Saul seduced under the fir-trees, embarked on 'the woman's road to hell', the destination, we're told, of many a bar-maid at 'The Lion' and the future, the poem infers, of Doxy Jane herself. The Ledbury burghers and those who contribute to the town's formless, godless low life are alike stifled beings, imprisoned either in *bien-pensant* stuffiness or pointless cruel pursuits; the ranks of the churchyard dead are better off. And Saul himself thinks:

> I wondered, then, why life should be,
> And what would be the end of me
> When youth and health and strength were gone
> And cold old age came creeping on?
> A keeper's gun? The Union ward?
> Or that new quod [prison] at Hereford?

Saul is spared all these; his later life is not sad to contemplate, life being as erratic in its rewards as in its bestowal of pain. (The religious will call this 'grace') But his very peace is maintained by his keeping a distance from the hurly-burly of life, by a self-release from the tangle of desires and aggressions which make it no surprise, for all the Neo-Platonist vocabulary here, to learn of Masefield's admiring preoccupation with Buddhism.

The central figures in *The Widow in the Bye Street*, not least the Widow herself, also most painfully illustrate waste in life. The Widow's years of gruelling self-sacrifice have as their reward the loss of her loved son and her own demented wanderings round her neighbourhood, under the impression she will see him again. Jimmy's strength as a navvy and all the misplaced ardour of his love for Anna end in his twenties, when he is hanged. Anna herself is granted (life's injustice once again) health and a normal span of years, but—as with Saul Kane—retreat is of her existence's essence.

> There, in the April, in the garden-close,
> One heard her in the morning singing sweet,
> Calling the birds from the unbudded rose,
> Offering her lips with grains for them to eat.
> The redbreasts come with little wiry feet,
> Sparrows and tits and all wild feathery things,
> Brushing her lifted face with quivering wings.

In *The Daffodil Fields* at the beginning of which we are told that 'tragic things came to pass', Masefield gives us brief biographies and character portraits of the protagonists in terms of the hopeful future they expect. Of Michael:

> ... the young student was a lively one,
> Handsome and passionate both, and fond of sport,
> Eager for fun, quick-witted in retort.
> The girls' hearts quick to see him cocking by,
> Young April on a blood horse, with a roving eye.

And of Lion:

> A well-built, clever man, unduly grave,
> One whose repute already travelled wide
> For skill in breeding beasts. His features gave
> Promise of brilliant mind, far-seeing, brave,
> One who would travel far.

These two, with such bright futures, with so much to give, die young, killing each other.

As for Dauber himself, a further instance of the injustice of life is given, curiously enough, if we contemplate his place of origin, Pauntley. From

Pauntley, just to the south of Ledbury, going towards Gloucester, came Dick Whittington, later the subject of a poem by Masefield, 'The Boy from Pauntley' in *A Letter from Pontus and Other Verse*:

> West, in the redlands, good for hops and corn,
> The famous Richard Whittington was born;
> Thence, when his parents died, the little lad
> Set off for London bearing all he had,
> A kitten and a bundle of small gear.

Whittington became thrice Lord Mayor of London and was buried 'in pride / Within the Abbey in a marble tomb'; Dauber is cast into the waters of the Pacific not even having achieved his ambition of coming 'after long months, at rosy dawn, / Into the placid blue of some great bay.'

Nor do these narrative poems present humankind, for all its pitiable multifarious misfortunes, in terms less alarming or greatly more sympathetic than unfeeling Nature and the universe of which it's part. The bystanders at Saul and Billy's fight, the townspeople woken up by the bell, the higher orders frozen in their conviction that all must be well in a world that keeps them in so secure a position; the other navvies and their boss (though some compassion is shown to Jimmy when he's arrested), the frequenters of the Ledbury pubs, those who carry out Justice; the ship-mates with whom the Dauber voyages—all are revealed, especially when acting in mass, as capable of, indeed relishing gratuitous destruction.

The Daffodil Fields, admittedly, does not show us the herd in the same way that the other poems do, but its message is, if anything, gloomier, more uncompromising still: that individuals, complex, decent, and bound to one another, can, and do, deal with each other in a manner no less unfeeling and punitive than that which characterises a wanton mob.

And in all four poems, in painful ironic contrast with the events unfolded, the beauty of the human form is paid tribute to, stands as a constant point of reference, particularly in its youthful manifestations — Masefield was after all comparatively young himself when he wrote these works. Continually we feel the vigour, sexuality, and hopefulness of the young male, the hopefulness that informs bearing and expression, and contrast it with what fate has in store.

3

> Daring as never before, wastage as never before,
> Young blood and high blood,
> fair cheeks, and fine bodies;
>
> There died a myriad,
> And of the best, among them,
> For an old bitch gone in the teeth,
> For a botched civilization ...

These often quoted lines are from Ezra Pound's *Hugh Selwyn Mauberley* (1920), and are a lament for the English dead of the Great War, part of a complaint against English—and European—culture responsible for carnage of such ghastly, unparalleled dimensions. The dates of Masefield's narrative poems are of vital importance here: *The Everlasting Mercy* dates from 1911, *The Widow in the Bye Street* from 1912, *Dauber* and *The Daffodil Fields* from 1913, the year before war was declared. Works of great literature—and I believe these narratives come into that category—feel the nerve of the times even if not overtly concerned with public or even social matters. They are prescient because of the writer's intensity of engagement with life—and with the life within his art. Masefield by all accounts was, in 1914, more aware than most of what was about to happen; Constance Babington Smith in her *Life* refers to a walk on the Berkshire Downs when Rupert Brooke (among others) laughed at him for thinking that the 'Austro-Serbian' business would explode into conflagration. But in a sense, to his credit though that is, this fore-knowledge is unimportant compared with that discernible in the poems themselves. Saul potentially, Jimmy Gurney and Michael and Lion and the Dauber are all representatives of the young men, the 'myriad' of them, who, teeming with hopes and ideas and sensations, had their lives cut off by the war, became no more than those stones falling into the abyss, so many of them indeed that individual echoes were largely undiscernible.

Dauber, Masefield told Muriel Spark, was about the artist 'compelled to obey the law of his own being'. Masefield himself followed this law in these extraordinary works, in a way he was never quite able to follow again. *The Widow* and *The Daffodil Fields*, it's true, have imperfections, occasional clumsinesses, momentary excursions into sententiousness out of anxiety to bring a point home; *The Everlasting Mercy* and *Dauber* seem to me very nearly perfect, marvellous marriages of technique and vision. But all four are thoroughly authentic works, with no kind of falsity, no capitulation to fashion or commerce or self-image marring them. They show terror and its inescapability as perhaps *the* truth about human life, and yet—in their rendering of feelings and of Nature—give a beauty to its context such as only D.H. Lawrence among his contemporaries had the boldness to achieve.

Art then was the means by which one could stare at the 'empty gorge' and—for as long as was permitted—survive while not living in a state of deception, of aversion from reality. The young man, Dauber, was right to have been as devoted to it as he was. In his 'being' he understood how to cope with existence.

CHAPTER SEVEN
Caesura: The Great War

Ten million men died in the Great War, three quarters of a million of them British and a further 200,000 from the British Empire. France lost nearly twice as many men as Britain. To these appalling figures, which assault one's reason even today, have to be added the wounded, the imprisoned and hospitalised—almost 3,000,000 from the British Empire alone, and the incalculable number of those whose lives were ruined by their experiences, who carried with them to their deathbeds what they had endured and what they had witnessed. Our century and Western culture haven't recovered from the trauma yet; what it demonstrated undermined faith of just about every kind in just about everything.

We look to creative writers to express for us what our intellects find hard to grasp, our morality hard to accommodate, and our imaginations hard to hold or even to envisage. The terrible years 1914-1918, with the vast, prolonged, historically unprecedented obscenity of the trenches, have bequeathed to British writers what can best be described as holy literary icons of the unholy: from whatever doldrums of artistic life that had existed, the calm of which Masefield's own early work shattered, combatants were galvanised by their outrage and their compassion into creating works at once revolutionary (if only in the subject) whilst drawing on tradition, the tradition of the sensitive and the civilised now seemingly going down forever in the blood and mud. As a result, to contemplate War now, for most educated Britons, is to remember the poetry of Wilfred Owen, Siegfried Sassoon, Isaac Rosenburg, Ivor Gurney, Edward Thomas, Robert Graves, David Jones. It has become a prism through which this whole human possibility—combined with the anti-human possibilities of the weaponry the human brain has invented—can be viewed. These anti-war icons in words, abundant in images taken specifically from the Great War though they may be (the trenches, the wires, the poison-gas) can be turned to for spiritual succour when other wars arise: in the Pacific, in Vietnam, in the Gulf, in the former Yugoslavia. To quote two examples, unfailingly powerful no matter how well-known:

> If in some smothering dreams you too could pace
> Behind the wagon that we flung him in,
> And watch the white eyes writhing in his face,
> His hanging face, like a devil's sick of sin;
> If you could hear, at every jolt, the blood
> Come gargling from the froth-corrupted lungs,
> Obscene as cancer, bitter as the cud
> Of vile, incurable sores on innocent tongues -
> My friend, you would not tell with such high zest
> To children ardent for some desperate glory,
> The old lie: Dulce et decorum est
> Pro patria mori.   Wilfred Owen; '*Dulce et decorum est*'

> Who died on the wires, and hung there, one of two -
> Who for his hours of life had chattered through
> Infinite lovely chatter of Bucks accent:
> Yet faced unbroken wires; stepped over, and went
> A noble fool, faithful to his stripes - and ended.
>   Ivor Gurney: 'The Silent One'

What enabled the human being to conceive, let alone carry out such horrors? How could he possibly survive them? Perhaps there is no more convincing answer than that given in *Aaron's Rod* by non-combatant D.H. Lawrence, whose loathing of the British Establishment during the War (exacerbated by his having a German wife) was such that he turned against his country, his culture for the duration of his life. Says his *alter ego*, Rawdon Lilly:

> "I knew the war was false; humanly quite false; I always knew
> it was false. The Germans were false, we were false, everybody was
> false ... Damn all masses and groups, anyhow. All I want is to get
> myself out of their horrible heap; to get out of the swarm. The

swarm to me is nightmare and nullity—horrible helpless writhing in a dream. I want to get myself awake, out of it all—all that mass-consciousness, all that mass-activity—it's the most horrible night-mare to me. No man is awake and himself. No man who was awake and in possession of himself would use poison gases: no man. His own awake self would scorn such a thing. It's only when the ghastly mob-sleep, the dream helplessness of the mass-psyche overcomes him, that he becomes completely base and obscene."

Masefield would have assented to much of this. His letters home to Constance from the Front show his shocked recognition of the betrayal of the deep human self, of its creative centre, that the War imposed. D.H. Lawrence and himself, I have tried to show, have much in common; not only did both contribute to Ford's *English Review*, both were—with perhaps equal misgivings—contributors to Edward Marsh's *Georgian Poetry* (first volume 1912), and at times surely the only writer the one can be compared with is the other. But their response to the War was, whatever abhorrences they shared, fundamentally different, so different that, as a result, their careers, their *oeuvres* from this point diverge very radically— which is why comparisons between them are so rarely made. When the question arises as to why Lawrence has been the writer who has enjoyed the greater and the wider critical appreciation in subsequent years, the answer must be sought in the War years. Ironically, the Masefield who so tirelessly met in France the casualties and fatalities of trench-warfare has less in common with the participant icon-makers, Owen and the others, than the Lawrence who spent the war-years in England, and whose bitterest times came as a result of both official and neighbourly paranoia down in Cornwall.

2

By 1914, Masefield was a famous, an admired man despite—or because of—the brouhaha *The Everlasting Mercy* and *The Widow* initially occa-sioned; he was widely read and discussed (and not only in Britain but in America, where his work won much praise). In June 1913, when the poetaster Poet Laureate, Alfred Austin died, Masefield's name came up, young though he was, as a possible candidate. (The Laureateship went to Robert Bridges, whom Masefield was in fact to succeed in 1930.) He was moreover married to a woman whom he loved as both wife and friend (whatever other limitations there may have been in the relationship) and he was the most devoted and attentive of fathers to Judith and Lewis. (Read the memoir of Lewis he wrote as an introduction to Lewis' *The Passion Left Behind* (1947) after his death while serving with the R.A.M.C. in 1942; paternal love can surely have nowhere more beautiful expression.) When war broke out, Masefield was living with his family in Lollingdon on the Berkshire Downs, not far from Wallingford. Thirty-six years old, he put his name down for active service, to be turned down on grounds of health. However, he became one of those many distin-guished writers—his friends John Galsworthy, Harley Granville-Barker among them, as well as Arnold Bennett, E.M. Forster, Somerset Maugham—whose talents officialdom utilised.

Lollingdon Downs is the setting for what is usually considered the only war-poem Masefield wrote, 'August 1914'. It is a poem at its best as moving and lovely and as charged with foreboding as the summer evening in southern England that brought it into being. But it also suggests, I think, certain incipient dilemmas—and maybe even weak-nesses—against which Masefield would have to struggle, and which go to explain why he never produced work of quite the raw vitality of his four pre-War narratives again.

> An endless quiet valley reaches out
> Past the blue hills into the evening sky;
> Over the stubble, cawing, goes a rout
> Of rooks from harvest, flagging as they fly.
>
> So beautiful it is, I never saw
> So great a beauty on these English fields,
> Touched by the twilight's coming into awe,
> Ripe to the soul and rich with summer's yields.

This is at once true to the poet's experience and feelings, and provides a metaphor of universal resonance. That endless-seeming valley ravish-ingly described—which is one Berkshire valley transmogrified by the fall of evening—stands, in its quietness and outreach, for all our needs and longings for a domain of peace, an inviolable one, to live in and to work. War is an unnatural obstance to our possession of such a place, unnatural because it goes against the better selves that we all carry and which propitious circumstances can develop (as that passage from *Aaron's Rod* later propounded).

The poem moves on to evoke the many times in England's past, even in the past of this very valley, when men had to leave their loved homes to fight, to suffer, and often to die elsewhere. So far so good, and so sympathetic!—but already a kind of equation of England with the good is palpable—with the good and the peace-promoting. This is converting an aesthetic response into a moral one; in truth a German or Austrian country scene would be no less peaceful, and exactly the same sentiments could be inspired by it. But already one can somehow sense that Masefield will not have this, is determined that there is something essentially spiritually favoured about his own country. (He thought this also, to be fair, about France). And in the later course of 'August 1914', Masefield—who had had the courage to face up to the bleakness of his basically Darwinist vision of existence he acknowledged and to posit ways of rising above it— falls into a kind of inclusive neo-Platonism, which seems to me not so much the blissful, rhapsodic state that promoted Saul Kane's, as a kind of comforting hold-all. (This is, for me, true at times of the war-time *Sonnets* for all their brooding power.) Take the opening of the third section of the poem, lines which at one time were feelingly quoted:

> If there be any life beyond the grave,
> It must be near the men and things we love,
> Some power of quick suggestion how to save,
> Touching the living soul as from above.
>
> An influence from the Earth from those dead hearts
> So passionate once, so deep, so truly kind,
> That in the living child the spirit starts,
> Feeling companioned still, not left behind.
>
> Surely above these fields a spirit broods
> A sense of many watchers muttering near
> Of the lone Downland with the forlorn woods
> Loved to the death, inestimably dear.

'*Must be*'? one protests. '*Surely*'? Why? Who says? What exactly *is* this 'power of quick suggestion' that can affect the soul, whatever that may be? And how about the 'influence from the Earth'? Fine sentiments, but shouldn't one expect more precision, and less noble sport with the ineffable, in a poem on a major subject concerning the opening of a new fearful epoch in human history. D.H. Lawrence, for all his interest in forces of Nature, would never have indulged himself as Masefield here; his rancour about England was too great.

3

Masefield spent his war-years actively, unsparingly and usefully, and in doing so joined the indisputable ranks of the great and good. They are rewarding and interesting ranks to be in, and not—as Vorticists and old-fashioned bohemians would have it—to be despised, but they are not always the best place for a creative artist, as they can cut him or her off from the muddled, stumbling, anonymous human beings who often inspire their most potent (and ultimately humanity-serving) works.

March 1915 saw Masefield in France, working as an orderly with the Red Cross. He tended men, and took part in their medical treatment, often facing horrific sights and hearing horrific sounds—the screams, the calls of distress, the curses, the brainstorms; he carpentered to make the men's lives more comfortable; he inspected hospitals, finding much in their organisation to complain of in the most serious terms.

Every day he wrote to Constance though the censor meant that not every letter reached her; *John Masefield's Letters from the Front 1915-17* (1984) gives a tremendously vivid account of battleground France and of his own presence there:

> My beloved Con wife,
> ... I have hated today here, not for the work, nor for the death, for when one sees it here, death does not seem so evil as what precedes it, but because of all the fearful pain I've watched and been unable to help ...
> The boy was not quite 21 ... The operation was very long and very very delicate, for they were all about his heart, and I marvelled at the skill of it, and thought of all the skill that had gone to giving him the wound, to making the wound possible, and then of the skill which was trying to heal the wound, and wondered at the strange lapse which was somewhere in the chain, some lapse of folly or stupidity or crime ... About half past three ... we had an alarm and I had to find the poor lad's father, who had gone to the garage, I think, to see the cars. I ran half over Arc in my shirt and trews to find him, but could not, though one of those whom I sent to hunt was luckier, so we got him in. The boy was lying with his eyes closed, gasping and the poor old father ... burst into tear, and I had to take him away

170

to another room and talk to him and to say that we had hope and that he must be calm. The poor old man was a farm labourer who worked in the fields, 'a hard life', he said, 'but pleasant', and his son was all he had, that he cared for, except for the grand girl in service at Fontainebleau. He cried again in his chair, sobbing 'Mon fils, mon fils', and 'C'est la faute de Guillaume' [the Kaiser] (I think this simply broke my heart, this last) and I could say nothing much, except that we hoped, and indeed we did, for his boy took a rally and did better. I got the old man some cigarettes and wine and water and left in Tonks' room, for I had to carry in wounded, and when I had finished that, the boy was dead.

At the last parting the boy wanted his father to kiss him and the old man bent and kissed him. I tried to talk to the old man and he talked of his little house, and how he had four hens, and loved his garden, and how the English were good gardeners, for there was one at Melun who had jolis fleurs.

How much this tells us of Masefield's responsiveness to others' plights, his deep humanity, his unselfishness. And how much it displays his descriptive powers, for the boy's death is as affecting as if it occurred yesterday.

Masefield's attitudes, however, were—perhaps a result of his new-found security—quite conventional. He blamed almost everything on the Germans, thought of Britain and France as righteous, civilised societies, and would have no truck with those who criticised the prolonged conduct of the war, such as his friends Goldsworthy Lowes Dickinson and George Bernard Shaw. (He branded the former a 'eunuch'.) Winning was what mattered. In August 1915, Masefield went out with the Red Cross to Gallipoli, the controversial campaign which he saw as a heroic enterprise and about which he wrote his famous propagandist study, *Gallipoli* (1916). In January 1916, he travelled, for the first time since the memorable voyage of his late adolescence, to the United States—on an official lecture-tour to rouse American support for the Allies (the course of which made him often highly critical of American mores and of the national preoccupation with money). He returned from America in July, only to go again to France in August, reporting on the American Ambulance Field Service at Verdun, still a battlefield. By October he had started work on another work of propaganda, this one about the Somme campaign. Work on this kept him in France until the June of 1917. *The*

Old Front Line was published that year, *The Battle of the Somme* in 1919, both books shorter than he would have liked, owing to his being refused access to official records and having to rely on hearsay and his own witness. In January 1918, he was back in the United States on another lecture tour.

☆   ☆   ☆

But what of his creative work. *Sonnets and Poems* appeared in 1916; these were subsumed in a larger collection, *Lollingdon Downs and Other Poems, with Sonnets* (1917), a book which constitutes his poetic testimony if not to the war itself, then to the grave climate of the years of its waging. (It should be noted that the numbering of these poems here follows that of this volume.) The volume surprises even now; after the story-telling force of the pre-War productions, poems chiefly contemplative; after the deliberate roughnesses and colloquialisms of *The Widow* and *Dauber*, an almost mandarin tone; inward wrestlings rather than external observations, an extension of the groping Neo-Platonism burgeoning in 'August 1914' rather than the sad, even angry Darwinism of the narratives.

The *Sonnets*—the majority 'English' or 'Shakespearean' sonnets: three quatrains and a final couplet—make up the greater part of the book, and should be read consecutively, to follow the poet's arguments with himself and with those interpretations or explanations of human life that have been offered to him. (The 'I' and his situation are recurrent, and given development.) Drawn to Platonic absolutes of Beauty and the Good, this 'I' is nevertheless haunted by the all-too-believable idea that a human is no more than an amalgam of cells (and the perishability of the amalgam must have come home to him, almost daily, in the ante-chambers to hell that were the French hospitals for the war-wounded). But does the reduction of life to cells, to atoms, mean a total negation of some immanent spirit? Poem III:

> Out of the special cell's most special sense
> Came the sensation when the light was sweet;
> All skill, all beauty, all magnificence,
> Are hints so caught, man's glimpse of the complete.
> And, though the body rots, that sense survives;
> Being of life's own essence, it endures
> (Fruit of the spirit's tillage in men's lives)
> Round all this ghost that wandering flesh immures.
> That is our friend, who, when the iron brain

172

Assails, or the earth clogs, or the sun hides,
Is the good God to whom none calls in vain,
Man's Achieved Good, which, being Life, abides;
The man-made God, that man in happy breath
Makes in despite of Time and dusty death.

Perhaps the heart of the volume is the sonnet that is Poem L, with its categorical statement that there can be no personal omnipotent being, and that the poet will not be tempted into such a mistaken belief, no matter the anguish of his inability to find philosophical rest:

There is no God, as I was taught in youth,
Though each, according to his stature, builds
Some covered shrine for what he thinks the truth,
Which day by day his reddest heart-blood gilds.
There is no God; but death, the clasping sea,
In which we move like fish, deep over deep,
Made of men's souls that bodies have set free,
Floods to a Justice though it seems asleep.
There is no God; but still, behind the veil,
The hurt thing works, out of its agony.
Still like the given cruse that did not fail
Return the pennies given to passers-by.
There is no God; but we, who breathe the air,
Are God ourselves, and touch God everywhere.

These poems are informed by a wholly exemplary honesty, and abound in many beauties of both courageous thought and language, the beauties often the greater when wedded to specifically personal apprehensions:

I could not sleep for thinking of the sky,
The unending sky, with all its million suns
Which turn their planets everlastingly
In nothing, where the fire-haired comet runs. (V)

How did the nothing come, how did these fires,
These million-leagues of fires, first toss their hair,
Licking the moons from heaven in their ires,
Flinging them forth for them to wander there? (VI)

Death lies in wait for you, you wild thing in the wood,
Shy-footed beauty dear, half-seen, half-understood ... (LXIV)

All the same, one has to admit that there is an almost late-Victorian earnestness in the sonnets that can run—even in those quoted in full—dangerously near sententiousness at times. This is because Masefield has banished the quirkily personal, the vernacular of his seasoned idiosyncratic self so thoroughly from these very literary performances (with Meredith somewhere in the background). Perhaps what one is saying here is that in the last analysis they represent his intellectual rather than his most deeply ceative self.

The old creativity is present in one poem in *Lollingdon Downs* above all its fellows and significantly it is a narrative, spare, contracted, ballad-like, the unmistakable fruit of a stimulated, moved imagination rather than of a mind intent on exercising its weightiness. This is 'No man takes the farm'(XXII), and significantly it reminds us of *The Widow* (Will's fate is the same as Jimmy's), of *The Daffodil Fields* and the Gloucester inset of *Dauber*—its farm background, the fate of unwanted or abandoned property. And though nothing of the War obtrudes directly into it, it is surely informed by something of the desolation Masefield had seen in the riven French countryside, and by sad re-appreciation of the extent of cruelty in life:

> No man takes the farm,
> Nothing grows there;
> The ivy's arm
> Strangles the rose there.
>
> Old Farmer Kyrle
> Farmed there the last;
> He beat his girl
> (It's seven years past).
>
> After market it was
> He beat his girl;
> He liked his glass,
> Old Farmer Kyrle.
>
> Old Kyrle's son
> Said to his father:
> "Now, dad, you ha' done,
> I'll kill you rather!

"Stop beating sister,
Or by God I'll kill you!"
Kyrle was full of liquor -
Old Kyrle said: "Will you?"

Kyrle took the cobb'd stick
And beat his daughter;
He said: "I'll teach my chick
As a father oughter."

Young Will, the son,
Heard his sister shriek;
He took his gun
Quick as a streak.

He said: "Now, dad,
Stop, once for all!"
He was a good lad,
Good at kicking the ball.

His father clubbed
The girl on the head
Young Will upped
And shot him dead.

"Now, sister," said Will,
"I've a-killed father,
As I said I'd kill.
O my love, I'd rather

"A-kill him again
Than see you suffer,
O my little Jane,
Kiss goodbye to your brother.

"I won't see you again,
Nor the cows homing,
Nor the mice in the grain,
Nor the primrose coming,

"Nor the fair, nor folk,
Nor the summer flowers
Growing on the wold,
Nor ought that's ours.

"Not Tib the cat,
Nor Stub the mare,
Nor old dog Pat,
Never anywhere.

"For I'll be hung
In Gloucester prison
When the bell's rung
And the sun's risen."

*   *   *

They hanged Will
As Will said;
With one thrill
They choked him dead.

Jane walked the wold
Like a grey gander;
All grown old
She would wander.

She died soon:
At high tide,
At full moon,
Jane died.

The brook chatters
As at first;
The farm it waters
Is accurst.

No man takes it,
Nothing grows there;
Blood straiks it,
A ghost goes there.

This is Masefield as his own man, the real creative artist, the poet whom we discuss in terms of his older contemporary, Walter de la Mare, and his own younger friend, Robert Graves, and—for prose comparisons—liken to J.M. Synge and Richard Hughes.

4

But being his own man, artistically, was to be no easy task—not after War-years when he'd used up so many energies on behalf of the Allies' cause, on behalf, as he saw it, of humanity itself, when he'd seen and done so much foreign to his previous experience and even inclinations. And he had to address a world that was in a state of stunned survival, which didn't know where to turn to make sense of the dreadfulness it had perpetrated.

> A crowd flowed over London Bridge, so many,
> I had not thought death had undone so many.

So wrote T.S. Eliot in the most influential work of the decade ahead, *The Waste Land*. To cope with that realisation, and at the same time encourage a sense that there was extant if battered, a sustainable culture—that was the problem.

Masefield was much preoccupied by Chaucer. Hadn't Chaucer years ago been a beacon to him in his darkness? Hadn't he named his own son after Chaucer's son, Lewis? Hadn't his finest performances been executed in Chaucerian mode? The organic England of Chaucer—that of St George, as he once put it, rather than that of John Bull. An England permeated by a faith that catered for all types and ranks of people and all ways of life should be sought, and, when found, recreated, not artificially but by drawing on what had been passed down from it through the centuries.

The Masefields moved to Boar's Hill, near Oxford, in 1919. For all the expected and enormous changes in literary fashion the next years were to be immensely successful ones for the writer—outwardly, that is. *Reynard the Fox* (1919) proved, and has continued to be amongst the most popular of his poetic works; the *Collected Poems* of 1923 sold spectacularly.

But from the point of view of realisation of his original and powerful imagination, however, the situation is much less certain, just as *au fond* Masefield was less certain. Those who knew him, those who met him often spoke of a pervasive sadness in his bearing. The equal of those four great narratives he would never produce again, but there was interesting and fascinating work ahead—and some of it English literature would be the poorer without. However *Reynard the Fox*—with which Masefield's name was at one time all but synonymous—is not one of these. It's a wrong turning, but to have taken a turning at all at this difficult time showed his habitual writer's courage.

CHAPTER EIGHT
After the Great War

The ambivalences in the poet's mind throughout *Reynard the Fox*—which are, in truth, irreconcilable tensions—are vitiatingly present in its very scheme, simple, bold and pregnant with imaginative possibilities though it may at first sight appear.

Part One presents the Meet, assembling outside 'The Cock and Pye'(in reality 'The Somers Arms' on the Ledbury-Eastnor road) and introduces us one by one to the various members of the Hunt in a fashion frankly, and almost didactically, bringing Chaucer's Canterbury pilgrims to mind. Here—we infer from the octosyllabic rhyming couplets—is just such another goodly company, at once individually full of foibles and faults (and some of these possibly grave) but healingly united in a common purpose, joyous and serious; here is another cross-section of English society, which can stand as a kind of paradigm for the country itself. After he has given his accounts of this diversity of people, the writer can let the hunt be off and away—over country which fuses Herefordshire and Berkshire—and before long, as they near Ghost Heath Wood, it picks up the scent of the fox.

In Part Two—for the most part also in octosyllabics, though breaking into 'heroic' (iambic pentameter) couplets for moments of heightened importance—there is a shift of point of view. It is now the fox's, though we are aware from time to time of the reactions of humans as he perhaps never could be. We are with the creature in his desperate flight zig-zagging across a countryside to a good measure based on that of the flanks of the Malverns' Herefordshire Beacon; we are with him trying to go to earth, and finding that, according to the atrocious practice of the fox-hunt, his natural refuges have all been carefully stopped up before-hand. Reynard eludes his pursuers, however; hounds pick up another scent, and in consequence another fox is killed (as far as we are concerned, out of sight and ear-shot). Our fox has survived, though exhausted in brain and body and having known desperate moments when he felt himself close to death, while the hunters return satisfied, feeling they have had a good day.

One is therefore put in the curious, and not uninvigorating, position of having the basically (though not exclusively) amiable English people of Part One—whom one is invited, if not exhorted to join—turning into a terrifying pursuing enemy, the many using all their strength and superior powers, intent on killing (not just catching, but killing—the word is emphasized enough times!) a single—and defenceless if resourceful—fellow-living being. Masefield's empathy with the fox—unsurprisingly in the light of his earlier productions—is such that readers' hopes are firmly pinned on his escape (and on the frustration of another set of hopes, those of the company they've been asked to see in terms of their country's pleasing traditions!). It would be a strange sensibility that read the following passage (one of the more sustainedly successful, in common with the other excursions into pentameters) with anything than horror and a catch at the heart:

> The fox was strong, he was full of running,
> He could run for an hour and then be cunning,
> But the cry behind him made him chill,
> They were nearer now and they meant to kill.
> They meant to run him until his blood
> Clogging on his heart as his brush with mud,
> Till his back bent up and his tongue hung flagging,
> And his belly and brush were filthed with dragging.
> Till he crouched stone-still, dead-beat and dirty,
> With nothing but teeth against the thirty.
> And all the way to that blinding end
> He would meet with men and have none his friend;
> Men to hulloa and men to run him,
> With stones to stagger and yells to stun him;
> Men to head him, with whips to beat him,
> Teeth to mangle and mouths to eat him.
> And all the way, that wild high crying.
> To cold his blood with the thought of dying,

The horn and the cheer, and the drum-like thunder
Of the horsehooves stamping the meadows under.
He upped his brush and went with a will
For the Sarsen Stones on the Wan Dyke Hill.

This is an account to chill *human* blood; its force can't be gainsaid, and the couplets as they succeed one another, contribute to our sense of the animal's plight (no crude anthropomorphism, this), of ghastly possibility after ghastly possibility suddenly becoming likelihood for him.

Can't then *Reynard the Fox* be read as a narrative showing that decent-seeming people can deliberately accomplish (and without, it would seem, any violation of their consciences) the most indecent cruelties, even though their victim is not wholly innocent (foxes are killers)? Can't also this fox-hunt be (remembering the poem's date of composition) an organic metaphor for the dreadful things good-living French, English and Germans were able to do to one another in the Flanders fields? As a passionate opponent of fox-hunting (and as a lover of foxes), I would like to uphold this interpretation (and it contains much that is tenable). But unfortunately the matter is not as straight-forward as this, for there are contradictions and inconsistencies that, far from making the work the richer, seriously undermine it—and point to confusions in the poet's stance (not only about hunting) that suggest difficulties for his subsequent work.

First, back to Part One, that written almost to earn the adjective 'Chaucerian' so lavishly bestowed on it both at the time and since. Some of the character-sketches of the Meet are pastiches of *The Canterbury Tales* 'Prologue' almost to the point of parody. Take the following (one of the more overtly critical and satirical):

The clergyman from Condicote.
His face was scarlet from his trot,
His white hair bobbed round his head
As halos do round clergy dead.
He asked Tom Clopp, "How long to wait?"
His loose mouth opened like a gate,
To pass the wagons of his speech.
He had a mighty voice to preach,
Though indolent in other matters.
He let his children go in tatters.

Manner has triumphed over the matter, as I believe it to have done in the greater part of the poem. Contrast this description with that of the parson accosted by Saul Kane in *The Everlasting Mercy*, paradoxically at once dishonest and honourable, both kindly and lazily sycophantic to his social superiors, and we find a caricature in *Reynard* imprisoned by the style the poet has too consciously adopted in contrast to a portrait of an autonomous flesh-and-blood individual. We don't really receive from this passage as we do from comparable ones in Chaucer a feeling of the poet's moral engagement with his subject's shortcomings and hypocrisies. There is something bland, too determinedly amicable here. This weakness is even more blatant in the accounts of the Hunt's young girls, a genus over whom Masefield was always apt to falter. Here is the youngest of the Squire's daughters:

> Blonde, with a face of blush and cream,
> And eyes deep violet in their gleam,
> Bright blue when quiet in repose,
> She was a very golden rose.
> And many a man when sunset came
> Would see the manor windows flame,
> And think "My beauty's home is there."
> Queen Helen had less golden hair,
> Queen Cleopatra paler lips,
> Queen Blanche's eyes were in eclipse
> By golden Carrie's glancing by.
> She had a wit for mockery
> And sang mild, pretty, senseless songs
> Of sunsets, Heav'n, and lovers' wrongs,
> Sweet to the Squire when he had dined.
> A rosebud need not have a mind.
> A lily is not sweet from learning.

Even remembering that the name of Masefield's beautiful mother (whose memory he so cherished) was Carrie, one cannot acquit this passage of a certain sentimentality, and sentimentality invariably leads to the vulgarity of such lines as 'And many a man when sunset came'. (A parallel here is the attempts at sweetness about the opposite sex in the Gilbert and Sullivan operas which Masefield, like so many of his contemporaries, enjoyed: 'Take a pair of sparkling eyes,' for example from *The*

Gondoliers.) But there is something else wrong here; it is not truthful, truthful, that is, to the poet's own feelings. Importing to literary criticism our knowledge of Masefield from his life, and how the women he was drawn to were without exception clever, complex, thoughtful, fiercely independent, formidable indeed, one can see from those last lines that he in fact despises the squire's daughter and her traditional Victorian-type wiles, thinks her deceitful, stupid and ignorant. But he isn't going to say so; he isn't even going wittily and openly to hint at that. He is going to soften his perceptions, both for literary and extra-literary reasons.

The lack of truthfulness is even more evident in the portraits of the men, the younger men not excluded. It is hard to believe in the light of Masefield's other writings (both earlier and later)—the foul-mouthed yobbos who form the 'crowds' of *The Everlasting Mercy* and *The Widow in the Bye Street* or the detestable young bloods later met in *Dead Ned*— that he has any high opinion of the likes of the three lads Nob, Cob and Bunny. But he is going to write about them nonetheless with a sort of hearty sweetness, or of the 'horse-mouthed' lad who acts as second whip, Kitty Myngs, of whom we read:

> His blood was crying for taming.
> He was the Devil's own chick for gaming.
> He was a rare good lad to box.
> He sometimes had a main of cocks
> Down at the Flags. His job with hounds
> At present kept his blood in bounds
> From rioting and running hare.
> Tom Dansey made him have a care.
> He worshiped Dansey heart and soul.
> To be a huntsman was his goal.

Admittedly there is accuracy enough in this particular portrait (more perhaps than in any of those of the males higher in the social class-system)—and here, as in the descriptions of the rhythms of the day, the preparations, the seeing to accoutrements, the country activities witnessed by the Hunt in motion, Masefield shows that Dutch masters' side of his art which is one of its finer aspects. All the same one has an uneasy feeling that in another work Kitty would have cut quite another figure—perhaps as egger-on of Saul's dirty fight with Billy, or as tormenter of Dauber on board ship.

There are two further marring faults in Part One, especially if one makes the comparison one is all but compelled to make with Chaucer. The company is neither a true cross-section, nor representative of English society—especially of the reduced, nerve-shattered society that followed the Armistice. Though England in the first two decades of this century was not that of the current '90s, there was nevertheless disapproval of the activity. (No members of my own family, for instance, all of whom lived in the country would have been at the Meet; my grandmother, living in such a rural community at precisely this time, made a point of sidetracking huntsmen from their quarry and forbade them access to her garden.) By confining himself to a sporting activity—rather than an ultimately spiritual one, as in Chaucer's case—Masefield limits his social franchise. By confining himself to one which excludes others because of ethical opposition, Masefield limits himself further still.

Such dissenters are not likely to be won over by the curious interpolations from the hunting party which occur in (the altogether superior) Part Two, and which read like emanations from Masefield's own disturbed memories, his uneasy conscience—for, whatever their verisimilitude (which may, alas, be pretty exact) they cannot but repel:

> "A dead fox or a broken bone."
> Said Robin, peering for his prey.

Or:

> "Mob him!" cried Ridden, "the wood's ahead.
> Turn him, damn it! Yooi! beauties, beat him!
> O God let them get him; let them eat him!
> O God!" said Ridden, "I'll eat him stewed,
> If you'll let us get him this side the wood."

And to this the second fault must be added. Chaucer's pilgrims after we have encountered them will reveal what makes them individuals, what makes them representative and what they have in common with one another as human beings—through the stories they'll tell and in their reception of those of others. Masefield's characters undergo no development at all; on the contrary they turn into an aggressive aggregate, that expresses itself only in cries and ejaculations such as the above, and in which many of those presented get completely swamped. Not only do we lose interest in them and their characters during the course of Part Two, we have the strongest feeling that Masefield himself has too.

But perhaps his interest was never so very great in the first place.

Style reveals a writer's sincerity and authenticity, and it must be said that stylistically—though not in its construction—*Reynard the Fox* is considerably the weakest of Masefield's longer works. After the lively deftness of the opening—with its evocation of a winter day beginning, and with it the necessary pre-Hunt activities—which does indeed create the requisite atmosphere of anticipation, the couplets too soon become coy, even, in the case of the introductions to the women, arch, with far too many self-conscious peeps at the Middle Ages. In Part Two, which attempts mimesis of the running, pausing, re-gathering of speed of both hunted and hunters, the effect is finally one of monotony; movement becomes over-dominant—as it doesn't in the progressions of *The Everlasting Mercy*—triumphing over emotions. The couplets then turn banal, even into doggerel. To the following examples many more could be added:

> He readied himself, then a soft horn blew,
> Then a clear voice carolled, "Ed-hoick! Eleu!"

> He hurried his trotting, he now felt frighted,
> It was his poor body made hounds excited.

> Then, as he listened, heard a "Hoy!"
> Tom Dancey's horn and "Awa-wa-woy!"

The strange truth is that, for all it is a poem dedicated to physical action, the best parts of which are distinguished by a kinaesthetic energy, *Reynard the Fox* is primarily a poem of the head—and it suffers from this. Masefield wanted to create a Chaucerian work, he wanted to celebrate a basically rural, pre-Industrial community close to Nature, in both its beauty and its harshness, of a kind denied to any modern society. He had affectionate memories of his own boyhood experiences of the Ledbury Hunt—which had alleviated a long period of loneliness and misery—and he possessed the (at times) unfortunate ability to elevate the past into romantic tableaux for contemporary delectation (as he had also done with periods of barbarous naval history). But by making a hunt stand in for a lost England, regardless of the complexity of his own feelings on the matter, of the bitter quality of many of his perceptions of the people and pursuits involved, he got himself into a morally tight corner. And when he came later to try and justify his subject in prose—in the essay, 'Fox-Hunting' of 1924—he was obliged to fall back on a sort of latterday Pre-Raphaelitism, on a morality drawn from aesthetics (for obviously he *did* find the spectacle of redcoat huntsmen, horses and hounds on hillside or in open country sensuously stirring) rather than from his own empathic powers and gift (for it was no less) of compassion:

> I have mentioned several reasons why fox-hunting should be popular: (a) that it is a social business, at which the whole community may and does attend in vast numbers in a pleasant mood of good-will, good humour and equality and during which all may go anywhere into ground otherwise shut to them, (b) that it is done in the winter at a season when other social gatherings are difficult, and in country districts where no buildings, except the churches, could contain the numbers assembled; (c) that it is most beautiful to watch, so beautiful that perhaps very few of the acts can be so lovely to watch nor so exhilarating. The only thing to be compared with it in this country is the sword dance, the old heroical dancing of the young men, still practised, in all its splendour of wild beauty, in some country places; (d) that we are a horse-loving people who have loved horses as we have loved the sea, and have made, in the course of generations, a breed of horse, second to none in the world, for beauty and speed.

Even at the time of *Reynard the Fox*'s great success, Masefield was troubled by what the activity he was apostrophising really meant. In *John Masefield: A Life*, Constance Babington Smith writes about this admirably:

> He confessed that he was saddened by the sombre fact that this fellowship involved the torment and possible death of an animal, and he wished that this was not so, but huntsmen had told him that hounds would not hunt unless they killed their fox fairly often. "I am not and never have been a fox-hunter," he wrote to St John Ervine [Irish dramatist and novelist (1883-1971)], "but it is the passion of English country people, and into it they put the beauty and the fervour which the English put into all things when deeply roused."

This is the voice of some self-appointed custodian of the English past speaking. And what if that last sentence *were* true? Does it, should it affect moral opinions?

Later, Masefield was to quarrel with hunting neighbours—and indeed with a Gloucestershire hunt itself, outraged by one of his cats being mutilated by hounds. He came, indeed, to detest the whole hunting set and what they got up to, and to attack them unequivocally in a novel *The Square Peg* (1937). In his moving tribute to his son, Lewis, after his death, he praised him for his hatred of any kind of sport that involved the distress and killing of animals.

But the real answer to how Masefield in the depths of his imagination thought of what happened in a hunt comes from one of the finest sections of the second part, from the fox's standpoint:

> Within, as he reached that soft green turf,
> The wind, blowing lonely, moaned like surf,
> Desolate ramparts rose up steep
> On either side, for the ghosts to keep.
> He raced the trench, past the rabbit warren,
> Close-grown with moss which the wind made barren;
> He passed the spring where the rushes spread,
> And there in the stones was his earth ahead.
> One last short burst upon failing feet -
> There life lay waiting, so sweet, so sweet,
> Rest in a darkness, balm for aches.
> * * * * * * * * * * * * * * * *
> The earth was stopped. It was barred with stakes.

How effective the quasi-enjambment—the breaking up the couplet by means of asterisks—is in conveying the agony of the animal, the hideous surprise that so unjustly awaits him, and which has such immediate and potent symbolic value! Reading it and admiring it is to realise afresh the danger of any kind of romantic-headed nationalism, no matter how politically benign. It always ends in evasion of truth and reality.

However, there were other ways of trying to recover and restore a shattered culture. And in *King Cole*, his narrative poem of 1921, which follows two other far less distinguished works in the genre, *Enslaved* and *Right Royal* (both 1920) he found one. The work is composed for the most part in *Troilus'* Rhyme Royal, but with regular excursions into heroic couplets (mainly for protracted dialogue) as if in this poem he were determined to bring together two different strands of his art: that which related from a distance giving it ironic perspective (*The Widow in the Bye Street*, *The Daffodil Fields* and *Dauber*) and a progression of which the reader becomes a part (*The Everlasting Mercy* and *Reynard the Fox*). He called the poem an 'adult fairy-tale'; this description must surely have turned readers' minds to the most famous adult fairy-tales of all, the last plays of Shakespeare: *Pericles* (1609), *Cymbeline*, *The Winter's Tale* (both 1610) and *The Tempest* (1611) with their theme of forgiveness and redemption and their use of non-realistic, magical properties to express it. In *King Cole* we have a child returning, grown-up, from the ranks of the missing/presumed dead, as in all four of these plays, and we have an old magician-figure who is like a less ambiguous Prospero. It was mythic matter that spoke very deeply to a war-wearied country. And Masefield, in his quest for material, went back to the period to which Shakespeare had journeyed for *Cymbeline*, a Britain where Romans and Britons were competing for power.

2

Not a reader who opened *King Cole* would be ignorant of the nursery rhyme:

> Old King Cole was a merry old soul
> And a merry old soul was he;
> He called for his pipe and he called for his bowl,
> And he called for his fiddlers three.

The second verse is less often sung:

> Every fiddler, he had a fiddle,
> And a very fine fiddle had he;
> Twee tweedle dee, tweedle dee went the fiddlers,
> There's none so rare
> As can compare
> With King Cole and his fiddlers three.

Soldiers in the Great War had sung parodies of the old song (many of them undoubtedly obscene), one ending:

188

AFTER THE GREAT WAR

> There's none so rare
> As can compare
> With Kitchener's New Armee.

And certainly the War would be read into the very opening lines:

> King Cole was King before the troubles came,
> The land was happy while he held the helm ...

No doubt in minds about what these 'troubles' were, or the happiness that was lost: a peace of mind, an absence of knowledge of the scale on which modern nations could slaughter one another or their hideous means of doing so.

King Cole as a semi-historical figure, beyond the song, appears in Geoffrey of Monmouth's *History*, of which we know the younger Masefield had been a keen reader. Little of the story Geoffrey tells has much foundation, and much of it is at variance with other legends, some of them Scottish (Robert Burns interested himself in them). Geoffrey's Cole was Duke of Colchester (which supposedly derives its name from him) before making himself king of Britain. His daughter Helena married Roman Constantius who also became king; these were the parents of the Christianising great Emperor, Constantine, born in Britain. Masefield does not use all this directly, (and transposes Cole's territory to the Thames Valley) and within his own poem shows different periods coexisting; now we seem to be in something resembling the third century of Cole's putative reign, now in the sad, bemused present.

Masefield allocates to Cole his proverbial benevolence and courage. After his death, as a reward for the goodness of his reign, he is offered, 'when he reached the judging-place', anything he cares to ask for. He chooses 'to wander earth, the friend of man.' And so he comes into modern times and moves among its ranks, and the stanzas in which Masefield describes the king's posthumous wanderings have a beauty unlike anything he had achieved before, and which heralds his later art (both in verse and prose):

> So, since that time, he wanders shore and shire
> An old, poor, wandering man, with glittering eyes,
> Helping distressful folk to their desire
> By power of spirit that within him lies.

Gentle he is, and quiet, and most wise,
He wears a ragged grey, he sings sweet words,
And where he walks there flutter little birds.

And when the planets glow as dusk begins,
He pipes a wooden flute to music old.
Men hear him on the downs, in lonely inns,
In valley woods, or up the Chiltern wold;
His piping feeds the starved and warms the cold,
It gives the beaten courage; to the lost
It brings back faith, that lodestar of the ghost.

To give 'the beaten courage'; who, even among the victorious nations, had not been beaten by the war? Who was not lost and in need of faith? Who did not have restoration of it as a 'lodestar'? Cole, it will be clear, is, to a significant degree, an avatar of Orpheus who descended to the world of the dead and then returned to the living, and whose music (a lyre in his case, a flute or 'pipe' in Cole's) moved animals, plants, even rocks, water and winds. Masefield brings a particularly English blend of sweetness and homeliness to his picture. Cole has powers but does not want Power; the nature he attracts to himself is susceptible to tenderness.

The figure of Orpheus occupied the post-Great War mind for reasons that scarcely need explaining; Rainer Maria Rilke (1875-1926)—a poet Masefield was to come to admire greatly—had already addressed his imagination to him, but was to do so more extendedly in the wonderful *Sonnets to Orpheus* of 1923, when he fuses his own feelings for a girl who died young with those for the ravaged continent beyond. Cole's music is in itself healing, in itself a bringer of faith (Masefield's assertion of his belief in its spiritual properties is adumbrated but never overtly expressed in *Dauber*). But so is his whole strange tatterdemalion personality, at once unworldly yet able to accommodate itself to every section of the world, from the high-ups (King, Queen, Prince) to the struggling and no-hopers.

The story takes us to one particular world which had always fascinated Masefield even as boy—and which was to continue to fascinate him into old age—the circus. (His nephew, William Masefield, who shared this enthusiasm, remembers conversations with Uncle John about the subject, and the special place *King Cole* had in his affections.) Obviously Masefield was drawn to worlds which were, for however short a span, self-sufficient, with laws, heroes, customs, a whole culture all of their own; he saw them as a kind of dowsing alternative to the humdrum one. (One can see, even with one's own moral disapproval, how the fox-hunt could have also been this for him in his youth.) In *Grace Before Ploughing* he writes of the circuses that brought happiness into his unhappy boyhood:

> Can I have written thus far about childhood without mention of the travelling circuses? There must have been more circuses on the summer roads then than now. They always pitched their tent in a field at the other end of the town, but always in fine weather they paraded through the town in the morning before giving a performance. The parades came as far along the road to our gate, halted briefly and turned near it, so that we saw it all in all its glory: the matchless piebalds, the floats of wonder, the unearthly beauty of the men and women, who were Red Indian Chiefs, perhaps, or Joan of Arc, or a Queen of somewhere, as matchless for beauty as for skill. All these wonders were there in full dress, promising to be more marvellous when they appeared in costume later to do their acts.
>
> The sight of these people, with their horses and costumes, filled the entire morning with rapture and the memory with splendour and expectation. In the afternoon, as we knew, we should see these marvellous people in action. Here we only saw them pretending.
>
> The true circus of my childhood was based on the talents of a few men and women and a few spotted or piebald horses. They performed with music, they were welcomed wherever they went in England, and travelled all over the land between May and September in a life that must have been hard, or indeed very hard.

It's harder still in the depressed post-War world of the poem. King Cole encounters a travelling circus troupe for whom nothing is going right; no one seems to want them, towns have other attractions, like visiting Royalty; maybe their acts are not as good as they were. The clown, once star of the show, Circus John, blames the failures of recent months to the infiltration of women into parts of the profession hitherto closed to them; the young boxer like juggler suffers from melancholy; the singer Molly burns for love of him, and this undermines her own performance. The Showman and his wife worry about money. While the rain is pouring down onto the miserable Oxfordshire country lane, he thinks to himself, obsessedly: "'This is the end; I'm ruined; I'm defeated.'" And to his misery about the economic situation can be added guilt about his son, who has disappeared (perhaps it was his fault as a father?) and whom he may never see again. Parallels with life in the society outside the circus will not be difficult to make.

To this sorry company—so much more adequately representative of the troubled post-War nation than the ossified county set and its hangers-on of *Reynard the Fox*—King Cole, incognito, brings comfort. His music, his whole being elicit performances from the dejected troupe-members—who are thus exhibiting in extreme form what their vocation has always asked of them (see the above passage): that they transcend themselves with all their limitations internal and external and become dazzling beings bringing joy to others, joy that makes life more bearable for them. The troupe's new excellences and changed demeanour even bring about unexpected response from the natural world, point to a new relationship with non-human creatures infinitely superior to that which informs *Reynard the Fox*:

> And with them, walking by the vans, there came
> The wild things from the woodland and the mead,
> The red stag, with his tender-stepping dame,
> Branched, and high-tongued and ever taking heed,
> Nose-wrinkling rabbits nibbling at the weed,
> The hares that box by moonlight on the hill, ...

Furthermore, Cole is responsible for thawing the coldness that officialdom/The Establishment has brought to bear on the circus people, greatly it must be said to the former's spiritual enrichment, and for restoring to the Showman and his wife their lost son who had enrolled himself as one of that establishment's servants, as a sergeant no less.

I said at the outset of this study that *King Cole* showed remarkable similarities with certain Modernist works, even though it is traditional in form and language. Puppets, circuses, mime, fairs, stage-companies—how they stalk, how they dominate some of the most vital works of the century's teens and twenties: Jean Cocteau's *Parade* with music by Satie and designs by Picasso, and his work for the famous clowns, the Fratellinis, *Le Boeuf sur le Toit* (The Ox on the Roof) (1920). The very year in which *King Cole* was published Pirandello's *Sei Personaggi in Cerca d'Autore* (Six Characters in Search of an Author) troubled audiences with its presentation of actors needing parts to be written in order to be themselves; otherwise they were lost, aimless. Rilke had already written his great Fifth Duino Elegy which celebrates Picasso's painting of circus-folk, *Les Saltimbanques*, and sees them as figures of regeneration, as possible conductors of the loveless back to a more loving world.

We saw how Masefield, in his presentation of the premature senseless deaths of young men—of Jimmy Gurney, of Michael Gray and Lion Occleve, of the Dauber—revealed his poet's prescience, anticipated the horror of the mass deaths of 'doomed youth' in the War. Now with the same prescience he, in his own very English way, showed what his continental peers were also imaging: that survivors of the disaster were like puppets, like partless actors wanting some script-writer or showman to step forward and create something for them, something which acknowledged their sadness but which gave them meaningful ritual, a public identity to disguise the ravaged private one, and the ability to arouse—and therefore possibly inwardly to feel again—if not joy, then a sort of magic happiness which could at least carry them through.

That magic—entertained against a world of such terrifying multiple misery—permeates the magnificent last stanzas of *King Cole*. The spiritual ecstasy on which they touch may remind us—different though vocabulary and manner is—of the close of *The Everlasting Mercy*, of the state Saul Kane attained:

King Cole is alone; the artistes he helped have moved on, are in their vans travelling along the Icknield Way:

> He watched the night; then taking up his flute,
> He breathed a piping of this life of ours,
> The half-seen prize, the difficult pursuit,
> The passionate lusts that shut us in their towers,
> The love that helps us on, the fear that lowers,
> The pride that makes us and the pride that mars,
> The beauty and the truth that are our stars.
>
> And man, the marvellous thing, that in the dark,
> Works with his little strength to make a light,
> His wit that strikes, his hope that tends, a spark,
> His sorrow of soul in toil, that brings delight,
> His friends, who make salt sweet and blackness bright,
> His birth and growth and change; and death the wise,
> His peace, that puts a hand upon his eyes.

All these pipings breathed of, until twelve
Struck in the belfry tower with tremblings numb
(Such as will shudder in the axe's helve
When the head strikes) to tell his hour was come.
Out of the living world of Christendom
He dimmed like mist till one could scarcely note
The robins nestling to his old grey coat.

Dimmer he grew, yet still a glimmering stayed
Like light on cobwebs, but it dimmed and died.
Then there was naught but moonlight in the glade,
Moonlight and water and an owl that cried.
Far overhead a rush of birds' wings sighed,
From migrants going south until the spring.
The night seemed fanned by an immortal wing.

But where the juggler trudged beside his love
Each felt a touching from beyond our ken,
Even that bright kingdom where the souls who strove,
Live now for ever, helping living men.
And as they kissed each other; even then
Their brows seemed blessed, as though a hand unseen
Had crowned their loves with never-withering green.

This may be *reminiscent* of *The Everlasting Mercy*, it may even suggest the same mind behind it, but it is not the same. It belongs to a different world which is demanding different responses. Masefield would never be able to unite his artistry with the particular stark apprehensions of those pre-War narrative poems again. He had given to readers something quite unrepeatable, and he as writer was but one factor in that unrepeatability. For someone as ceaselessly creative, as industrious, as principled and as successful as Masefield was at the start of the War, the post-War world presented particularly onerous problems as practitioner of the art of literature. He had a public which expected things of him; he had also an awareness of a change in perceptions infinitely greater and more challenging than those expectations. More than before he must follow his inclinations to work in the mythic and magical to achieve the truthful, to ponder, for instance, the mysteries of Troy and the Arthuriad in order to come to fresh understanding of the world around him, to contemplate Gautama Buddha as intently as the West's own saviours, to re-enter the provinces of childhood perhaps in preference to those of more mundane prestige, to see beyond the sophistications of the society in which he himself cut so increasingly successful a figure the vast ranks of so-called primitive societies which his had violated, annexed, exploited.

☆   ☆   ☆

In *The Midnight Folk* (1927) and *The Box of Delights, or When the Wolves Were Running* (1935) Masefield was to create what have proved—to date—his most durable and widely appreciated works, and not only among their intended young readership. Both books—the second a sequel to the first—are impregnated to the intensest degree by the atmosphere of rural England at particular seasons: summer nights in woodland in *The Midnight Folk*, Christmas-time in a country house and a cathedral city in *The Box of Delights*, with bitter cold, falls of snow and freezing fog—and the reiterated suggestion (becoming a motto for the whole story) that, as in some northern realm, 'The Wolves Are Running'. The success of both books derives not a little from projection on the author's part into the character and situation of their boy-protagonist, Kay Harker, who in the first book leads a lonely life in a huge rambling old mansion, Seekings—in part The Priory, in part Woollas Hall. His governess of hated memory, here called Miss Pouncer, turns out to belong to a coven of witches, affiliated with forces of darkness who are trying to appropriate the Harker family treasure. The story of this treasure connects up with events in the imaginary South American country of Santa Barbara as related in *Sard Harker* and *Odtaa*, and the way violence from the past constantly impinges on and disturbs the present gives the book a strange, unforgettable dimension. Descendants of the original adventurers are found living in Kay's locality, often in possession of their ancestors' characteristics; the past and its evils cannot lightly be laid to rest.

All the same, perhaps the most memorable aspect of *The Midnight Folk* is not that concerned with villains and their foiling, but rather its loving intimate re-creation of the nocturnal life of animals: the cats, especially Nibbins, the fox, Rollicum Bitem, the owl, the otter, the bat. One senses in some of its most joyous passages that for Jack Masefield as a boy there was no greater route out of loneliness than his empathy with the creature-world.

The Box of Delights is as rich in encounters and incidents as its title would suggest. Once again innocence is under threat from the unscrupulous who have dark forces on their side, but innocence also has magic as

195

an ally—a metaphor surely for the redemption by imaginative activity of the misery of the author's earlier years. Cole Hawlings, the Punch-and-Judy man with the box of the title, with whom Kay makes friends, is a most poetic character, undoubted kin to King Cole himself; he has been tramping the road, century in century out, since pagan times. *The Box of Delights* makes (highly individual) excursions into British lore, none of them more beautiful than the appearance of Herne the Hunter (who appears in Herefordshire's own folklore) who changes Kay, for his delectation and his spiritual enrichment, into stag, wild duck and fish, to provide one of the finest instances in all children's literature for that *participation mystique* with Nature for which all of us in our childhood (and many of us later) long.

The young readers who enjoyed *The Midnight Folk* and *The Box of Delights* could well have grown into the first readers of *Dead Ned* and *Live and Kicking Ned*. If there is a weakness in the two books for younger children, it is that their amazing prolixity of invention, tends, in its very exuberance, somewhat to reduce narrative tension. In the Ned novels, on the other hand, there is total accord between the linear progression of Ned's story—which in that part of *Dead Ned* dealing with the day of Admiral Topsle Cringle's murder attains a near-unbearable relentlessness—and the copiously detailed solidity of the world in which it unfolds. Solidity, that is, in the sense of its geographical and social composition, with which, one feels, the author has a bottomless familiarity. In other respects, however, it is a most precarious world, terrifyingly lacking in the certainties decent humanity has surely a right to expect. (It is surely not fanciful to see in the impending inescapable doom of *Dead Ned* the impending inescapable horror of war against the Fascist powers that was to come so shortly after its publication.)

An elderly man, a good one for all his cantankerousness and changeability of mood, the crusty Admiral who befriends Ned is murdered; a good younger man, Ned himself, idealistic, principled, kind-hearted, is not merely charged with his murder but hanged for it (though from the hanging he is revived into life). Men of obvious ill intent prosper, and are seen to do so; ordinary folk, pleasant-seeming on the exterior, collude with a dark fate and have little shame in doing so. And behind an often deceptively placid-faced England, the land- and cityscapes of which are so surely drawn by Masefield, loom both the cruel life of sailors on the ships that make the country rich and strong, and, too, the huge-scale cruelties they themselves help to inflict—in the form of the slave trade, the heinous rape of the black inhabitants of the west coast of Africa (especially the Bight of Benin also known as the Coast of Dead Ned), whose sufferings the perpetrators have still to this day not fully acknowledged or atoned for.

Live and Kicking Ned ends with its hero living in quiet useful happiness, with his affections and morals vindicated, but with unease, a sense of life's mammoth unfairness hanging over him and filtering his prose in the novel's fine last pages. Who can doubt that John Masefield was pondering here the strangeness of his own destiny, of all destinies?

> And since it's only Ned,
> Who was alive and is dead,
> There's no more to be said.

But indeed, until his death, John Masefield never died; there was always more to be said. He tried to come to terms with his own life, and the courage and vitality of his attempts—*In the Mill*, *New Chum*, *So Long to Learn* and *Grace Before Ploughing*—have been shown, I hope, in the ample quotations from these books given in the course of this study. Nor was he ever content merely to present himself. There was always the endless quiet valley reaching out to suggest worlds beyond the immediate.

Selected Bibliography of works by John Masefield

(dates of British publication only)

Salt-Water Ballads (poems) 1902
Ballads (poems) 1903
A Mainsail Haul (prose) 1905
A Tarpaulin Muster (prose) 1907
Captain Margaret (novel) 1908
The Tragedy of Nan and other Plays (drama) 1909
Multitude and Solitude (novel) 1909
Ballads and Poems (poems) 1910
Martin Hyde: The Duke's Messenger (novel) 1910
A Book of Discoveries (children's novel) 1910
The Tragedy of Pompey the Great (drama) 1910
Jim Davis (novel) 1911
William Shakespeare (criticism) 1911
The Everlasting Mercy (poem) 1911
The Widow in the Bye Street (poem) 1912
The Daffodil Fields (poem) 1913
Dauber (poem) 1913
Philip the King and Other Poems (poems) 1914
Good Friday (dramatic poem) 1916
Sonnets and Poems (poems) 1916
Gallipoli (prose) 1916
Lollingdon Downs and Other Poems, with Sonnets (poems) 1917
The Old Front Line (prose) 1917
The Battle of the Somme (prose) 1919
Reynard the Fox; or the Ghost Heath Run (poem) 1919
Enslaved and other Poems (poems) 1920
Right Royal (poem) 1920

King Cole (poem) 1921
Collected Poems 1923
Recent Prose 1924
Sard Harker (novel) 1924
The Trial of Jesus (play) 1925
Odtaa (novel) 1926
The Midnight Folk (children's novel) 1927
Midsummer Night and Other Tales in Verse (poems) 1928
The Wanderer of Liverpool (prose and verse) 1930
Minnie Maylow's Story and Other Tales and Scenes (poems) 1931
The Bird of Dawning (novel) 1933
The Conway from her Foundation to the Present Day (prose) 1933
The Box of Delights (children's novel) 1935
A Letter from Pontus and Other Verse (poems) 1936
Eggs and Baker (novel) 1936
The Square Peg (novel) 1937
Dead Ned (novel) 1938
Live and Kicking Ned (novel) 1939
Gautama the Enlightened and other Verse (poems) 1941
The Nine Days Wonder (prose) 1941
In the Mill (prose) 1941
Wonderings (Between One and Six Years) (poems) 1943
New Chum (prose) 1944
St Katherine of Ledbury, and Other Ledbury Papers (prose) 1951
So Long to Learn: Chapters of an Autobiography (prose) 1952
The Bluebells and Other Verse (poems) 1961
Old Raiger and Other Verse (poems) 1964
Grace Before Ploughing: Fragments of Autobiography (prose) 1966

Index

INDEX

ALSO FROM LOGASTON PRESS

Monuments in the Landscape Series

Vol. III Castles of Radnorshire

by Paul Remfry. 160pp with some 35 photographs, plans and maps.
£7.95
ISBN 1 873827 54 7

The history of the centuries of warfare and changing alliances in Radnorshire is covered in some detail for it provides the background to the construction of the castles; indeed, much of the recorded history is about the sieges and capture of castles. Detailed information is also given about all the castle sites.

Vol. IV Prehistoric Sites of Monmouthshire

by George Children and George Nash. 144pp with 40 photographs, plans and maps. £7.95
ISBN 1 873827 49 0

An introduction to the history and archaeology of Prehistoric Monmouthshire, followed by a detailed description of the main sites, including arrangements for access. The guide is in layman's English but with reference to the language of archaeology for those either in the know, or who wish they were.

Vol. V Neolithic Sites of Cardiganshire, Carmarthenshire & Pembrokeshire

by George Children and George Nash. 160pp with 50 photographs, plans and maps. £7.95
ISBN 1 873827 99 7

This uses anthropology to develop ideas of how Neolithic society operated in south-west wales, whilst also using the archaeological evidence, and giving detailed site descriptions of the 37 remaining monuments.

ALSO FROM LOGASTON PRESS

Arthurian Links with Herefordshire
by Mary Andere. 160pp with maps and photographs. £9.95

ISBN 1 873827 44 X

Enthused by reports of a friend who felt she had had an 'experience' near the site of St. Dubricius' seminary at Hentland, Mary sets the scene by analysing what we do know of the Arthurian period in general, what is myth and legend, and where such myths and legends could contain germs of the original truth. Spreading out from Hentland, she details the possible basis for Mordred's connection with Mordiford, for Gawain's connection with both Hereford and the old kingdom of Erging; with Uthyr Pendragon's possible siege of Vortigern at The Doward and for the same area to be the site for Arthur's eighth battle. Includes details of the early British and Welsh kings and families, and of the Roman Empire.

The Civil War in Hereford
by Ron Shoesmith. 176pp with maps and photographs. £8.95

ISBN 1 873827 34 2

This book uses documents from the Civil War to largely tell the history of the four sieges of Parliament of Hereford. Ironically the best prepared army led by one of the most experienced generals of age, that of the Scots led by Alexander Leslie, Earl of Leven, was the one which failed with much loss of life. Two earlier attempts succeeded after brief skirmishes, with resultant court martials for some of the Royalist officers; the final attempt resulted in a pamphlet entitled *A new tricke to take Townes*.

Alfred Watkins - A Herefordshire Man
by Ron Shoesmith. 160pp paperback, 80 photographs. £5.95

ISBN 0 9510242 7 2

It chronicles the life of the author of *The Old Straight Track*, the book which gave birth to ley lines. But Watkins had varied interests—his family ran the Hereford Brewery, he invented the first exposure meter, became a successful archaeologist, was a fan of steam cars, bee-keeping and Free Trade. The book includes 80 photographs, many of them taken from Watkins' original glass plate negatives stored in Hereford's city library.

ALSO FROM LOGASTON PRESS

A View from Hereford's Past
by Richard Stone. 80pp with 44 photographs, maps and illustrations.
£9.95
ISBN 1 873827 34 2

This tells of the excavation and finds in the precincts of Hereford Cathedral in preparation for the building of the new exhibition centre for the Mappa Mundi and Chained Library. It relates several surprising finds, including over 1,100 complete skeletons and charnel of an additional 5,000 bodies. The excavation has also shed new light on the road layout and style of buildings of the Saxon city; of the diseases that prevailed amongst the medieval population and much besides. Whilst serving as the interim archaeological report, the text is written in a way that anyone interested in finding out in substantial detail what has so far emerged from the archaeological work can do so.

JAMES WATHEN'S HEREFORDSHIRE 1770-1820
His sketches and paintings
by David Whitehead & Ron Shoesmith, 228pp,
90 colour illustrations. £65
ISBN 1 873827 04 0

A high quality production, this details the life of James Wathen, including his early years in Hereford's gloving industry before his turning to watercolour painting. The paintings show the city gates before demolition, street scenes now disappeared, country houses as they were being rebuilt with the profits from a buoyant agriculture, the Wye at the time of the Wye Tour and rural scenes and villages before mechanisation. Also included are some of his contributions, turned to engravings, for *The Gentleman's Magazine*, together with his descriptions of antiquities and churches.

ALSO FROM LOGASTON PRESS

The Man in the Moone
by Francis Godwin, bishop of Hereford between 1617 and 1633. 80pp,
hardback, with photographs. £8.95
ISBN 1 873827 64 4

A science fiction story that predates Jules Verne by some two centuries
and, despite Godwin's appreciation of gravitational theory, the birth of
Newton by at least ten years. A Spaniard, set ashore on St Helena to recu-
perate, starts to train the tame wildlife to lift loads with a series of pulleys.
He uses a white signal to encourage the birds to rise and, after a few adventures *en route*, he is whisked off to the ultimate white signal—the Moon.
A modern introduction sets Godwin's scientific views against the knowledge of the age, and also considers the wider implications of the book
which appears to have been both a cover for scientific debate as well as a
political call for greater seaborne exploration. It might also have inspired
Swift as the two families were related.

Dear Pamela
by Taffy Prothero, 64pp, 6 illustrations. £5.95
ISBN 1 873827 10 5

A series of letters written years later to a friend which tell of life on a farm
at Hundred House, near Builth Wells, in the early twentieth century.

Haber Nant Llan Nerch Freit
An upbringing on a Radnorshire Hill Farm
by George F. Lewis, 144pp, 35 illustrations. £7.95
ISBN 1 873827 25 3

The story of a hill farming community in the Ithon Valley near Llanbister
in the 1920s and 30s. Drovers still took stock to market, ploughing was
still done by horse, hay-making by scythe or mower. Hours were long,
money always a worry, clothes passed down from the eldest to the
youngest, luxury a piece of bread with butter *and* jam. George evokes the
life of the period, both on the farm and in the wider community with its
various characters.